MARY BURRITT CHRISTIANSEN POETRY SERIES

V. B. Price, Series Editor

Also available in the

UNIVERSITY OF NEW MEXICO PRESS

MARY BURRITT CHRISTIANSEN POETRY SERIES

*Miracles of Sainted Earth,* Victoria Edwards Tester

Mary Burritt
Christiansen
Poetry Series

POETS OF THE NON-EXISTENT CITY

# POETS OF THE NON-EXISTENT CITY

## Los Angeles in the McCarthy Era

*Edited by*

**Estelle Gershgoren Novak**

UNIVERSITY OF NEW MEXICO PRESS

ALBUQUERQUE

LIBRARY OF CONGRESS CATALOGING-IN-PUBLICATION DATA

Novak, Estelle Gershgoren.
    Poets of the non-existent city : Los Angeles in the McCarthy era /
Estelle Gershgoren Novak.
       p.   cm.— (Mary Burritt Christiansen poetry series)
Includes bibliographical references and indexes.
    ISBN 0-8263-2951-9 (alk. paper) — ISBN 0-8263-2952-7 (pbk. : alk. paper)
      1. American poetry—California—Los Angeles—History and criticism.
      2. Los Angeles (Calif.)—Intellectual life—20th century.
      3. American poetry—20th century—History and criticism.
      4. American poetry—California—Los Angeles. 5. Los Angeles (Calif.)—In literature.
      6. American poetry—20th century. 7. Los Angeles (Calif.)—Poetry.
        I. Title. II. Series.
    PS285.L7 N68 2002
      811'.5409979494—dc21

                                             2002006406

DESIGN: Mina Yamashita

In memory of
Thomas McGrath,
the guiding spirit

# Contents

List of Illustrations / xiv

Acknowledgments / xvi

Foreword / xvii

Introduction / 1

**You Can Start the Poetry Now!!** / 59

    First Editorial Statement: *California Quarterly* / 59

**Thomas McGrath** / 60

    Homage to Thomas McGrath: E. P. Thompson / 61

    Statement to the House Un-American Activities Committee / 61

    Mr. and Mrs. Foxbright X Muddlehead, At Home / 62

    All the Dead Poets / 63

    A Note on Tom McGrath—the Early 50s: Gene Frumkin / 65

    Escape / 66

    The Roads into the Country / 66

    On Writing "Letter to an Imaginary Friend" / 67

    Letter to an Imaginary Friend / 68

    from Letter to an Imaginary Friend / 74

    Entry in Ann Stanford's Diary on Tom McGrath / 78

    Complaint / 78

    Successions / 78

    *Longshot O'Leary Says It's Your Duty to be Full of Fury: Alice McGrath* / 80

    Alabanza para Thomas McGrath: Sergio Ramirez / 80

**Edwin Rolfe** / 83

    from "Foreword," *Permit Me Refuge:* Thomas McGrath / 83

    Sentry / 84

    Bon Voyage / 85

    Editors of *The California Quarterly* on Rolfe's death / 85

    Elegy for a Soldier of the Spanish Civil War: Eugene Frumkin / 86

    "Dedication," *Coastlines,* spring 1955 / 89

    "A Note on Independent Publishing" from the Editors of *The California Quarterly* / 89

    Poem / 90

    Idiot Joe Prays in Pershing Square and Gets Hauled in for Vagrancy / 91

    Editorial: *The California Quarterly* / 91

**Don Gordon** / 92

    The Dissenter / 93

    The Travelers / 94

    the investigation / 94

    At the Station / 96

    Consider the Meaning of Love / 97

    The Middle Passage / 98

**Naomi Replansky** / 100

    Ring Song / 101

    Housing Shortage / 102

    The Art Editor on Art in *The California Quarterly* / 102

    Night Prayer for Various Trades / 103

    You Walked a Crooked Mile / 104

    Epitaph: 1945 / 105

**William Pillin** / 106

    "Statement," *Epos*: *Poetry Los Angeles:* A Special Issue / 106

    Alvaro Cardona-Hine on William Pillin / 107

    Sabbath / 108

    Aubade / 109

    Two Jewish Poems / 110

    Ocean Park / 112

    That which is good is simply done / 113

    Miserere / 114

**Henri Coulette** / 115

    Migration / 116

    The Head's Dark House / 117

    The Problem of Creation / 118

**Curtis Zahn** / 119

    The People's Choice / 120

    Unposed Photograph of I. I. Freitag, Esq. / 121

    Josephine Ain on Curtis Zahn / 122

    Officers, Gentlemen, Reluctant Violence / 123

    Tijuana / 124

    One Star for "P.R." / 126

    Southern California as the State of the Union / 128

    Announcement for Poetry Reading: McGrath, Boyer-May, Spingarn,
        Ain, and Zahn / 129

**Lawrence Springarn** / 130

 Night in the Funeral Range / 131

 The Ship of Fools / 132

 an imperial fragment / 132

 Rococo Summer / 134

 Jack of Diamonds / 135

 The Grammarian: Parts of Speech / 136

**Burt Meyers** / 137

 Letter: Bert Meyers to John Haines / 137

 In the Alley / 138

 "The Daily Reality," Bert Meyers's *Early Rain.* Reviewed by Gene Frumkin / 139

 I Dreamed / 141

 Picture Framing / 141

 Because There's So Much Speed / 142

**Mel Weisburd** / 143

 Editorial: First Issue of *Coastlines* / 144

 My Father / 145

 A Crow Black With Purpose / 146

 On *Coastlines*: From an Interview with Mel Weisburd / 148

 When I Go Down to That Sleep / 148

 Dreamsong: a Sirvente for Mel Weisburd: Thomas McGrath / 149

 Editorial / 150

 "Lysergic Acid and the Creative Experience" / 152

 Commentary from "The Merchant of Venice" / 160

 Between Chicago and St. Paul / 160

 Report From Evanston / 162

 Announcement for *Coastlines*-Forum concert / 161

 Letter: Mel Weisburd to *Coastlines'* Final Issue / 164

**Eugene Frumkin** / 166

 "A Note on Tom McGrath—the Early '50s" / 167

 Elegy for a Tailor / 168

 The Waiting Room in the County Hospital / 168

 Regarding a Proposal to Merge *Coastlines* and *The California Quarterly* into One Magazine / 170

 Iowa, Kansas, Nebraska / 170

 The Clue / 171

 "A Birthday Editorial," *Coastlines* / 174

The Debt  /  175

Men Fail in Communion  /  176

"The Great Promotor: A Hangnail Sketch of Lawrence Lipton"  /  177

**Alvaro Cardona-Hine**  /  189

Three Personal Poems of Grandeur and Magniloquence  /  190

Vindication  /  196

Letter: Cardona-Hine on *Coastlines*  /  198

Doomsday and Components  /  198

Letter: Cardona-Hine on Editing *Coastlines*  /  199

The Train of the Wounded. Miguel Hernandez—translation by
　　　　Cardona-Hine  /  199

**Stanley Kiesel**  /  201

Gregg  /  201

Joey  /  202

Seven Children  /  203

**Josephine Ain**  /  204

You There, Weeping  /  205

Magdalen  /  206

Don Quixote  /  207

Seven Haiku  /  208

Aspects  /  208

Letter: Alvaro Cardona-Hine on Readings at the House of Josephine Ain  /  212

Number XVI from *The Flesh of Utopia* to Bob Chuey: Cardona-Hine  /  213

**Sid Gershgoren**  /  214

The Frugal Repast  /  214

Cleaning Woman  /  216

The Trouble with the Times  /  217

**Estelle Gershgoren Novak**  /  218

Legend  /  219

The Time Machine of War  /  219

Hiroshima Woman  /  220

The Shape of a Pear  /  221

Scars  /  221

**Ann Stanford** / 222

    Pandora / 222

    The Burning Glass / 223

    The Weathercock / 224

    The Bear / 225

    A Summer Walk / 226

    The Window / 228

**Peter Yates: Reading Poetry Aloud** / 229

**Two Poets on the Beat Fringes** / 235

    The Pocket Poet Series, Reviewed by Thomas McGrath / 237

**Lawrence Lipton** / 240

    Lawrence Lipton on "America's Literary Underground," *Coastlines* / 240

    rainbow at midnight / 241

    Night Flight / 242

    Poetry, Jazz, Etc., by Thomas McGrath / 247

    I Was a Poet for the FBI / 251

    Lipton's Message in *Coastlines'* Final Issue / 253

**Charles Bukowski** / 254

    Dow Jones: Down / 255

    everything: / 256

**Moved On, by Alexandra Garrett: *Coastlines* Saying Goodbye** / 257

***Coastlines*: a Post-mortem** / 259

Complete List of *Coastlines* Contributors / 259

The Artists / 263

Title Index / 267

Index of First Lines / 270

Works Consulted / 273

# List of Illustrations

In Order of Appearance

1. Thomas McGrath, ca. 1950s. Photo by Alice McGrath. / **vii**
2. *Coastlines* and Len Harris's "Community Forum": Bard Dahl, Mel Weisburd, Len Harris, and unknown *Coastlines* contributor, ca. 1955. / **3**
3. *Coastlines* editor-in-chief Mel Weisburd, 1956. / **7**
4. Josephine Ain (Chuey), mid-1960s. / **10**
5. Estelle Gershgoren in Barnsdall Park. / **16**
6. Keith Gundersson, Mel Weisburd, Gene Frumkin, Stanley Kiesel, 1969. / **23**
7. Alvaro Cardona-Hine, 1969. / **46**
8. Estelle Gershgoren and Sid Gershgoren, ca. 1959. / **48**
9. Cover: *Coastlines* 4, nos. 2 and 3 (spring 1960). / **56**
10. Cover: *The California Quarterly* 1, no. 1 (autumn 1951). / **58**
11. Cover: *The California Quarterly* 3, no. 3 (1954). / **82**
12. Advertisement for Edwin Rolfe's *Permit Me Refuge,* from *The California Quarterly* 4, no. 1 (1956). / **88**
13. Cover: *Coastlines* 1, no. 1 (spring 1955). / **90**
14. Cover: *The California Quarterly* 3, no. 1, (autumn 1953). / **91**
15. Cover: *The California Quarterly* 4, no. 1 (1956). / **99**
16. Mario Casetta, Woodcut: "Car Barn" in *The California Quarterly* 4, no. 1 (1956). / **100**
17. Mario Casetta, Woodcut: "War Orphan" in *The California Quarterly* 4, no. 1 (1956). / **101**
18. Mario Casetta, Woodcut: "Deportation Hearing" in *The California Quarterly* 4, no. 1 (1956). / **102**
19. Mario Casetta, Woodcut: "Apprentice," in *The California Quarterly* 4, no. 1 (1956). / **103**
20. Martin Lubner, Four Drawings, *The California Quarterly* 3, no. 4 (1955). / **104–105**
21. Polia Pillin, linoleum block cut: *Epos* 9, no. 4 (summer 1958). / **107**
22. Cover: *The California Quarterly* 3, no. 4 (1955). / **113**
23. Morton Dimondstein, Engraving: "Gerry," the *California Quarterly* 3, no. 2 (1954) also used as the cover for *The California Quarterly* 3, no. 1 (autumn 1953). / **117**

24. Morton Dimondstein, Engraving: "View from Toluca" *The California Quarterly* 3, no. 2 (1954). / 118

25. Morton Dimondstein, Engraving: "Musicians," *The California Quarterly* 3, no. 2 (1954). / 120

26. Morton Dimondstein, Engraving: "Street Musicians," *The California Quarterly* 3, no. 2 (1954). / 122

27. Cover: *The California Quarterly* 4 (summer 1952). / 129

28. Cover: *The California Quarterly* 3, no. 2 (1954). / 134

29. Arnold Mesches, Four Drawings: "Seamy Side," "The Boners," "Coronation," "Vernon Trucks," in *The California Quarterly* 3, no. 1 (1953). / 138–139

30. Obituary for *The California Quarterly,* in *Coastlines* 2, no. 2 (winter 1956). / 141

31. Cover: *Coastlines* 5, no. 4 (1963). / 142

32. Cover: *Coastlines* 1, no. 4 (spring 1956). / 145

33. Cover: *Coastlines* 3, no. 2 (spring–summer 1958). / 151

34. Announcements of *Coastlines*-Forum concert. / 163

35. Cover: *Coastlines* 4, no. 1 (autumn 1959). / 165

36. Announcements of *Coastlines'* parties. / 188

37. Cover drawing of Josephine Ain (Chuey): *Coastlines* 5, no. 1 (1961). / 202

38. Cover: *Coastlines* 2, no. 2 (winter 1956–57). / 212

39. Cover: *Coastlines* 4, no. 4 (autumn 1960). / 215

40. Announcement for jazz and poetry at LA Jazz Concert Hall. / 250

40. Cover (final issue): *Coastlines* 6, nos. 21 and 22 (1964). / 258

# Acknowledgments

I would like to thank the many people who assisted me with this anthology. In particular I owe thanks to Mel Weisburd, Gene Frumkin, and Alvaro Cardona-Hine for sharing their memories of *Coastlines* and *The California Quarterly* with me; to Alice McGrath for her memories of her husband and the years of the Marsh Street Irregulars; to Naomi Replansky for her description of her time in Los Angeles; to Tina Gainsborough for memories of her father, Don Gordon; to Roseanna Norton for her memories of her mother, Ann Stanford; to the late Odette Meyers for sharing her memories of her husband, Bert Meyers; and to all the poets for allowing me to collect their poems. For information on the artwork and its appearance in the magazines I owe thanks to the late Morton Dimondstein. I am grateful to the librarians at the Huntington Library for opening the yet uncataloged papers of Ann Stanford to me and to the librarians at the Department of Special Collections at the University of California at Los Angeles for allowing me access to the oral histories of Don Gordon and Alice McGrath, to the Alexandra Garrett Papers, and to copies of *The California Quarterly* and *Coastlines* in their collection. I also wish to thank my husband, Max Novak, for his patience with this project and his support.

# Foreword

*"As a literary magazine, our first duty is toward the things of the world, for without these there is no literature, no art—just desolation. Among these things are the timeless human problems, public and private. We must try to see them honestly, from the inside, in the material we publish and in our own commentaries. We must try to see them freshly too, for otherwise we cannot see them honestly. But originality should not be our only value; it dare not be accepted as an abstract value cut off from the world's images."*
—GENE FRUMKIN, "A Birthday Editorial," *Coastlines* (spring 1960)

Gene Frumkin, a poet, creative-writing teacher, and mentor at the University of New Mexico for over thirty years, spells out here what seems to be the essence of a little-known American poetic movement in the "non-existent city" of Los Angeles, California. Beginning in 1951, and perhaps earlier, this worldly and humanitarian vision of poetry was embodied by writers and teachers enduring the dangerous and depressing political climate of the McCarthy era and the black-listing machinery of the House Un-American Activities Committee (HUAC).

The literature that this sensibility of conscience and engagement produced was recorded most clearly in two magazines: *The California Quarterly,* published from 1952 to 1956, and *Coastlines,* published from 1955 to 1964. Gene Frumkin was one of the editors of *Coastlines* in 1960.

Reading Frumkin, we see that the poetry of these Los Angeles writers is set off from modernism's fetish of originality as well as from the "inhumanist" philosophy of California's most famous poet, the disenchanted though severe naturalist Robinson Jeffers. Their work seems less aligned with the cultural revolution of the contemporary beat movement in San Francisco than with the spirit of the human rights, populist, and antifascist perspective of European refugees who had settled in Los Angeles after the war, among them Thomas Mann and Aldous Huxley.

Few Americans are aware of the great poets of this period in Los Angeles or even that Los Angeles had a poetic fluorescence in those dark years at the beginning of the cold war. Names like Tom McGrath, Don Gordon, Edwin Rolfe, and Gene Frumkin are regrettably not common in anthologies of American poetry. It is as if the country's hypocrisy about Hollywood—its passion for the distractions of movies alongside its snobbery about "non-existent" southern California and the sneered-at lower-caste culture of popular fantasy that the film industry created— just swallowed these poets up. Or is their long absence from recognition simpler to explain than that? Was their work, along with some of their jobs, erased by the frightening and sensationalized association of having been interrogated and blacklisted by HUAC witch hunters? That seems at least as likely.

Estelle Gershgoren Novak's handsomely thorough and annotated anthology of these mostly forgotten poets is an indispensable first effort in lifting the veil of hypocrisy and fear that has obscured their work for so long.

Her scholarship and editorial selection reveals to contemporary readers invaluable perspectives on the all-but-invisible world of American letters in the 1950s outside New York, Chicago, and San Francisco. Novak demonstrates the unpublicized heroism of poets who lived on the fringes of Hollywood and were persecuted as ruthlessly as any moviemaker by right-wing zealots in the federal government. She makes available the deeply compassionate, socially realistic, and humanitarian poetry being produced in Los Angeles under enormous political pressure. And she shows what it takes to survive and flourish creatively in a climate of political oppression, a topic especially relevant in our times of diminished civil liberties in the wake of the terrorist attacks on New York and Washington, D.C., in September 2001.

As a young teenager growing up in the Hollywood community in the mid-1950s, I experienced, personally, the terrifying insecurity and insidious sense of threat that actors, screenwriters, directors, and their families felt when HUAC spread its vile curtain of suspicion over the Los Angeles Basin. Academy Award-winning actors, like Anne Revere, were blacklisted and never worked in Hollywood again. My father was "gray listed" as a "premature Anti-Nazi Sympathizer" along with many others because he made a Christmas recording to raise money for Russian war relief before the Soviet Union was invaded by Hitler. My whole family and most of the people they knew were unable to get work or further their careers for years. The secrecy and sense of helplessness was demoralizing and enervating. And now, because of Novak's work, we are reminded again of how widespread the black-listing was and how courageous poets like Tom McGrath were in the face of it.

McGrath was the leading figure in Los Angeles poetry after World War II. Originally from North Dakota, he had written and worked all over America, from the West Side docks of Manhattan to Louisiana State University, where he studied. In 1951, McGrath was hired by Los Angeles State College to teach creative writing. Two years later he was subpoenaed by HUAC to appear before its hearings. As Novak writes, "He was what they called 'uncooperative.' He betrayed no one: not himself, not his friends. And for that he was fired from his job at Los Angeles State College in 1954 and forced into various and sundry occupations, the flotsam and jetsam of the work world."

McGrath's statement to HUAC is an inspiration in an era like ours in which wilderness advocates, conservationists, antiglobalization activists, environmentalists, and dissenters of all kinds are being associated, by some Bush administration officials and others on the far right, with supporters of "terrorism."

McGrath told the menacing committeemen of HUAC in 1953,

> As a poet I must refuse to cooperate with the committee on what I can only call esthetic grounds. The view of life which we receive through the great works of art is a privileged one—it is a view of life according to probability or necessity, not subject to the chance and accident of our real world and therefore in a sense truer than the life we see lived all around us. . . . Then, too, poets have been notorious non-cooperators where committees of this sort are concerned. As a traditionalist, I would prefer to take my stand with Marvell, Blake, Shelley and García Lorca. . . . I do not wish to bring dishonor to my tribe.

Frumkin remembered the encounter, writing later, "The House Un-American Activities Committee (HUAC) came to the City of Angels looking for devils. . . . Tom, who has been politically involved in the Left for longer than I've known him, was among those subpoenaed. . . . His responses to questions were as forthright as they customarily are; although they didn't get him thrown in jail for contempt . . . they did get him fired from his teaching post . . . despite a strong student petition campaign urging his reinstatement."

In a poem "editorial" in *Coastlines* called "The Debt," Gene Frumkin wrote that he was trying "to make an important event of our time a personal matter. The problem of the poem is to get beyond Premier Castro's beleaguered truculence and the ignorant floundering of the U.S. Government vis-à-vis Cuba to a relationship with a long-victimized people."

The first stanza of that poem goes as follows:

"When I read of worms slipping / through the skin of children's feet, / swimming in their blood with open mouths, / damning the currents of their lives, / my muscles thunder and my eyes / become the bells of a burning city."

For many younger New Mexicans writing in the late 1960s and 1970s, a teacher like Frumkin, who could write a poem like "The Debt," would set the moral tone for much of their work. And, in the strange ways of history, a dire and forgotten time in Los Angeles would inspire students in New Mexico to take the problems of the world and its people as "a personal matter."

The great value of Estelle Gershgoren Novak's anthology is that it not only presents a wide range of poetry by twenty long-overshadowed Los Angeles poets, along with a detailed introduction to the period and illustrations and relevant documents throughout the text, it also shows us clearly once again the importance of poetry in a free society. One of the reasons why HUAC hounded poets in Los Angeles is that even the sharklike mentality of its members recognized that poetry is the surest of all antidotes to propaganda. Its danger is that it encourages people to read precisely, to analyze language, and to think for themselves, especially if poets are writing about "timeless human problems, public and private." And nothing is more threatening to a repressive society than people who take what happens in the world personally, people like Solzhenitsyn, who, surviving Stalin's gulags, argued years later that "the salvation of mankind lies only in making everything the concern of all."

I believe that's what the poets of the McCarthy era in Los Angeles were doing when they concerned themselves with "the things of the world" and why, perhaps, in an ongoing "us or them" cold war culture like our own, they've been buried in obscurity for such a long time.

V. B. PRICE

Albuquerque, 2002

# Introduction

Los Angeles is the city of the angels, a city that has long been connected to the glitter of Hollywood and the crass commercialism that always emanates from the movie capital. A city without a center, it has often been called a city without a soul, a nonexistent city. This is the Los Angeles that outsiders imagine before they settle down near the ocean in Venice, or in Westwood, or downtown near Alvarado, or in Hollywood around Vermont Avenue. Yet Los Angeles is a city that outsiders built, and there is substance under the superficial glitter. Almost all Angelinos came here from somewhere else. In the 1940s, before and after the war, expatriate writers, musicians, artists, and intellectuals came fleeing Nazi Germany. After the war easterners came to worship the sun, find jobs, and live a better life in the new bungalows going up in the wake of the wartime Quonset huts.

And among these sun worshipers and refugees were the poets: Edwin Rolfe came to Los Angeles after fighting in the Spanish Civil War, Thomas McGrath came to Los Angeles from the colder regions of North Dakota after a sojourn in Europe, and some like Don Gordon had lived here since childhood. In a city that had no center, they got together with other refugees or native Angelinos and made poetry.

But they found themselves in the midst of the McCarthy anticommunist witch-hunt that had begun only a few years before, in a city where Hollywood screenwriters were being blacklisted and unemployed by those among them who "named names" and by the House Un-American Activities Committee, which had made it all possible. Edwin Rolfe, who had fought the battle against fascism in Spain and written poems about that struggle, was now thrust into a new conflict against those who would, if they could, silence poets like him. Thomas McGrath had fought in the Aleutians, but this battle would be, even for him, a different one. Don Gordon, living in Los Angeles and a reader for the studios, found himself blacklisted and fired after having been called before HUAC. McGrath, who at that time had no connections to Hollywood, was also brought before the committee and then fired from his teaching job at Los

Angeles State College as a result of his failure to cooperate. Both Gordon and McGrath lost their jobs because of their politics, not because of their poetry. Yet it was poetry that McGrath used in his statement before the committee, arguing an Aristotelian view of literature. Of course, he also refused to answer on the grounds of the Fourth, the First, and the Fifth Amendments to the United States Constitution.[1] Poetry and politics were closely entwined for the poets who had been affected by the depression and World War II. And for these poets in the 1950s, with liberal sentiments and socially conscious attitudes in their writing, the McCarthy period was a particularly difficult one. But it was difficult even for those who had no direct leftist associations and did not personally suffer the persecution of the committee. Ann Stanford, a sympathizer with the suffering of those persecuted by McCarthy, was certainly nervous about the "guilt by association" practiced by the House Un-American Activities Committee. She remarks in her diary entry for Saturday May 14, 1955, "The 'Epilogue' to my Magellan was read at the Unitarian Church Festival of Arts this evening. I had had some hesitation when they asked me to submit something because of the blacklisting of people who even associate with people who are suspected of leftist leanings these days, and Tom McGrath and his wife always participate so prominently in these affairs, in fact, Alice McGrath was in charge of this one. Such an association might impede Ron's clearance in case he had the chance to design any government building."[2] Stanford and many others who sympathized with the sufferings of those brought before the committee were nervous about their own safety and professional futures. But she concludes in her diary entry, "However, I decided to participate because you can't live inside a barrel and even went down with the Yerkes, who are now publicly acknowledged ex-Communists."[3] By the time she attended the arts festival, McGrath had already appeared before the committee and had lost his job.

But what was the response of these poets to the repression of the period? They did what poets do. They founded literary journals. Most journals lasted for only a few years. That was the norm for little magazines in America. But although *The California Quarterly* only lasted from 1951 to 1956, *Coastlines*, which followed in its wake, lasted for nearly ten years, from 1955 to 1964. The editors of *Coastlines* were sympathetic to many of the sentiments of *The California Quarterly* but saw themselves as more individualistic, less a part of

*Coastlines* and Len Harris's "Community Forum" participated in joint activities at Coastlines Headquarters at Bard Dahl's house, 1753 No. Virginia Road, Los Angeles. Photo taken ca. 1955. From upper right, clockwise: Bard Dahl, Mel Weisburd, Len Harris, and unknown *Coastlines* contributor. Photographer unknown.

a political movement. Gordon, in an interview about the blacklist, described his early poems as "social minded, of course, leftist" and his later poems as "more in the middle of things, more social minded."[4] In 1951 *The California Quarterly* published its first issue. The managing editor was Philip Stevenson, who began the journal, and the editors, from the beginning, included poets like Thomas McGrath and Lawrence Spingarn. Poets who published in its pages included Edwin Rolfe (for the last few years of his life), Thomas McGrath, Naomi Replansky, Don Gordon, Curtis Zahn, and younger poets like Bert Meyers, Gene Frumkin, and Mel Weisburd. Gene Frumkin, a young poet and student of McGrath's, was working on *The California Quarterly*'s editorial board when he and Mel Weisburd brought out the first issue of *Coastlines*, dedicated to Ed Rolfe, who had died the year before. Thomas McGrath had encouraged these young poets to begin another Los Angeles quarterly in 1955, and that had become *Coastlines,* its first issue gathered together in mimeograph sheets.[5] *Coastlines* would later acquire *The California Quarterly* and with it Edwin Rolfe's posthumous book of poems, *Permit Me Refuge*, which *The California Quarterly* had published. Early on in the history of *Coastlines* there was talk of uniting the two journals, but they remained separate, and when *The California Quarterly* died, *Coastlines* continued.[6] Mel Weisburd had also been the editor of the Los Angeles State College journal *Statement*, where Thomas McGrath was the faculty adviser, and to a certain extent *Coastlines* was the child of that journal as well. Henri Coulette, Mel Weisburd, Gene Frumkin, and Stanley Kiesel, among others, were products of Thomas McGrath's writing class at Los Angeles State College. And it was *Coastlines* that published the first sections of McGrath's long poem *Letter to an Imaginary Friend* in its spring-summer 1957 issue. In hindsight it was McGrath's personal charisma, warmth, knowledge, talent, and sensitivity to people and writers that was the attractant necessary to create a community of writers. When McGrath lost his job at Los Angeles State College, hundreds of students came out to protest and to hear him speak. As poet and personality he held everything together at the beginning, the journal, social activities, readings. When the *Coastlines*-Community Forum developed, it further amplified these community activities. Thus there was a literary community developing that was very much independent of the movie industry in Los Angeles during those years.

In its winter 1956 issue the editors of *Coastlines* mourned *The California Quarterly*'s demise.[7] One of the associate editors of *Coastlines*, Gene Frumkin, had been an editorial assistant on *The California Quarterly* in 1955 just after *Coastlines* produced its first issue. He then became one of the editors for the volume 4, number 1, 1956, issue of *The California Quarterly*, doing double duty for both magazines. Poems by *Coastlines* poets appeared in *The California Quarterly* both in 1954 and 1955. They included poems by *Coastlines* editor Mel Weisburd, one of its associate editors, Gene Frumkin, and Bert Meyers. After the death of that journal, *Coastlines* published many of the same writers and newer ones for almost ten years, and those poets continued to write and to represent the tradition they had shared. The poets who started the journal in the early 1950s had come full circle. After *Coastlines* other literary journals appeared in Los Angeles, like *Ante, Momentum, Bachy, Santa Monica Review, Omnibus,* and *Poetry L.A.,* to name just a few. But it was with the publication of *The California*

*Quarterly* in 1951 and *Coastlines* in 1955 that Los Angeles poetry took root in the city and became its literary and social conscience.

## Gathering Places for Poets

In the fifties and sixties, poetry was alive and well in Los Angeles. *Coastlines*, in its autumn 1957 issue, listed at least six or seven different poetry venues existing simultaneously. Events in San Francisco (later to be called the San Francisco Renaissance by some) were mirrored in Los Angeles. *Coastlines* reports that the Los Angeles police seized works appearing in Wally Berman's *Semina*.[8] Writers met at Larry Spingarn's house on Agnes Avenue, according to the *Coastlines* report, "every Tuesday night."[9] Spingarn was a poet and fiction writer, and that particular group was a fiction and playwriting group. Again, according to the *Coastlines* report, Lawrence Spingarn was fired from his teaching assistant job at the University of California at Los Angeles (UCLA) for a story he printed.[10] In the Los Angeles of the fifties and sixties there were so many local gathering places for poets that it is difficult to list them all. William Pillin, at the house in Hollywood that his poetry shared with his wife's (Polia) pottery and his son's (Boris) music, gathered poets around him. He would stay in that house until he died, and he would continue to nurture a new generation of poets.[11] Then there was Thomas McGrath, who would collect a group of poets around him imbued with both a mission to write great poetry and to keep a social conscience with his "every-other-Wednesday-night poetry sessions."[12] This group came to be called "the Marsh Street Irregulars"[13] by Tom after the name of the street on which he lived at the time. The group included close friends and mature writers like Don Gordon and Naomi Replansky. Replansky had brought out *Ring Song*, a book of poems nominated for the National Book Award, and Gordon had published *Displaced Persons*, his third book of poems. And there were students like Henri Coulette, Gene Frumkin, Mel Weisburd, Bert Meyers, and later Alvaro Cardona-Hine, Sid Gershgoren, and Estelle Gershgoren. Many poets learned from McGrath, who was probably as great a teacher of writing as he was a poet. He never imposed his own way of writing on any of his students but seemed to bring out the best in them all. Alice McGrath said of those meetings, "They would read to each other and make comments, and I have the recollection that the comments were always made in the most generous spirit. . . ."[14] Some of the poets who had gathered around McGrath not only met at his bimonthly Wednesday night meetings, but also met in North Hollywood Park with their families on Sunday afternoons. This was the late fifties. Bert Meyers, Alvaro Cardona-Hine, Stanley Kiesel, Gene Frumkin, and Mel Weisburd were all there with their families. While their various children screamed, ran around the grass, and swung on the swings, the poets talked about and read poetry. New poems came out of people's mouths. All the problems of poetry and the vast military-industrial complex, traffic, and smog were discussed. But the sun shone and the park was beautiful and poetry dominated. And then, of course, there was the patron of *Coastlines*, Alexandra Garret, whose house in Santa Monica Canyon was opened for parties and readings to help keep *Coastlines* financially afloat. As Mel Weisburd tells it, Alexandra Garrett and Barding Dahl purchased the magazine from him and Gene Frumkin for a dollar and then kept it going.[15] It was Garrett and Dahl who were the editors when the quarterly finally died in 1964 after almost ten years.

## Poetry Readings

Don Gordon recalled that poetry in LA was always being read aloud in those years. Readings went on at Barnsdall Park in Los Angeles, where writers like Bert Meyers, Thomas McGrath, James Boyer May, and Lawrence Spingarn appeared.[16] In fact, the publisher who printed *Coastlines* (Villiers Publications) printed *Poetry Los Angeles: I* in 1958, which collected some of the poetry read at Barnsdall Park.[17] Unfortunately no second volume of *Poetry Los Angeles* was ever printed. Under the direction of Peter Yates, poet and music critic, poetry readings were given at the Wilshire Ebell theater.[18] Curtis Zahn conducted readings at his house in Malibu. Josephine Ain, married to the artist Robert Chuey, held regular poetry readings at their house, where Chuey's paintings hung on the wall and lay scattered on the floor of his huge studio space. *Coastlines* also reports monthly readings at Sol and Mae Babitz's house in Hollywood. Apparently these poetry readings alternated between the Babitz house and the house of Peter and Frances Yates. Poets who read there were Peter Yates, Naomi Replansky, Gene Frumkin, Stanley Kiesel, and Melissa Blake. Both Allen Ginsberg and Kenneth Patchen were read in absentia and published in *Coastlines*. It was at these meetings that Ann Stanford first read from her long dramatic poem *Magellan*.[19] And, as I have already mentioned, the "Epilogue" to *Magellan* was read in a more formal setting

*Coastlines* editor-in-chief
Mel Weisburd at benefit
concert February 12, 1956.
Photographer unknown.

by the actor Jeff Corey at the First Unitarian Church's Festival of the Arts in 1955. At that same festival, poets from the *California Quarterly/Coastlines* group, Frumkin, Gordon, Kiesel, Replansky, Spingarn, Yates, and Zahn were also read. Because this festival was held after Edwin Rolfe's death, poems from his last book were read along with a memorial commentary.[20] Several Writers' Workshops announced their readings for 1958, where Alvaro Cardona-Hine joined Bert Meyers and Ann Stanford. These organized festivals and workshops were held in Los Angeles and produced mimeographed programs of the readings.[21]

In 1962 some of these Los Angeles poets found themselves joining San Francisco poets reading at the San Francisco Museum of Art's Poetry Festival. There Ann Stanford, Henri Coulette, Lawrence Spingarn, and Gene Frumkin assembled with Kenneth Rexroth and Brother Antoninus to read. This particular festival was dedicated to Dag Hammarskjöld of the United Nations by Adlai E.

Stevenson, who noted in the program, "The purpose of a Poetry Festival is as noble a one as there can be: to rouse our spirits to a new life; to make us rejoice through the mighty power of beauty; to allow to each of us a glimpse of our nature and destiny, and thus to make us more deeply human."[22] However, not all the readings were quite as formally organized. At some of the gatherings, not only did the poets read, but they talked and argued, the discussions sometimes waxing furious. Politeness often evaporated. Curtis Zahn, for example, complains in the 1957 issue of *Coastlines* about Lawrence Lipton and his Venice West buddies (whom Zahn calls "the Great Ungifted"). Zahn says that they are "hamming up the reading, falling on their asses, spilling drinks or getting into a corner and talking animatedly to somebody they would never talk to if there wasn't a reading going on which they drove 50 miles to attend."[23] Curtis Zahn wasn't the only one who publicly quarreled with Lawrence Lipton. Mel Weisburd, editor of *Coastlines,* appeared on CBS radio with Lipton, talking about the famous poetry reading when Allen Ginsberg took off all his clothes.[24] Weisburd had been one of the first to try LSD and had written a coolly scientific article about the experience.[25] Lipton had ridiculed Weisburd as a "Sunday Slummer in Paradise," and Weisburd, in a *Coastlines* article, had referred to Lipton as the "Merchant of Venice," while Frumkin had called him "The Great Promotor."[26] The split was never entirely healed between these two groups, but they functioned simultaneously in LA. The Los Angeles poets around *Coastlines* were, to a great extent, buried by the publicity around the beats, both the publicity generated by the San Francisco poetry scene and the artificial publicity created by Lawrence Lipton in Los Angeles itself. Gene Frumkin's article in *Coastlines* called into question Lipton's view of the poets at the magazine and Lipton's memory of Allen Ginsberg's poetry reading in LA in his book *The Holy Barbarians.* Lipton had referred to the *Coastlines* group as attached to the "Movement" and reading only what was put out by the "Party" or "Cryptoparty" publications.[27] Frumkin's response was that this was not a time to be labeling writers as *red,* certainly not during the period of the blacklist.[28] In fact, although *Coastlines* published many poets with left-wing sentiments, it was not itself a radical journal.[29] It was far more individualistic and experimental than the old left would have found palatable. And, as has been mentioned, *Coastlines* published Lipton and poets from his group.

Lawrence Lipton headed the Venice West Poetry Center. Listed in *Coastlines* among the group at the center were Stuart Perkoff, Charles Newman, Charles Foster, Saul White, and Bruce Boyd. In 1957 these poets were talking about mixing poetry with jazz, and Stuart Perkoff had written "Round About Midnight," which *Coastlines* says "uses four voices, music and dance." At Venice West, poetry of the San Francisco poets Rexroth, Ginsberg, and Ferlinghetti was read along with the Los Angeles poetry of Lipton. *Coastlines* reports the "credo of this community of writers" as "(1) an emphasis on on the vocal tradition in poetry, (2) the numinous/religious/magical nature of the creative process, (3) the functional writer/reader/listener relationship, designed to 'transform' the audience, (4) total engagement of the writer in total rejection of the Social Lie and the lifeways that flow from it; disaffiliation and cultivation of the art of poverty."[30] Despite the differences between the *Coastlines* group and the Venice West group, both had grown out of the radical tradition of the thirties and forties. Kenneth Rexroth had published poems in the *New Masses* in the thirties. Others have written much on the beats, but it seems to me that a distinction must be made between the propaganda that was spread about them in the mainstream press and the reality of their origins. The beats had at first represented what was a disaffiliation from the bourgeoisie, but not wholly a disengagement. With Lawrence Lipton the Venice West group chose to present itself as more and more disengaged, and its path separated from the group around *Coastlines,* so much so that when *Coastlines* published its final issue, Lipton was quoted in it as saying that he would have continued publishing in the journal had it "not pursued such a narrow sectarian policy."[31]

### Poetry and the Arts

Venice West was not the only group that tried to connect poetry to the arts. From the beginning of *The California Quarterly* and through the life of *Coastlines,* there had been a connection among the poets and local artists and local musicians. Peter Yates, the writer, was also Peter Yates the music critic. He held concerts at his house on Micheltorena Street in the Silver Lake district. He and his wife, Frances Mullen, the pianist, called those concerts "Evenings on the Roof" because they were held in a studio that had been built by the well-known architect R. M. Schindler expressly for that purpose.[32] The studio was in a privileged

Josephine Ain (Chuey),
Los Angeles, mid-1960s.
Photographer unknown.

visual position overlooking on one side the Los Angeles City Hall, on another the Griffith Park Observatory, and on still another the Pacific Ocean in the distance. It was at these concerts that works by Igor Stravinsky, Arnold Schoenberg, and Ives were played and where musicians like Gregor Piatagorsky and Jascha Heifetz performed.[33] But the concerts were coming to an end at Yates's house at the time *Coastlines* was beginning, and Yates was becoming more involved with writing poetry. The Ashgrove, a Los Angeles club, held poetry readings with jazz.[34] In the winter 1957 issue of *Coastlines*, McGrath reviewed a jazz and poetry performance at the Jazz Concert Hall,[35] and Peter Yates wrote an article on the art of reading poetry aloud for *Coastlines*.[36] While other groups might have pursued poetry and jazz, *The California Quarterly* and *Coastlines* actively connected themselves with graphic art. Artist Morton Dimondstein was art editor of *The California Quarterly* and produced all of its covers from 1953 onward. Inside its pages woodcuts by Mario Casetta, engravings by Dimondstein, and drawings by Martin Lubner, David Lemon, and Arnold Mesches could be found. Covers of *Coastlines* included works by Manual Santana, Lemon, Milton Gershgoren, Mesches, Lubner, and Dimondstein among others.[37] A special issue of *Epos* coming out of Florida in 1958 was dedicated to Los Angeles Poets and contained linoleum cuts by Los Angeles potter and artist Polia Pillin (wife of poet William Pillin).[38] Alvaro Cardona-Hine wrote poetry, painted, and composed music.

There were connections among all the arts, and poetry was at the center. Bert Meyers, an early contributor to *Coastlines*, made frames for the Landau Gallery on La Cienega Boulevard. Two of the women poets who published in *Coastlines* were married to artists and architects. Josephine Ain was married to architect Gregory Ain and then to artist Robert Chuey. She also had painted. Ann Stanford was married to one of the consulting architects on Disneyland, Ronald White.

In Los Angeles, Hollywood was never far away, even after it had been torn apart by the prosecution of the Hollywood Ten. In the summer of 1953, *The California Quarterly* devoted an entire issue to publication of Michael Wilson's screenplay of *Salt of the Earth* along with articles by its producer, Paul Jarrico, its director, Herbert Biberman, its actors, and members of the crew. The devotion of a full issue to the publication of a screenplay was defended by the editors on the grounds that the film was under attack and since it might not be seen, it should be read.[39] During the midforties, a journal called *Hollywood Quarterly* had been published by the University of California Press with the Hollywood Writers Mobilization. In the July 1946 number the motion picture advisory committee still lists Michael Wilson along with the later-to-be-blacklisted Abraham Polonsky. This was Hollywood, where film was an important medium for writers.[40] Some poets, like Thomas McGrath, even wrote for the movies. He wrote scripts for documentary movies in New York for a while, and one of those movies was presented at the World's Fair. He also worked for a time with film director Michael Cimino. During the years following World War II, Los Angeles was the place where poetry, art, music, and film made connections.

## Literary and Social Philosophies: *California Quarterly*

The editors of *The California Quarterly* had argued in 1952 that "the most enduring art is an imaginative re-creation of real life, it will reflect not only the complexity and contrariety of immediate experience, but also the simplicity underlying the turbulent history of men in whatever period, their unquenchable will to make a better life, and their capacity to progress toward it."[41] Commenting on the pall that the "clang of prison gates on Hollywood screenwriters" cast on writing in Los Angeles and literature in general, the editors express "an openness to new talent and to established writers" and present a basic humanistic attitude toward art founded in left-wing philosophies of equality of the races and the support of the oppressed. The editorial for the first issue of *Coastlines* expresses no such clearly articulated philosophy, even though some of its writers were a part of the same socially conscious tradition. That tradition, however, for the *Coastlines* poets did not simply reproduce the decidedly left ambience of *The California Quarterly*. Both journals were opposed to the disaffiliates, or beats. However, *The California Quarterly* was more in the tradition of those literary journals of the period with a definite and focused leftist orientation toward politics and social realism. The editors of *The California Quarterly* were older than those of *Coastlines* and were informed by their experience with the labor strife of the Great Depression. Quite a few of them were Marxist oriented, were blacklisted in the fifties, and came from radical-left backgrounds. The editors of *Coastlines*, on the other hand, were young children during the depression, had no formal affiliation with left-wing movements, and were part of the nondoctrinaire left. They focused on McCarthyism and antiwar movements and were influenced by many and varied literary movements and poets, the New Criticism of Cleanth Brooks and Robert Penn Warren, and poets like André Breton, Ezra Pound, and Wallace Stevens as well as Bertolt Brecht, Hart Crane, and Rainer Maria Rilke.

### Coastlines

The editors of *Coastlines* were in the unique position of being able to look back toward the thirties and forties through their relationship with older poets like Thomas McGrath, Don Gordon, William Pillin, and, briefly, Edwin Rolfe. But the journal was able to filter the literary experiments and social humanism of those earlier decades through the lens of the fifties and to look toward the future. As editor, Mel Weisburd was interested in incorporating the technology of the future into his thinking about poetry in the present. The fifties was a period marked by the red scare and a renewal of nativism. It was a time when UCLA was routinely referred to as "the little red school house." Literary coteries like the influential New Critics avoided the social and political and encouraged a revival of the metaphysical conceit and concentration on excitement in language. Just as some of the experimental poets of the thirties were able to combine the techniques of T. S. Eliot with their own radical politics, the poets of *Coastlines* were able to put together the new literary experiments with a humanistic philosophy that was not narrowly sectarian either to the left or right, but one that resisted both the constraints of the McCarthy period and the constricting social realism advocated by the left. At the same time those poets resisted the disengagement advocated and publicized by many of the beat poets. Thus *Coastlines* moved poetry in Los Angeles toward the sixties, pushing the individual into the midst of the social without the negativism that accompanied the beats and the disaffiliates, but also without the restrictive and sectarian quality of much of the earlier radical literature. The editors were interested in accessibility, surrealism, the metaphysical conceit, liveliness, relevance, and experimentation. They reacted to the stodginess and ingrown nature of both the academic journals and the left wing journals. They were, perhaps without knowing it, halfway between the editors of *The California Quarterly* and Allen Ginsberg.

Responding to a proposal to merge *The California Quarterly* and *Coastlines*, the editors argued that "there should be no attempt to integrate a political base to the magazine. The humanistic philosophies of both magazines are apparently compatible." But in conclusion, the editors say that their "attitude is aimed to improve the left wing press, and the right wing press for that matter, in order for literature to reassert its leadership for the society as a whole. It is our aim to write what is appropriate for the '50s, not for the '30s and '40s."[42] Thus it was difficult for the editors at the time to understand how Lawrence Lipton could call them "sectarian" or to describe them as a radical "movement." When asked about it today, *Coastlines'* first editors, Mel Weisburd and Gene Frumkin, attribute his remarks to Lipton's public relations campaign. After all, Lipton had been a part of *The California Quarterly,* where narrow political sectarianism had been more prevalent. The FBI had shown an interest in *The California Quarterly* and was not far away during the McCarthy years, when *Coastlines* was published. Among the other things that McGrath's second wife, the political activist, Alice McGrath, found in her FBI file was a copy of the first issue of *Coastlines,* its cover design, and the poem she had contributed.[43] Despite the FBI's records, the editors and poets of *Coastlines* were always much broader and more diverse than Lipton imagined.

The first *Coastlines* editorial said that "Los Angeles is undergoing a vast social revolution whose shape, though sometimes causing despair, is not yet altogether clear."[44] Whether or not that social revolution came to pass is up to historians to decide. Although not taking a doctrinaire political line, *Coastlines* would be a political and social forum for writers in Los Angeles. In the summer 1956 issue of the quarterly, Barding Dahl did a profile of Tijuana, quoting directly from news releases about the strikes, the infant mortality rates, and the tourists in Baja California, talking about its "clogged trickle-down economy."[45] In 1961 *Coastlines* published an Anti-War issue with everything from poems to interviews with the Peace Pilgrim. Gene Frumkin in his editorial on the fifth anniversary of the magazine declared, "As a literary magazine, our first duty is toward the things of the world, for without these there is no literature, no art—just desolation. Among these things are the timeless human problems, public and private. We must try to see them honestly, from the inside, in the material we publish and in our own commentaries."[46] Meanwhile the poets wrote about the city, around it, and inside of it, and poetry in Los Angeles began to rival and surpass what was going on in San Francisco to the north. The main emphasis of the editors throughout was the quality of the poetry. By 1973 an editor in Denmark had put the poetry of America into one volume called *San Francisco Renaissancen,* and though the anthology bore the title of the northern city, a section was reserved for what the editor called the "Los Angeles Gruppen." There was a place for Los Angeles between San Francisco and the Black Mountain Group.[47] At least in Denmark, Los Angeles was recognized as a place for poetry by the 1970s. In 1960 *Coastlines* produced its own Los Angeles poets issue, calling it "The Non-Existent City."[48] There most of the poets writing in Los Angeles at the time appeared. As early as 1958, when *Epos* published its "Poetry Los Angeles" special issue, William Pillin wrote in its introduction, "Actually the number of poets in Los Angeles area is as great or greater than in the northern city."[49] More poets were yet to come.

### After Coastlines

Poets in Los Angeles never stopped writing. Some of the poets in the *Coastlines* group disappeared into other parts of the country. Thomas McGrath eventually went to Minnesota, taking with him Alvaro Cardona-Hine and Stanley Kiesel for a time. Gene Frumkin went off to teach at the University of New Mexico. Years later he would find his fellow poets Alvaro and Stanley with him, along with newer and different poets like Paula Gunn Allen, who was commuting to teach at UCLA, settling into the sands of New Mexico. Meanwhile the first editor of *Coastlines,* Mel Weisburd, had left Los Angeles for Evanston, Illinois, in 1962, two years before *Coastlines* folded, only to return in 1966 and stay. Bert Meyers stayed, eventually gave up frame making, and entered academia, teaching at Pitzer College in Claremont, an hour or more commute from Los Angeles. There he created a following of young poets until his death. Gene Frumkin, before leaving Los Angeles, taught poetry workshops for UCLA Extension and left in his wake a group of dedicated younger poets like Robin Johnston and Helen Sorrels, the latter publishing in the last issues of *Coastlines.* For a time, before departing Los Angeles, Alvaro Cardona-Hine also taught workshops, leaving behind younger and newer poets like Holly Prado. William Pillin remained (along with his wife, Polia, who continued to make decorative pots) and collected new poets around him. Poetry workshops continued to create new poets and new groups. The world around *The California Quarterly* and *Coastlines* in the fifties belonged almost exclusively to men. But from the standpoint of poetry, with those journals, that was beginning to change. There have always been fine women poets in Los Angeles. They had often been pushed aside by the men who controlled the poetry scene, regarded as secondary or mostly decorative. Poets like Ann Stanford, Naomi Replansky, and Josephine Ain were representative of the women poets in Los Angeles. Ann Stanford reports in a diary entry for 1956 that when she suggested organizing a collection of woman poets to Yvor Winters, poet and professor of creative writing at Stanford, he found it an occasion for laughter.[50] In the fifties, as a young woman who had been writing poems for just a few years, I remember reading poems at the Pepper Tree Cafe near Los Angeles City College. A man from the audience came up to me and told me, in no uncertain terms, that women shouldn't write poems like that. They should write about kitchens and children. And I don't remember saying a word. But, of course, neither I nor any other woman poet of the period intended to take his advice. *Coastlines* was one of the journals in LA that helped change those attitudes.

Estelle Gershgoren in Barnsdall Park, the venue of many *Coastlines* poetry readings. Photo by Meyer Greenberg.

The poetry scene changed as Los Angeles changed. The editors of *Coastlines* may have been correct: Los Angeles was undergoing "a vast social revolution," which in 1955 was still in its infancy. Los Angeles became larger, more multicultural, more interracial, and despite, or perhaps because of, the first rebellion in Watts and the uprising associated with the beating of Rodney King, it is no longer the same city for poets that it was when the editors made that statement. The city had also extended its borders. Ann Stanford taught at a new campus of the California State University system in Northridge that opened in the late 1950s. Larry Spingarn taught at Valley College, and his Perivale Press published volumes of poetry. Presses publishing poetry sprang up all over. As I have already mentioned, while it was still functioning, *The California Quarterly* had a press and published Ed Rolfe's last book of poems. Papa Bach Books and the journal *Bachy* both came out of Papa Bach bookstore in the seventies. Larry Edmunds's bookstore on

Hollywood Boulevard had lent its imprint to *First Love and Other Poems,* by Edwin Rolfe, in 1951. Papa Bach bookstore is now gone, but Larry Edmunds is still there. *The California Quarterly* may have died in 1956, but *Coastlines* continued its tradition and lasted for over nine years, longer than most little magazines. The final issue in 1964 was titled "Los Angeles Writers." It never forgot its mission, to publish Los Angeles poets and to chronicle the literary world of a city. And it produced a whole bushel full of wonderful poems. The poetry lasts. Old issues might still be found on the shelves of used bookstores; volumes of poetry no longer at Papa Bach's are at the Midnight Special or Book Soup bookstores. And the old *Index of Little Magazines* still chronicles the poems and magazines that made Los Angeles a center of good poetry.

This anthology cannot possibly include all the poets who lived and wrote in Los Angeles in the years when *The California Quarterly* and *Coastlines* were publishing and in the time afterward, when many of these poets continued to write in Los Angeles. Even though some have since moved away from the city and some have died, their poems and their memory still resonate here. Although they never referred to themselves as a movement, they all inherited the tradition of social activism and tried, in the painful silence and paranoia that was nurtured by the McCarthy period and followed in its wake, to continue producing a poetry with a social conscience. The poems they wrote give the reader not only a good sense of the poetry that came out of the city, but an understanding of what writing and living in Los Angeles in those years meant to the poet.

■

Of the poets who lived and wrote in Los Angeles for a time, some are no longer with us. Dying youngest of all was Edwin Rolfe, who died in 1954 at the age of forty-five. Many said his experience in the Spanish Civil War pursued him to Los Angeles and finally claimed him. Thomas McGrath died in 1990, ending his struggle with the world and finishing his long poem, *Letter to an Imaginary Friend.* When Don Gordon died in 1989, neither he nor McGrath had allowed the House Un-American Activities Committee to stop them from living and writing their own honest poetry. And Henri Coulette, student of McGrath and member of the "Marsh Street Irregulars," who some years later taught at Los

Angeles State College (now California State University), died in 1988. Ann Stanford, having quietly taught and written poetry, is gone, along with Curtis Zahn, who passed away in the same year as McGrath. Bert Meyers, one of the young followers of McGrath, died young in 1979. Poets on the fringe of this group like Lawrence Lipton, who published poems in *The California Quarterly* and both published in and feuded with *Coastlines,* and Charles Bukowski, who contributed some of his earliest poems to *Coastlines* at the age of thirty-five, are now dead. Lawrence Spingarn, having outlived many of the older poets, died a few years ago in Los Angeles. Naomi Replansky is still alive and living in New York, having brought out *A Dangerous World: New and Selected Poems* in 1994. Josephine Ain still lives and writes in Los Angeles in the house where she and her husband Bob Chuey held poetry readings in the fifties and early sixties. And the younger poets, Gene Frumkin, Mel Weisburd, Sid Gershgoren, Estelle Gershgoren, Alvaro Cardona-Hine, and Stanley Kiesel, now live variously in New Mexico and California.

### Thomas McGrath

Of these poets, Thomas McGrath stood at the center of the community of poets in Los Angeles in the 1950s and of the community of poets that continued after his departure into the early 1970s. The 1962 issue of *Coastlines'* "Notes on Contributors" has this to say of McGrath: "Now living in North Dakota, THOMAS MCGRATH for a number of years was a leading influence on Los Angeles poetry. . . ."[51] And he continued to exercise that influence from a long distance. He was a poet whom the poetry establishment refused to acknowledge because he was antiestablishment, because he was a communist, or because he was irreverent.[52] Alice McGrath, his second wife, found the following statement about her former husband in her own FBI file: "Besides being a teacher, he claims to be a poet and a writer."[53] McGrath, despite the misgivings of the FBI, was definitely a major poet. Although McGrath was anthologized in the first Donald Hall, Robert Pack, and Louis Simpson anthology, *New Poets of England and America,* in 1957, in his lifetime his genius was not fully acknowledged. Philip Levine, writing his memories of McGrath, recalls reading "Ode for the American Dead in Korea" in that anthology and noting that it was the only poem on that war in the entire anthology.[54] The poem opens, "God love you now, if no one else will ever, / Corpse in the paddy, or dead on a high hill / In the fine and ruinous summer of a war / You never wanted . . ."[55] and is a signature for the kind of poetry McGrath was writing in *Figures from a Double World,* though he later retitled it in that collection "Ode for the American Dead in Asia."[56]

Thomas McGrath was born in 1916 near Sheldon, North Dakota, to Irish Catholic parents who were poor farmers. He studied for a while at Moorhead State University in Minnesota and then at the University of North Dakota, where he graduated with a B.A. in 1939. After graduation he was awarded a Rhodes scholarship. But first he would study at Louisiana State University for an M.A. in English, Louisiana State, where the Southern Agrarians, Cleanth Brooks, Alan Tate, and Robert Penn Warren, had their academic home. There he met Alan Swallow, who founded Swallow Press and published McGrath's first book of poems, *First Manifesto.* In New York City he worked at the Kearney Shipyards until 1942, when he entered the army. It wasn't until after he had fought in the Aleutians in World War II that he would pick up the Rhodes scholarship and study at New College, Oxford in the academic year of 1947–1948. Finishing everything but his thesis for the B.Litt. degree, he traveled to the south of France, wrote his first novel, *All but the Last,* published as *This Coffin Has No Handles,* and then returned to the United States. The way McGrath tells the story, his professors at New College were not receptive to his desire to write on either Christopher Caudwell or on Stephen Duck, the Thresher Poet. Stuffed shirts of Oxford academia, they thought he was joking. So he decided to give up the scholarship rather than stay on and deal with them.[57]

McGrath did not like to think of himself as an academic, even though he definitely had the tinge of one from his years at Louisiana State and Oxford. He had worked on the West Side docks of Manhattan in 1941 and had been a farmworker, logger, and shipyard welder, and though often referred to as a union organizer, what he really did was write for a union newspaper.[58] His poetry, which he began publishing in the forties against the background of the Depression and World War II, reflects both the traditions of English poetry going back to Marvell's "Garden," American poetry back to Whitman, and left-wing politics of all stripes from Agrarian populists to Wobblies to communists. The voices one hears in the *Letter to an Imaginary Friend* are the voices of ordinary people, voices from McGrath's own experience. He could write satiric, technically traditional poetry attacking the tradition from which he learned a good deal, and he could incorporate that tradition into the style he would eventually create as his own.

He was capable of employing political prophecy and the language of the Catholic Church (with which he grew up) to make his statement. In *Longshot O'Leary's Garland of Practical Poetry* he uses the traditional ballad, wryly observing the world somewhat in the manner of Brecht and the early Auden. And in a 1956 issue of *The California Quarterly* he could write the Kenneth Fearing-like poem "Mr. and Mrs. Foxbright X. Muddlehead, At Home," whose second stanza begins:

> Meanwhile Mrs. Muddlehead, erotic in blue jeans
> To Foxbright X, is answering three phones—
> The Book Club, Christ Inc., Rebels Ltd. . . .[59]

But unlike Fearing's work, the poem does not rely solely on satiric devices. There is a sense of lament about the world in which the Foxbrights live, and McGrath's images often come from the natural world outside the Foxbrights' living room. The poem ends, "To Duty. The goldfish swims. The moon / Provokes the bird. O lovers, pity, pity, / Pity them, who, in some lost summer, loved, were young."

McGrath's poems are informed with a political understanding and slang picked up from real experience on the waterfront, on farms, and on logging teams. All of that comes to make up his most serious contribution, *Letter to an Imaginary Friend,* its early parts published first in *Coastlines.* But McGrath was capable of writing the amusing poem as well, as in "All the Dead Poets," published in *The California Quarterly* in the 1950s.

> How vainly men themselves bestir
> For Bollingen or Pulitzer
> To raise, through ritual and rhyme
> Some Lazarus of an earlier time:
> The thought that died upon the page;
> The attitude stiffened with its age;
> The feeling, once appropriate
> Now, like honesty, out of date.[60]

And he could write the little poems with Zen-like power:

The crow:
Coat black as an undertaker's
His song . . .
Even darker
He wants to be judge
Of the dead![61]

His poems, large or small, always managed the striking image and the powerful emotion. And he could shock and surprise as well as move deeply, as he had in 1955 in "Ode to the American Dead in Korea," with lines like, "Your scarecrow valor grows / And rusts like early lilac while the rose / Blooms in Dakota and the stock exchange / Flowers. . . ."[62] He had a real pleasure in language, and that made him into a poet. In an interview with Reginald Gibbons and Terrence Des Pres (January 30–February 1, 1987) in answer to Gibbons's question, "What 'strategic' value do those poems have?" he says,

It doesn't matter to me if they don't have any! I want to take everything that comes. I'm very greedy in that way. This is 'Welcome,' which I wrote for Etheridge Knight:

One and one are two
Two and two are four
Pipsissewa and sassafras
Grow at my front door.

Now, that's not especially tactical or strategic or whatever, but I like it. . . . We ought to honor ourselves and the natural world and our fellows in every goddamn way we can![63]

Like Whitman, McGrath's poems contained multitudes, both great and small.

McGrath used to talk about two kinds of poetry, the tactical and the strategic. The first was a political poem that concentrated on an immediate event, and the second was one that might absorb the event into a larger consciousness of the political and personal. That is, of course, how Reginald Gibbons came to ask the question he did. When he wrote "McGrath on McGrath" for the 1982 issue of the *North Dakota Quarterly*, which was devoted to him, McGrath said, "All of us live twice at the same time—once uniquely and once representatively. I am interested in those moments when my unique personal life intersects with something bigger, when my small brief moment has a part in 'fabricating the legend.'"[64] And it was just that combination of the personal and the political he accomplished in his long poem *Letter to an Imaginary Friend* and that same combination he offered up to his students in Los Angeles.

McGrath's *Letter* is autobiographical, political, lyrical, and elegiac. The poem begins with Los Angeles, "'From here it is necessary to ship all bodies east.' / I am in Los Angeles at 2714 Marsh Street,"[65] but then goes backward toward North Dakota, childhood, and early adulthood. Its beginning is like a commentary on westward expansion and includes his own expansion both west and east. He is not only wryly comic about the world of HUAC, but painfully comic and serious about the growth of nuclear power in the Dakotas and elsewhere, Hiroshima, the Battle of Wounded Knee, and Vietnam, all of history compressing and expanding around the personal and the political. In this long poem he calls back the voice of Whitman and echoes the voices of workingmen and -women whom he had known. Whatever he is writing, whether in the long poem or in the lyrical satire, he is always deflating power, pulling down the high-handed authority from its seat in the hierarchy. It is that element of McGrath that Alice McGrath evokes in her poem "Longshot O'Leary Says It's Your Duty to be Full of Fury."

Thomas McGrath ended up in Los Angeles in 1950, making the full journey westward. He helped to edit *The California Quarterly* along with Lawrence Spingarn, Philip Stevenson, and Sonora Babb. There he was a friend to Edwin Rolfe, who lived his last years in Los Angeles after the Spanish Civil War. First he made a living by publishing stories under several different pseudonyms in a pulp western magazine. Then in 1951 McGrath was hired to teach at Los Angeles State College. But his teaching there was to be short-lived. In 1953 he was called before the House Un-American Activities Committee. He was what they called "uncooperative." He betrayed no one: not himself, not his friends. And for that he was fired from his job at Los Angeles State College in 1954 and forced

Clockwise from upper left: Keith Gundersson, Mel Weisburd, Gene Frumkin, Stanley Kiesel, 1969. Photographer unknown.

into various and sundry occupations, the flotsam and jetsam of the work world. Alice McGrath remembers that ironically one of those jobs was marking up prices of stocks at the stock market.[66] McGrath suffered from the loss of his teaching job in Los Angeles because he loved teaching and did it well. He taught in a secondary private school and wrote film and television scripts, but mostly he worked for a while at odd boring jobs. He was hired by a friend and wood sculptor, Stanley Schwartz, to work in his shop, Artforms, a place everyone called the "animal factory," where, at least, he was among like souls.[67] After a while McGrath returned east to Manhattan, teaching at C. W. Post College. But he didn't stay. In the 1960 special Los Angeles issue of *Coastlines* the editors remark in "Notes on Contributors" that "Thomas McGrath has returned to Los Angeles after a year in New York City which he says is God's country. But he's still not a believer."[68] Two years later he would go to North Dakota, where he spent five years teaching at

North Dakota State University in Fargo, and Moorhead State University in Minnesota, where he himself had studied, would also hire him to teach. He started teaching at Moorhead in 1969 and stayed until he retired in 1983.

At Los Angeles State College he was the teacher of many poets and faculty sponsor for the college literary journal *Statement,* edited by Mel Weisburd. There McGrath's writing classes gathered together a group of fine poets: Henri Coulette, Gene Frumkin, Stanley Kiesel, Mel Weisburd, Stanley Kurnik, and others. And at the fringes of the campus Bert Meyers, who was not a student, would learn from Tom and begin writing poems. Tom encouraged the young poets in his writing classes to publish in *The California Quarterly.* Eventually Gene Frumkin would join that journal's editorial board. And then McGrath would gather together poems with the help of his wife, Alice, in the hopes of starting still another magazine. Simultaneously Mel Weisburd and Gene Frumkin were trying to raise funds to start a magazine. In 1955 *Coastlines* was launched. Thomas McGrath, the poet and teacher who encouraged poets and poetry around him, was at the center of this activity. As Alice McGrath remembers it, "The people who are on the masthead there are all students or former students. It was just a homemade affair. . . ."[69]

McGrath wasn't happy in Los Angeles, mostly because he was dumped from a job he loved and attacked by the committee. In Part II of *Letter to an Imaginary Friend* he wrote: "Ten years—doing time in detention camps of the spirit, / Grounded in Twin Plague Harbor with comrades Flotsam and Jetsam: / Wreckage of sunken boats becalmed in the Horse Latitudes / Windless soul's doldrums Los Angeles Asia Minor of the intellect / Exile."[70] While he was in Los Angeles, he broke off with his first wife, Marian, married Alice, and divorced her also. He met his third wife, Eugenia, in New York in 1959; they were married in Los Angeles in 1960 and stayed for seven or eight months before McGrath left Los Angeles again. He had gathered his "Marsh Street Irregulars" around him and left a circle of poets to carry on his work. Gene Frumkin would later recall seeing Tom on Marsh Street with Mel Weisburd and others, and Tom himself would recall them with some pleasure in Part II of the *Letter,* "Inventing again the commune and round / Song gathering the Crazy Horse Resistance and Marsh St. Irregulars, / Building the Ramshackle Socialist Victory Party (RSVP) / And Union of Poets."[71] Frumkin would also remember Tom's founding of the open university, the Sequoia School, where young poets learned from both

Tom and once or twice from Edwin Rolfe.[72]

Although McGrath loved the idea of poetry and jazz and was briefly entranced with the West Coast Renaissance, he wanted more. For him all the social consciousness had disappeared as the beats developed. After he left Los Angeles, he wrote "After the Beat Generation" and published it in his own journal, *Crazy Horse*. The poem begins, "What! All those years after the Annunciation at Venice / And no revolution in sight?" and ends, "From enormous imaginary loud cap pistols of infinitely small caliber / Anarcholunacy—how long, in that light, to read what signposts? When all that glows with a gem-like flame is the end of Lipton's cigar."[73]

Thomas McGrath wanted more. He wanted revolution, but lacking that, he would take poetry as a way to be, at the least, a "witness to the times." His students gathered some of his poems in a collection protesting his firing at LA State. McGrath wrote in the preface to that collection, "The poet always has this task, it seems to me: to bear witness to the times; but now especially when the State is trying by corruption, coercion, and its own paltry terror to silence writers, or dupe them or convert them into the bird sanctuaries of public monuments— now especially the artist should be responsible to the world."[74]

### Edwin Rolfe

And the poets in this anthology heard that message and struggled to heed it throughout the difficult McCarthy years of the fifties and the Vietnam and antinuclear protests of the sixties. But before all of that, and not living to see much of that future, Edwin Rolfe had come to Los Angeles to write his last poems and, by his example and sometimes his tutelage, to teach those younger poets to write in the world that was to come. Born in 1909, he died of a heart attack at age forty-five in Los Angeles in 1954, but not before *The California Quarterly* had published some of his last poems in the journal and his last book, *Permit Me Refuge,* the one book that came out of its press. A few years before he died, he had produced *First Love and Other Poems* in 1951, published by himself on subscription but carrying the name of the Larry Edmunds Book Shop in Los Angeles and illustrated with drawings by Los Angeles artist Lia Nickson, wife of poet Richard Nickson.

Edwin Rolfe was born Solomon Fishman.[75] His parents were Russian immigrants and radicals. He himself was a member of the Communist Party and the Young Communist League and in his youth published stories, drawings, and poems in the *Daily Worker.* In 1933 Rolfe published poems in *We Gather Strength,* an anthology including poets like Sol Funaroff and Herman Spector, poets who also published in the *New Masses.* He was among those who published in *Dynamo* magazine, alongside Kenneth Fearing, Muriel Rukeyser, Sol Funaroff, William Pillin, and others. Some of the best and most experimental poetry of the Left was written in the 1930s by the Dynamo poets.[76] In 1936 Dynamo Press, a press organized by the experimental poets of the Dynamo group, published his first book of poems, *To My Contemporaries.* Those poems are the revolutionary poetry of the 1930s, very direct, what Thomas McGrath would later call tactical poems. Like the other talented poets of the Dynamo group, he could produce striking images: "This is the sixth winter: / this is the season of death / when lungs contract and the breath of homeless men / freezes on restaurant window panes. . . ."[77] In what was to become the turning point of his life and poetry, he went to Spain in 1937 and became editor of *Volunteer for Liberty,* published in English and representing the brigades of volunteers who came to fight against Franco in Spain. The most famous of these was the Abraham Lincoln Brigade. The journal and Rolfe went to Barcelona in March 1938, and in April he went to the front lines. He was part of the offensive at Ebro. Afterward Spain hovered over his poems like a lost mistress.

After coming to Los Angeles in the early forties, following his wife, Mary, he continued to write of Spain. Poems in *First Love and Other Poems* (1951) remembered the Spain that was always on his mind. "A City of Anguish" is a powerful poem about the war that is both narrative and guidebook for the reader to the battle in Madrid. Among the people who populate the poem is the "beggar" who "sings among the ruins." And he sings about the destruction of the city, "Trees became torches / lighting the avenues / where lovers huddled in terror / who would be lovers no longer."[78] The most famous poem in the volume, "Elegia," first published in Spanish in Mexico in 1949, is published here in English for the first time in *First Love and Other Poems.* It is a true love poem for the city: "Who is not true to you is false to every man / and he to whom your name means nothing never / loved / and they would use your flesh and blood again / as a whore for their wars and their wise investments." And he echoes the

Old Testament's promise to Jerusalem in his promise of memory and love: "I promise: Madrid, if I ever forget you / may my right hand lose its human cunning."[79] In his poem "Survival Is of the Essence" he opens, "Survival is of the essence, but only after submergence / completely in chaos, in combat as clearest eyes see it." The sentiment is in praise of those who died in Spain, but it contains Rolfe's efforts at his own survival until his untimely death. He submerged himself in the life and death around him.

Although Rolfe always wrote against the backdrop of Spain (his "first love"), during his time in Los Angeles he also wrote of the world around him. He wrote of Theodore Dreiser on his death and of Chaplin on his art. In his "Essay on Dreiser (1871–1945)" he is confounded by "what casts the malignant mote in mankind's eye / why did he gibe the English, bait the Jew?" and finds no answer. In his last stanza he answers much the way Auden answered the question for himself about Yeats, that "Dreiser / was what he was. No judgment is complete. / Much as we wish he had been surer, wiser, / we cannot change the fact. The man was great / in a way Americans uniquely understand / who know the uneven contours of their land." And he writes of Charlie Chaplin in "The Melancholy Comus," saying, "Mimic of the small dry crumbs of our joy / and the inedible shoestrings of our indignation / and the hurled pie of outrage and of hurt / and the sudden soul-washing sight of the lovely girl / he mirrors the true motions of our regimented lives, / our nerve-ends, our goose-stepping muscles. And he sings / our unwavering happiness and unchanging sorrows / and our loneliness from which there is no escape." No one, I think, has written better of Chaplin's gift.[80] But at the end of the poem we see why Rolfe is so pained. "And in anger I cry to those who will listen: What kind of world is this where he who speaks of man, / and man's sorrows, and man's deep longings, / and man's unmitigated loneliness, / is looked at as a leper." This is, of course, what Chaplin was always portraying in his films. But at the moment of Rolfe's death in 1954 *The California Quarterly*'s editors, announcing Rolfe's untimely death in the first paragraph of their notes, remark in the second paragraph that Los Angeles "is the only major city of the United States whose citizens have not yet been permitted to see Charlie Chaplin's masterpiece, *Limelight*."[81] Red-baiting and anticommunist feeling were particularly strong in Los Angeles, and theaters could not withstand such pressure.

Rolfe's poems were published in *The California Quarterly* before and after his death. He had contributed to the first issue of *Coastlines* but died before it was published. So many of his poems were about Spain that it is difficult not to think of him only as the poet of the Spanish Civil War, but he was capable of writing other poems with the same seriousness and wry humor about the world around him in Los Angeles. In the summer 1952 issue of *The California Quarterly* he published "two mysteries," a two-part piece describing a world like W. H. Auden's or Kenneth Fearing's. It opens, "The corpse is in the central square, in the spring sun. / The hilts of two jeweled daggers tremble on her breasts. / The blood is cold, corked, on her black and rigid nipples. / Her face in death is beautiful. She has obviously been raped." And Rolfe's poem "Idiot Joe Prays in Pershing Square / And Gets Hauled in for Vagrancy," a poem about the Los Angeles response to the world around it, appears in the first issue of *Coastlines.* The prayer, which is the poem itself, is a powerful and painful commentary on the world in which Rolfe lived his last years. "Let us praise, / while time to praise remains, / the simple bullet, / the antique ambuscade. . . ." In that issue *Coastlines* also published the poem "And if you don't see what you want / Ask for it," whose refrain is what had become the watchword of the McCarthy period: "If you don't like it here go back where / you came from!" The issue contains one of the most touching poems Rolfe ever wrote, called simply "Poem." It ends with these lines, "And loveless girls have called me love. / These do I most enshrine / because their simple longing builds / love amid lovelessness, and gilds / even the tarnished feelings till they shine—/ yes, theirs and mine." Rolfe's last volume of poems, *Permit Me Refuge,* whose working title had been *Words and Ballads,* was the first and only publication of *The California Quarterly.* It was there he published the fullest of his commentaries on the McCarthy hearings, "Ballad of the Noble Intentions." In the beginning of the poem the man vows to stay true to his ideals: "I'll answer with anger, go down, if I must, / hurling pearls of defiance." But in the end he says, "And there were some living men too that I named. / What harm could it do them, after two decades? / Besides, as I've reason to know, it was all—/ after all—in the records." Rolfe concludes with a real sense of betrayal and loss. "And that was your crime; in the noon of your life / you resigned from the living."[82]

Edwin Rolfe was buried in 1954 in the Hollywood cemetery on Santa Monica Boulevard, what Thomas McGrath would come to call "that bone yard on Santa

Monica." He left friends behind him like McGrath and Don Gordon. Don Gordon would write in his poem "The Middle Passage" of Rolfe as one who "lived among us by reflection for a time."[83] But Rolfe also left grateful and admiring younger poets whom he had touched briefly. On the cover of the 1954 *The California Quarterly*, Morton Dimondstein's woodcut of Rolfe has pride of place, and in the first pages there is a brief tribute by the editors. They write, "His best work speaks to us personally, helping us to remember not merely what we are but what we have yet to become."[84]

And that brief tribute is followed by "Elegy for a Soldier of the Spanish Civil War," by Eugene Frumkin. There Frumkin not only praises him as "a man with Spain / in his blood, a sane Quixote—" but celebrates him as a man who built poets as well as poems. "Apprentices of the craft of words, / Listened, the moon-webbed seas enfolded / The living, dying men and birds / Of barb-wire beaches, and held the shore / In gentle sway until my heart / Could feel the world at ebb no more, / But all, all caught in his calm art, / The seas of peace coming on, molded."[85] Those who survived him in Los Angeles remembered him with love. The dedication to the first issue of *Coastlines* is to Edwin Rolfe. The editors write, "Edwin Rolfe was a man whose friends and even brief acquaintances can find satisfaction in remembering."[86]

And he was remembered by many, though his poetry has not had the recognition it has always deserved. In "Bon Voyage" (published in *The California Quarterly* right after his death and the last poem in his posthumous volume *Permit Me Refuge*, a volume that takes its title from the first line of the poem) he asks for refuge in the memories of his friends. "My wake and rail attend you, welded and wed, / through the dark tunnels of the years ahead."[87] And many Los Angeles poets gave him "refuge" in his last years and in their own poems tried not to betray him through the different and difficult years that followed.

### Don Gordon

One of the close friends of Edwin Rolfe and of Thomas McGrath was Don Gordon, born in Connecticut but spending most of his life in Los Angeles. He wrote quiet poems quietly and without fanfare, but because his politics were suspect, he too was brought before the House Un-American Activities Committee. Donald Gordon was born on November 21, 1902, in Bridgeport, Connecticut, to

Sadie Levy Gordon, who was American born with English parents, and Morris J. Gordon, a Lithuanian who had immigrated to the United States as a boy. The memory of his father that Gordon carried with him into his poems was, "The thing I always remember about him was 'hiding in the attic till the Cossack terror passed.'"[88] In 1912 his family came to Los Angeles, where he lived out his life. He was with the first class that attended what was to become UCLA, then called the Southern Campus of the University of California. Getting his B.A. from Pomona College, he thought he would become a lawyer like his father but spent only a year at USC Law School. He married Henriette Goldfinger in 1931. During World War II he was a corporal in the California National Guard. He found various kinds of work and ended up first a law clerk and then a reader of books that might be made into scripts for movies. He worked for Republic Pictures, Universal, RKO, Paramount, and Metro-Goldwyn-Mayer. His mother and sister had both acted briefly in Hollywood. He became a part of that world, though he said that he never liked it. He did it to earn a living and write poems.[89]

Like Rolfe and McGrath, Gordon was a member of the Communist Party. He also belonged to the Friends of the Abraham Lincoln Brigade and the Hollywood Democratic Committee and was one of the organizers of the Screen Readers Guild. For the most part he lived in Los Angeles, but he spent 1927 in New York City, where he ran into anti-Semitism. As early as 1941 he was being fired from jobs because he was thought of as a "red." In 1947 the blacklist began officially with the accusations against the Hollywood Ten. In 1953 he was brought before the House Un-American Activities Committee and lost his job as a reader for the studios. As he tells it to his interviewer, Larry Ceplair, in the records of the UCLA Oral History Program, he refused to have a lawyer present after he saw how another attorney representing someone else was treated by the committee. He had been advised like the others to take the Fifth Amendment, and he took both the Fifth and the First.

After he lost his job at the studios, his wife, Henriette, began doing interior decorating. She knew and worked with well-known Los Angeles architect Rudolf Schindler. Gordon later found work in day care centers for the mentally ill. In the end, according to his own account, he found such labor more satisfying than working as a script reader.

And Don Gordon wrote poems all through those years. His first published book, *Statement,* came out in 1943 and the second, *Civilian Poems,* after the war, in 1946. During the 1950s he published *Displaced Persons* (1958) with Alan Swallow; his next books didn't come out until the late seventies and eighties. Asked about his early poems, he says that they were "about hunger marches, strikebreakers, things like that, real direct themes."[90] He had published poetry early on in the *New Masses.* Even in his later years Gordon's poems were always quietly commenting on the world around him.

Don Gordon came from the same poetic world as Edwin Rolfe and Thomas McGrath. In 1988, commenting on Los Angeles and the poets he remembered, he remarked, "Yes, poetry has been read a lot in Los Angeles, read aloud. And now there's more of it than ever being read, from what I've heard of it, of course it isn't very good."[91] Gordon recalled meeting with friends and reading poems. And among them he remembered Edwin Rolfe: "But no, not a group, but a few friends of mine would meet and read some stuff. One of them was a stool pigeon, and one was not . . . and one died. Eddie, Edwin Rolfe, fought in Spain. I don't know what he fought. He was there with the Lincoln Brigade. He died— here—I'm sure as a result of the Spanish Civil War.[92] Gordon, Rolfe, and McGrath were of the same generation and the same political sympathies.

Don Gordon didn't write manifestos nor comment much on his own or other people's poetry. He wrote poems and had strong convictions, which he quietly retained. About his poetry he said, "I wrote more like conversation, much as Jeffers [Robinson Jeffers] often did or Walt Whitman. But the influence I can't really trace, because I was never much influenced by anybody. Even my friend, Tom McGrath, who's the best poet I knew of—I liked his work, but he never influenced me at all. He was so unlike what I was doing. No, I suspect the whole political movement had a lot more to do with it than other poets, in the sense of the content, in the thirties."[93] What he says is true. His poems were not directly influenced by Thomas McGrath. But they share some of the same conversational tone of the poems of Auden and Spender and the same political content. In a poem with the title "Spain," he wrote, "Respect is not enough: we are the sons they / could not have, / The daughters they did not see. We inherit / graves and guns."[94] And of Lenin in a poem by that name he wrote: "He caught the first rumble / in the throat of time. / He said: act."[95] And about the "Unemployed" he wrote, "The man breathes (a reflex, a solemn irony), /

The tool was trimmed / To one edge and use: tool without task is / for the moment dead. / The man is in himself, the seed rattles in / the house unbroken."[96] Even in his early poems he had the quiet respect for the image and the quiet conversational tone, even when writing about revolution, Lenin hearing the "rumble in the throat of time," and an unemployed man whose breathing is the irony of his existence.

In 1952 in "the investigation," published in *The California Quarterly,* the investigators who are the powers of the city try to pull out the secret that no one knows: "The bailiff in his gray corner, / The gendarme at the door like a public statue, / cowled or bare, the committee is always in session: / tell / tell the secret / tell us before we go." The poem has obvious references to the McCarthy period: "On a morning of sun and birds he was heard / whistling in his house. / A whistle can be dangerous: it could lead / to singing. / The budget unbalanced the deficit mounting / what if they danced in the streets?"[97] The ordinary and the political come together in Don Gordon's poems.

In 1958 in *Displaced Persons* he writes not only of the displaced persons behind barbed wire in the opening poem, but of people everywhere displaced by war, exile, death, and neurosis. In "The Kimono" he writes about a woman after the atomic bomb has fallen on Hiroshima, "Ended the age of natural love as the / bomb bay opened / On the burned shoulders: she is now / the memorable one."[98] The woman is at the center of the poem even though she is now simply a newsreel. In "The Destroyers" he writes again about the atomic bomb, this time not of Hiroshima but of Bikini. "They blew up the island like a fish in a hole / in the killer Pacific: / That was the day the world embraced itself, / That was the day for lovers under the sign / of the active cloud."[99]

And he writes about dissent and deportation in two separate poems. "The Dissenter" opens with, "People will turn the middens we bequeath: / the hunters / or the hunted / express the age," and ends with, "When the air is burning and the cloud / signals unbearable change, / The dissenter is born alive on the edges / of the weather."[100] Here he combines the terror of the cloud and weather of the nuclear age with the isolation of the man who dissents. But he gives him life outside the terror of the times. And in "The Deportee" he ends with the lines, "tell him / in the country / of the blind / the one-eyed man / is always murdered."[101] Turning the proverb that says, *En la tierra de los ciegos, el hombre con un ojo es rey* ("In the land of the blind the one-eyed man is king"), Gordon expresses the reality of the dissenter who cannot be tolerated by the blind society from which he has to be deported. And the blindness of the city is expressed in that poem by the line, "The metropolis closes its concrete eyes." Not only do the buildings refuse to see, but their concrete expresses the absolute hardness and coldness of their sightlessness.

The generation of the fifties had been dubbed "the silent generation," and Gordon used that phrase to title a poem about the young around him that ends, "A country of silent youth / Is an old man whose sons / Have not come back from war, / An old man dry as an insect / At the end of the napalm summer."[102] The young in his poem are without language and the old are those who remember the deaths in the war, "the stones of the foreign graves." And Gordon could write beautifully about the old and their loss in "The Middle Passage." He writes, "My mother and father went too often to funerals; / Their lives seemed bleak to be so fond of ceremony. / Later I knew they simply went to say goodbye: / When they were old I saw they had no friends." But this is only a preface to his own losses, "the physician, my friend back from war / With the unexploded mine in his breast," or about Edwin Rolfe, "the poet, his sun blackened in Spain, / who lived among us by reflection for a time."[103] The quietness and sureness of Gordon's poems is revealed most clearly in the image he uses at the end of this poem. "You are not the axle on which the world turns / Abstract yourself like a number from the scene, / The landscape with its motions will not quiver." Don Gordon was able to both abstract himself and bear witness to what he saw and at the same time put his voice securely inside the poem so that we would never forget what he said. Although he is right that his poems are conversational, they are more like Muriel Rukeyser and W. H. Auden than Robinson Jeffers, probably because those poets shared Gordon's political landscape.

### Naomi Replansky

Another poet who shared that same political milieu and wrote for *The California Quarterly* and for *Coastlines* was Naomi Replansky. She had published a volume of poetry titled *Ring Song* in 1952. Her great talent lay in an ability to compress whole worlds into a couplet. *Ring Song,* published by Scribners, was nominated for a National Book Award. But soon the book would be out of print, and for many years this brilliant poet would be forgotten by all but a few. She had begun writing very young, at the age of ten, and had been first published in *Poetry* at the age of sixteen. By 1988 she would bring out a chapbook titled *Twenty-One Poems: Old and New,* and forty years after *Ring Song* she would bring out *A Dangerous World: New and Selected Poems, 1934–1994,* the title taken from lines by William Blake, which she quotes as an epigram. "My mother groan'd! my father wept. / Into the dangerous world I leapt." If Replansky can be compared to any poet in the power of her lines, it is definitely William Blake. She herself counts him among her major influences as well as George Herbert, African American spirituals, nursery rhymes, and work songs, Emily Dickinson, and Japanese poetry.

Replansky's poetry is spare and precise, packing tremendous power into a single line or a couplet. She published some poems in *The California Quarterly* that appeared in *Ring Song* and contributed to the first issue of *Coastlines.* In *The California Quarterly* she published a free-verse poem titled "Housing Shortage." The poem relies on the central metaphor of living in cramped spaces. She creates the image of the body spreading itself out, taking up room to breathe and dreaming of even larger spaces. It begins, "I tried to live small. / I took a narrow bed," and ends with her dream of "a landscape, unbounded / And vast in abandon."[104] The first stanza minces along in its smallness, while the last spreads out into endless space. But all along in the poem, as her lungs are expanding and taking in air and the body's needs are multiplying, the poet is aware of the other person and her needs. The poem ends with, "You too dreaming the same."

Replansky often centers her poems in the "I," but like William Blake, the "I" of the poem always comes up against the world outside. The best example of this is "Ring Song," the title poem for her first book and one of the most Blakean of her poems. Her couplets here work wonders by connecting the ideas through the rhymes. "When the thorn brings no reprieve / I rise and live, I rise and live." The reprieve itself should allow for living, but in this couplet the living itself comes despite the failure of reprieve. After offering herself for sale, "Nude in the marketplace," she concludes, "When I stand and am not sold / I build a fire against the cold."[105] The final couplet of the poem returns to the joy that has been lost in the first. Replansky is a careful craftsman. She always chooses the precisely right word and never says more than she needs to. What she says either startles or pains, but in the end the poem always gives pleasure.

The poem she published in the first issue of *Coastlines,* "Night Prayer for Various Trades," reflects her compassion for those who do the work of the world. In many of her poems she writes about the hardworking("Factory Poem") or about the homeless ("The Street") with compassion and true empathy. And there is the poem about the Holocaust, "The Six Million," or the poem about the bombing of Hiroshima. The poems are always about living, suffering, and the fragile individual surviving in the world around her with determination.

Naomi Replansky had spent a year in Los Angeles in 1946 and 1947. During that time she worked with Bertolt Brecht, translating some lyric poems. Between 1948 and 1951 she lived in Paris. When she returned to New York for a visit in 1952, her passport was lifted. It was not returned to her until years later. She had no idea what specific reason there was, if any, for such an action. She had been, in her teens and twenties, a member of the Young Communist League. And she had been associated with people like Bertolt Brecht and others on the left and, when asked, she says that such people were "persona non grata to the authorities."[106] After her book *Ring Song* was accepted by Scribners, she left New York for Los Angeles.

Replansky was on the periphery of the group around Tom McGrath. She had met McGrath first in New York, and she visited Tom and Alice in Los Angeles. There she met poets Bert Meyers, Gene Frumkin, Mel Weisburd, and Alvaro Cardona-Hine. She lived in Venice and found it difficult to drive. At first she was working full time in a machine shop, and then she went to UCLA to study and worked part time at General Telephone in Santa Monica. But the poets around *The California Quarterly* and *Coastlines* remembered Naomi Replansky and counted her among their number.

### William Pillin

Among the poets who had begun writing in the 1930s who contributed to *Coastlines* was William Pillin. Like Edwin Rolfe, between 1934 and 1936 Pillin had been a contributor to *Dynamo* magazine. Pillin was born in 1910 in Alexandrowsk, Ukraine. He came to the United States like many others from the Jewish villages of Russia, escaping hunger, disease, and pogroms. He was fourteen years old. In 1917 his family moved to Chicago, where his father worked as a pharmacist, and Pillin worked with him. While in Chicago he became acquainted with novelists Richard Wright and Nelson Algren. By the time he was nineteen, he was married to Polia, who made her living as a milliner but was studying painting and sculpture. She was eventually to produce wonderful pots, prints, and paintings, and the two of them would live in front of their studio on Hollywood Boulevard in Los Angeles and make pots and poetry. In the "Notes on Contributors" to the spring 1960 issue of *Coastlines* the editors wrote, "WILLIAM PILLIN also went hungry before he discovered that his wife, Polia, had a gift for making ceramics. Now he is chief kiln-lighter and supervisor of shipping. Will soon open a gallery featuring ceramics and poetry."[107] The poetry, of course, was not sold for enough money to keep the family alive. The ceramics were.

William Pillin's poetry came out of the world of the Jewish villages in Russia but also out of the American depression. He shared the interest in experimental poetry that the Dynamo poets had and much of their radical politics. When in Los Angeles, the story goes, he threw the Southerner James Dickey out of his house for making a racist remark.[108] Poets in Los Angeles remember long political discussions at his house as well as poetry. But his poetry was primarily lyrical. One of his poems, titled "Fugue," published in *Coastlines* in its summer 1956 issue, uses the mechanical image of the natural, an effect that was so popular among the Dynamo poets. "Under the plastic wheel / a metal tiger purrs; / explosive teeth devour / the wavering wind and thrill / with lubricated grace" describes a drive out into the countryside. But it's not a poem about a summer's drive that is purely rose colored. Pillin writes, "and we cannot escape / accumulated trash; / garages, tourist shacks / follow our tracks."[109] He would publish a poem in *Coastlines* about the way he kept the Jewish sabbath secularly, noting: "I can spare but a few hours / for this evening's silence / as I can't afford a whole day without labor."[110] He would also publish poems about the world at the beach in "Ocean Park," calling up the usual bevy of demons and purveyors of magic that he liked to use in his poems culled from Jewish and Russian folk traditions and any others he could find.[111]

Although he didn't contribute a poem to the Anti-War issue of *Coastlines*, one of his most moving poems, "Miserere," published in 1958 in the special Los Angeles issue of *Epos*, is about the Holocaust. He writes, "I will spare my tears for the / loudmouthed unhappy conniving / Jews / the usurious lenders / tuberculous hunchbacked / scum of the ghettos (the sweeping of Europe)," and the last lines, "I want them / back as they were, piteous, ignoble, / instead of these gray ashes / that like a winding sheet settles on shivering Europe."[112] And in his poems he was always trying to fight a war against the soul-destroying world of the bosses, as in "Prelude and Dance on Quitting a Rotten Job," which begins, "The hours of paid labor involve / an absolute smile of the Boss / on pins, pads, paper clips; / fate hanging on nimble telephone wit."[113] Pillin was both seriously lyrical and wonderfully inventive. He had become a figure in Los Angeles poetry among the young poets. He was probably the last of the poets who came directly out of the radical poetic tradition of the 1930s. But that tradition was carried on among the younger poets through Thomas McGrath's teaching. McGrath encouraged young poets to read Christopher Caudwell, who said that the best of capitalism would shape the Marxist worldview. And he particularly tried to encourage those poets to make socially conscious poetry lively and exciting.[114] Many of them did.

### Henri Coulette

The other writers who congregated around *The California Quarterly* and *Coastlines* may have been less radical because they were younger and not part of the thirties tradition that had shaped Rolfe, McGrath, Gordon, Replansky, and Pillin. But they never rejected the primary obligation of a humanistic commitment to poetry as the voice of the social world. At a time when much poetry was becoming solipsistic, they rejected the commitment to a personal vision that ignored the sufferings of others. Henri Coulette, born eleven years later than McGrath in 1927 and dead in 1988, two years before McGrath's own death, may not have wholly shared McGrath's radical politics and wrote poetry mainstream enough to allow him to publish in *The New Yorker.* But his early poems in *The California Quarterly* are centered in the world of ordinary working people; his images come from the idea of revolution. In "Migration," published in the winter 1952 issue of *The California Quarterly,* he writes, "Fatigued, the workers lie in coffin rooms / And listen while the birds parade the streets / Of midnight sky, and mingle sweat / And grief with contemplation of time."[115] The workers in their tiny rooms that enclose them like coffins listen to the migrating birds. And later in the poem he talks about the poor and a kind of migration of revolution,

"And measured, too, these dreams, for they will end / With poor men rising, leaving poverty / Wrapped in the wilted winding sheet of their / Long suffering innocence, and rising. . . ."[116] Coulette takes the migration of birds in autumn and makes it into a poem of revolution in "the factory towns." This is surely a radical poem of the kind that Sol Funaroff or Muriel Rukeyser might have written for *Dynamo* in the mid-1930s.

But Coulette could also compose poetry on more conventional subjects. When he published *Wars of the Secret Agents,* he was writing about a world in which no one could find the enemy, not a world in which the enemy was so clearly defined by the roll of dollar bills in his hand and his gold stickpin. Because Thomas McGrath did not interfere directly in the poetry of his students, a poet like Coulette could develop and learn from McGrath but at the same time write a very different kind of poetry.

And there were McGrath's other students who made up a community of poets in Los Angeles that continued even after his departure from the city. When *Coastlines* published its final issue in 1964, Mel Weisburd, its first editor and a student of McGrath, wrote, "We're scared as hell at publishing our real feelings, our real beliefs. That's the real problem. *Coastlines* has always wanted to, but was never willing to truly represent itself."[117] The political paranoia and repression of the fifties extended for most of these poets well into the 1960s. Despite McCarthy's growing disrepute, McCarthyism had already done its work. Although the mainstream news media has always pictured the 1960s as the time of cultural revolution, it was always a revolution for personal freedom, not for responsibility and social and economic change. It reflected the energies of people like Allen Ginsberg, Gregory Corso, Charles Bukowski, and Lawrence Lipton, who were interested in the sexual revolution or the private transformation of the self and rejected the politics of one of its own progenitors, Kenneth Rexroth, who had been a leftist in his time.[118] Poets like Thomas McGrath were more often than not interested in the political and social revolution that would change the conditions of life for working people. His students who founded *Coastlines* took from McGrath the belief in personal manifestos, which, because they were uniquely personal, must therefore be radical. They were what at the time was described as "progressives," nondoctrinaire leftists or "liberal" Democrats. Articles appeared in *Coastlines* about Tijuana and the conditions there, about Faulkner's racism, and about nuclear war. The poets and editors were not, as Lawrence Lipton labeled them, narrowly sectarian, but they never gave up their obligation to write about the conditions of the world around them. *Coastlines,* after all, not only occasionally published Lawrence Lipton, but published Judson Jerome, Eve Merriam, George Abbe, and Kenneth Rexroth as well as translations of Rimbaud, Neruda, and Miguel Hernandez. Even when they were not writing about radical politics, they revealed in their poetry the feelings of pain and loss experienced by those around them. Mel Weisburd's reflections after the demise of *Coastlines* demonstrate how difficult it was to write social poetry of any kind in the repressive atmosphere of the fifties and sixties.

Much of the early poetry of the older poets, the poems of McGrath, Replansky, Gordon, and Rolfe, had been influenced by the experimental poets of the 1930s, Kenneth Fearing, Sol Funaroff, or Muriel Rukeyser. For example, Curtis Zahn, who was one of the older poets, wrote in a satiric style much influenced by Kenneth Fearing and very much political in orientation. Zahn himself was a pacifist, a conscientious objector who had been imprisoned for his refusal to serve in the armed forces. Some of the thirties tradition remained in the poems from *The California Quarterly* and in occasional poems published in *Coastlines.* But Thomas McGrath's students would reflect their world differently.

### Bert Meyers

Bert Meyers, a young disciple of McGrath, was born in 1928 in Los Angeles and died there at the age of fifty-one in 1979. He grew up in Los Angeles and was mostly self-educated. First working as a housepainter and then as a picture framer and gilder, he eventually entered academia as an instructor at Pitzer College. He had become a graduate student and had finished everything but the dissertation for the Ph.D., even though he had never completed a bachelor's degree at any university.[119] In fact, he had never received his high school diploma from Marshall High School in Los Angeles. Meyers had been one of McGrath's "Marsh Street Irregulars." From the very beginning he published in *The California Quarterly* and then in *Coastlines.* Kenneth Funsten begins a series of articles on Los Angeles poets with one about Bert Meyers. He refers to him as having been "accepted into that group of poets known as the 'Coastliners,' who then gathered around Thomas McGrath, teaching at Cal State L.A., and

Gene Frumkin, an editor of *Coastlines* magazine."[120] Meyers married Odette Miller, a survivor of the Holocaust, in 1957. In 1960 his first book of poems, *Early Rain*, was published by Alan Swallow. His second book, *The Dark Birds*, was put out by Doubleday. But despite an Ingrim Merrill Foundation award given to him in 1964 and again in 1967, Bert Meyers's poetry was little known in his lifetime. Late in his life Marianne Moore praised his poetry. By the end of his life Denise Levertov had also discovered the beauty of his work, and after his death his students, poets themselves, attempted to spread the word about just how good his poetry was. In the 1954 issue of *The California Quarterly*, Meyers published an early poem titled "The Cougar Has Been Shot." In it the "weekend hunters" shoot a cougar and the whole landscape is "brought to life by their guns." But as Meyers tells us, "the weekend hunters worry: such mountain breaking, making passion, / in a living thing is dangerous."[121] Through the image of the hunters against nature, Meyers evokes the world of the hunted as a world where life itself and its passions are dangerous. Although the poem itself is not political, it mirrors the world of 1954 and the McCarthy period, albeit indirectly, and it reflects the contrast between the human passions of these poets and the colder world in which they lived. And in the next 1954 issue of *The California Quarterly*, dedicated to Edwin Rolfe, Meyers has the poem "Pity the Child," in which a child loses hope and love in an uncaring world where we, "Blame the weather that keeps/letters of love unsent," and another where the man and woman who make love and explore each other's bodies before they marry "wear each other's breath / and only fear love's death."[122] Early on Bert Meyers wrote poems that were close to the bone, tightly woven, and exact in their language.

In a 1962 issue of *Coastlines*, Gene Frumkin reviewed Bert Meyers's first book, *Early Rain*. Frumkin says about Meyers's poetry in general, "Bert Meyers's poetry is founded on the daily reality and makes no effort to soften the grimness."[123] And later in the review he quotes the poem "In the Alley," which has these lines in its third stanza: "Later, a man / gray as gravel, / comes up the alley. / At a garbage can / an alarm of flies / goes off in his face." About this poem Frumkin says, "This is a social poem in the best sense, one that pays heed to the sound and language of the 'content.' It is a poem of surprises, the kind that stun us with their truth."[124] The editors of *Coastlines*, like their teacher Thomas McGrath, were always looking for this kind of poetry.

And Meyers could compose the directly political poem also, using much the same techniques as in his other poems. Writing in "I Dreamed," published in the Anti-War issue of *Coastlines,* where he portrays a demonstration for peace, he says, "At last the generals / were beaten with ploughshares / and you and I became / two hammers with one blow that builds."[125] Although those who wrote about Meyers after his death often talked about the closeness of his imagery, the tightness of his poems, and his attention to the ordinary, they often saw him as not connected to the political world around him. This is far from the truth. Meyers was always writing political poetry about people who work for a living, pay rent, and try to get by in a world that uses them up. In his poem "L.A." he describes the city as "the place that boredom built. / Freeways, condominiums, malls, / where the cartons of trash and diamonds / and ideologies / are opened, used, dumped into the sea." What was particularly important to Bert Meyers as a poet was the precise image, the only one that could describe the world he saw before him, the thing itself. And his content was about the ordinary, the ordinary suffering of ordinary people in poems like "Paris" or "Old." Denise Levertov remarks that "he did not like 'engaged' poetry, feeling that it violated what he believed was the essentially evocative and nondidactic nature of the art. . . ."[126] But even she can see political statement in poems like "Arc de Triomphe" and "Saigon." I think, in the end, what one can observe in each of Meyers's poems is the statement of the political become personal. Lines like, "Their smiles are gun belts, / their brains, nuclear clouds; / and they speak a dialect / that sounds like money . . ." are certainly political, but even lines that do not at first seem to be about politics are about the politics of living, for the poor, the homeless, the old, the worker. Certainly the poetry he wrote for *Coastlines* was a socially conscious poetry of the best kind. Meyers is a good representative of the poetry of the group around *Coastlines,* a poetry that was able to combine a social consciousness with an imagistic approach to the poem and to make the personal political and the political personal.

## Editors of *Coastlines:* Mel Weisburd and Gene Frumkin

### Mel Weisburd

The editors of *Coastlines,* Mel Weisburd and Eugene Frumkin, were students of Tom McGrath and were influenced by the tradition of social relevance that he carried with him as well as by his notions of poetry as the language of surprise. They emphasized excitement of language in the poetry they published and in the poetry they wrote. By 1963 Barding Dahl and Alexandra Garrett were the editors, and Barbara Harris took over as poetry editor. From the beginning Mel Weisburd was the editor, with associate editors like Gene Frumkin and Carol Zimmerman. Not until the spring/summer issue of that first year was there a poetry editor, and that seat was occupied variously by Gene Frumkin, Mel Weisburd, Stanley Kiesel, and Alvaro Cardona-Hine. Mel Weisburd would write poems for *Coastlines* during his tenure as editor and even after he had given over the journal to Barding Dahl and Alexandra Garrett. During his time as editor he was the main organizer of materials, in charge of managing the daily workings of the magazine as well as writing editorials and special articles. Although he would not publish any collection of poems during that time or later because he was involved in working full time for the Los Angeles County Air Pollution Control District (the forerunner of the Air Quality Management Bureau) and would later open an environmental protection company, he continued to write. He published early on in *The California Quarterly* in its issue devoted to Edwin Rolfe. In his poem "My Father" he writes lovingly about his father's old age and his body corroded by labor and love. "My father, a laborer, forty eight, divorced three times, timid / And always tired, comes home with the furnace blast in his ears / And speaks in an empty egoless voice."[127] Weisburd's image of his father's "empty, egoless voice" is the image of the worker worn down by his life, and the "furnace blast in his ears" reminds one that his labor has taken over his body. Weisburd was always interested in machines and predicted to McGrath in those years that computers would reshape the world. He was able to write a poem like "Descendant Robot" in the first issue of *Coastlines* that described the machine as human rather than the human as machine. It begins, "The trumpet of his voice / Bleeds in its rusted organ."[128] He could also write in "The American" about the American destiny and the exhaustion of the American reality: "Then one day arrested in his vagrant dream, while / A thousand-eyed facelessness gaveled for order / In the electric darkness of its justice, / Scanning the withered truths scarred along his body."[129] And he could examine time and the image of space ending his poem "The Sixth and the Seventh Sense of Men" with these lines about the atomic bomb: "In all of nature but that gross stupidity. / Blundering mushrooms rising from the missile slopes. / In the mass acres of universal death."[130] He could write about the natural world and poetry and his neighbors in "A Crow Black With Purpose," hoping that in some future world, "Before it is too late—in time, when thought will / Set the thinking / Mass ablaze, . . . we will break our appetite with our will." In the Anti-War issue of *Coastlines,* Weisburd contributed "Firestorm," a piece from a novel in progress about the World War II bombing of Hamburg.

By the final issue of the journal Mel Weisburd had moved to Evanston, Chicago, where he remained between 1962 and 1966. From there he sent in his final poem and his final message to *Coastlines.* The poem, "Report from Evanston," says, "Cities are rarely made from joy / And nothing lasts," but continues, "On quite an ordinary day / The Mayor lights a candle for peace / And nobody resists."[131] Mel Weisburd had started *Coastlines* in his days as a young poet, and had moved on to publish poems in other journals. It was mainly through his effort and the effort of Gene Frumkin that the journal continued as long as it did. Even when they had to give it over to Barding Dahl and Alexandra Garrett, they would keep in touch.

### Gene Frumkin

Gene (Eugene) Frumkin began writing while studying with Thomas McGrath at Los Angeles State College. By 1963 he had published a volume of poems, *The Hawk and the Lizard,* with Swallow paperbacks. He joined the writers who contributed to *The California Quarterly* and helped found *Coastlines* with Mel Weisburd. He had received a degree in English from UCLA and had been editor of the university newspaper *The Daily Bruin.* His editorship had occurred at an interesting and decisive moment for that student newspaper. The paper was dismembered by the university administration because it had attacked the racism in the campus fraternities. The editors held a very public funeral for the newspaper as a form of protest. Gene Frumkin was certainly equipped to become one of the editors of another socially conscious publication, this time a literary journal. And it was Gene Frumkin who eventually helped get some of the early issues of *Coastlines* printed at his place of employment, the Fashion Press. He was always a socially conscious poet, low-key, very much more in the mold of Don Gordon than of his teacher, Thomas McGrath. He pushed for socially conscious and lively poetry at *Coastlines* and felt that he had learned much from the earlier poets at *The California Quarterly.*

In *The California Quarterly* he himself had published poems that had in them a sense of humanity and compassion for the individual sufferer of circumstance. In "The Waiting Room in the County Hospital," published in the 1954 issue of *The California Quarterly,* he writes, "No microscope sees / These poor shuttling in the culture / Of the charity-raw room, / No stethoscope hears / The cyclone of hearts in the silence," about the patients in the clinic of the county hospital. It is a poem that might be written today about Los Angeles County Hospital, but its concluding stanza expresses not only compassion, but a hope for the future. "Then, doctor, do as you must. / Your love, not in teaspoons / At appointed hours, but always, / By the whole bottle, must tonic / All these patients, who wait / In the chemical air for the day / When a better solution prospers."[132] In the same issue of the quarterly, Frumkin published "Elegy for a Tailor" about hard work. It opens with an image of the narrow world of the tailor: "Myopic old tailor, you poked at life / As at the eye of a needle," and goes on to describe the ever present work of the tailor even in sleep: "While your face hung limp in Cyclopean sleep. / The twelve lizard hours you daily pursued / In sewing circles tired you. . . ." The tailor's one-eyed, "Cyclopean sleep" was never satisfying but always pursued by the "humid clouds of press / machines" and the "sweat of walls." But it is the last line of this poem that tears at the reader because it is not about the tailor, but the poet: "You are the chalk that scrapes my mind's gray slate."[133]

For the most part Frumkin's poetry is personal and compassionate. But he can also be directly political in his focus. The poem he published in the Anti-War issue of *Coastlines* in 1962 is a directly political statement about apathy and suffering. The second stanza of "Men Fail in Communion" is most effective. "A man starves within sight of flowers. / A king lies drunk on the mountain. The black man, / darkest leaf on Alabama's autumn tree. / Whisper it: Men fail in communion."[134] Frumkin's statements are direct and to the point, his images always apt. The lynched black man in Alabama becomes a dark leaf on a tree, the darkest.

Frumkin was also both an editor and a poet, and in "The Debt" he used a poem to make an editorial statement while keeping the poem true to itself. The poem is about Cuba, about Castro and the American embargo. But it is not a tactical poem that directly addresses the political issue. It is a poem that describes the suffering of the Cuban people. At the end he makes the connection between the political and the personal that makes the poem so powerful. "People, ploughed like soil. / Because they are the hands of my clock / I must wear their clothes, / eat their food, think their thoughts / or I will forget /—forget I owe them doeskin slippers, / grapes and apples, cigars, wine, poems."[135] In fact, Frumkin, making an editorial comment on the poem, states, "This poem of mine is an attempt to make an important event of our time a personal matter."[136] Frumkin was always a poet, but he and Weisburd never forgot their editorial functions on *Coastline*. He wrote in "Speech to the Silent Generation" in *The Hawk and the Lizard* about the danger the generation of the fifties felt about speaking out. "We are china dolls / who stand upon our mantels quietly, / not daring to oppose what we dare not see."[137] Yet he himself continues to write about political events and personal suffering. In "Budapest, October 1956" he writes "Red October 1917 / meets its progeny in this October. . . ."[138] And Frumkin could always create the image that seemed to fit into the ordinary proselike line. For example, in "The Hawk and the Lizard" he writes, "Attacking heaven, the hawk loses his prey, / melting into the sun, / at first a sparrow then a midge / and finally the wind. / Heaven becomes / a mountainous solitude."[139] The hawk's disappearance into the landscape becomes a metaphor for the great solitude of nature, and it all seems so natural that we hardly notice it.

Gene Frumkin was one of the associate editors of *Coastlines* with Mel Weisburd from its beginning in 1955 and became the editor from the winter 1957–58 issue until the 1963 issue, when Barding Dahl and Alexandra Garrett took over. His voice was a strong one for poetry with a social conscience, and he himself practiced the art in his poetry, his editorials, and his reviews.

Alvaro Cardona-Hine, Los Angeles, 1969. Photograph by Layle Silbert.

### Alvaro Cardona-Hine:
### Occasional Poetry Editor of Coastlines

Alvaro Cardona-Hine, who himself became one of the "Marsh Street Irregulars," returned to Los Angeles in 1957 and was one of the group that consisted of McGrath, Meyers, Frumkin, Weisburd, and many others. He was born in Costa Rica, his brother a well-known Costa Rican poet who subsequently moved to Mexico. Cardona-Hine was involved in painting as well as poetry. At present he runs a gallery and continues painting and writing poems in New Mexico. In the late fifties his poetry was much influenced by the Japanese haiku as well as by Pablo Neruda and García Lorca. Like Meyers, he was able to create the single image that startled, but his poems were more fluid and tended to be more descriptive. His first book of poems, published by Swallow, was a collection of haiku, *The Gathering Wave*. But he could also write the politically conscious poem and did so for *Coastlines* in its Anti-War issue. The poem, "Doomsday and Components," begins, "there is more than one skeletal eruption / one brutal eyelash tattooed upon our sight / while hunger stretches off in vast horizons / this fat and blinded land prepares for war."[140] Hunger becomes vast like the land and the land itself is fat while the people starve. He continues to describe "the cross" that children learn to make as a letter, the cross that sits on tombstones where the war dead lie. In the Los Angeles issue of *Coastlines* he writes a poem on a "sudden death" called "Vindication" describing the way death turns life upside down: "for death is a kingdom in reverse / or a mirror where you part your hair to the right."[141] Cardona-Hine at times also acted as a translator. He published a translation of a Miguel Hernandez poem in *Coastlines,* and his poems in *Flesh of Utopia* (a poem by that title appeared first in *Coastlines*) were much influenced by the South American poets. In the year after the demise of *Coastlines* he was the editor, along with Stanley Kurnik, of a special issue of *Ante* magazine in Los Angeles in 1965 that published *Coastlines* poets, and he would, some years later in the seventies, write about Los Angeles poetry in *Bachy* magazine.

### Still Other Poets

Other poets populated the pages of *The California Quarterly* and *Coastlines.* Like Gene Frumkin and Mel Weisburd, Stanley Kiesel was a poet who published in *The California Quarterly* and then in *Coastlines.* He was part of the group that congregated around Thomas McGrath. He would teach kindergarten and publish wryly humorous poems about the children he saw every day. Lawrence Spingarn, an older poet, was one of the founders and early editors of *The California Quarterly* whose poems could be found in the pages of *Coastlines* up to its end. Curtis Zahn was an outspoken member of the *Coastlines* fraternity, and his poetry continued the tradition he shared with McGrath, Replansky, and Pillin while he wrote plays and organized groups to read at his home in Malibu. Ann Stanford, making a reputation for herself at the time, was very much involved in the Los Angeles poetry world that produced those two quarterlies. Stanford was of McGrath's age and had been a student of Yvor Winters at Stanford. Like McGrath and others, she was published by Alan Swallow. Other poets, less well known, Josephine Ain, Sid Gershgoren, and Estelle Gershgoren, contributed to the pages of *Coastlines* from the middle and late fifties onward. Poets like Stanford and Ain were not directly involved in the political climate that had produced some of the other poets. But Spingarn had begun in that tradition with *The California Quarterly* and, though his poems were not always overtly social, was part of that world. Other poets like Charles Bukowski and

Estelle Gershgoren and
Sid Gershgoren ca. 1959,
Vista Street, West Hollywood.
Photographer unknown.

Lawrence Lipton seemed to represent the fringes of *Coastlines* territory. Lawrence Lipton had begun by publishing in *The California Quarterly* but had, during the 1950s, grown away from the radical impetus that had spurred on that journal. He organized his own group at Venice West, often quarreled with the *Coastlines* group, even while contributing to its pages, and finally judged it too far to the left. Charles Bukowski, after early publication in *Coastlines*, eventually staked out a poetic territory very different from what *Coastlines* and its poets represented.

## Conclusions

By its last issue in 1964 *Coastlines* had cast a wide net for poets. But its reflections backward on the socially conscious poetry of the poets of the 1930s and 1940s, its resistance to McCarthyism's suffocating effect on literature, and its effort to publish technically exciting and socially aware poetry have not been entirely forgotten. Many of the poets who began as the *Coastlines* group around Thomas McGrath continued to write both a socially responsible poetry and a poetry that found astonishment and pleasure in language. Although the McCarthy period may have tried to silence the voices of protest, the poets were not silent about the painful social issues of their day, and they continued to speak up long after *Coastlines* had died and many of them had left Los Angeles behind. The distinction of the Coastliners was that they refused to join the easy rebellions of the sixties in personal disaffiliation but rather continued to see poetry as centered in a combination of rich language, experiment, and social awareness.

No literary journals could honestly replace *The California Quarterly* and *Coastlines*. The poets who had published there and who had been involved in the culture of those two journals still wrote into the seventies and beyond, but only McGrath's *Crazy Horse* and Mark Vinz's *Dacotah Territory* would give space to that kind of poetry again far from Los Angeles itself. One poetry annual, *Pemmican,* published in Washington State by Robert Edwards, continued to publish some of the poets who wrote in those years, but it has recently folded.[142] Although in time other poets rose up, Los Angeles had returned to smog and to Hollywood.

The poets collected here all had an influence on the poets who would write in Los Angeles after them. And they all were nurtured by the tradition that had preceded them, the tradition of radical poetry that began in the 1930s with the Dynamo poets and was carried on by its participants and descendants: Thomas McGrath, Naomi Replansky, Edwin Rolfe, Don Gordon, and William Pillin. Although the younger poets did not always share the most doctrinaire politics of the earlier generation, they received a tradition of poetry that combined a devotion to the craft and an insistence on quality with a socially conscious humanism that never wavered in its attention to the things of this world and its people, both in praise and condemnation. And they made it their own in the most unlikely of places, Los Angeles.

Estelle Gershgoren Novak

Los Angeles, 2002

# Notes

All interviews are with the author.

1. Thomas McGrath, Statement to the House Un-American Activities Committee, 1952. Reprinted in *The North Dakota Quarterly* 50 (fall 1982). See selections from McGrath's remarks to the committee reproduced in these pages.

2. Ann Stanford, pages from her diary for Saturday, May 14, 1955. Ann Stanford's husband was Ronald White, a local architect. See her further commentary on the difficulties of the times reprinted in these pages. The pages from the diary cited here can be found among Ann Stanford's papers in the manuscript collection at the Huntington Library in San Marino, California.

3. Ibid.

4. Larry Ceplair, interviewer, *Hollywood Blacklist: Donald Gordon.* Oral History Program, UCLA, pp. 78–79, tape number I, side II, 20 August 1988.

5. By the October 1955 issue of *Trace* (a journal that provided continually updated listings of little magazines) *Coastlines* was listed in "A Directory Supplement" as follows: "*Coastlines*, 1753 Virginia Rd., Los Angeles 19, Calif., U.S.A. (D. I.; stresses individualism, now open to all forms) 35¢., '55." *Trace* no. 14 (October 1955): 18. In the February 1956 issue *Coastlines* was noted as having a "vigorous individualistic social outlook." *Trace* no. 15 (February 1956): 12.

6. See "Regarding a Proposal to Merge *Coastlines* and *The California Quarterly* into One Magazine" in these pages. Alexandra Garrett Papers, Special Collections, UCLA.

7. See the black-bordered memorial statement on the death of *The California Quarterly* in these pages.

8. "Blunderbuss . . . what's going on around L.A.," in *Coastlines* 2, no. 4 (autumn 1957): 36.

9. Ibid.

10. Ibid.

11. Thomas McGrath, Gene Frumkin, Bert Meyers, Alvaro Cardona-Hine, Sid Gershgoren, and Estelle Gershgoren were among those who would come to those gatherings.

12. "Blunderbuss . . . what's going on around L.A.," in Coastlines 2, no. 4 (autumn 1957): 36.

13. Gene Frumkin, "A Note on Tom McGrath— The Early '50s," *North Dakota Quarterly* 50 (fall 1982): 48.

14. Michael Bolter, interviewer, *The Education of Alice McGrath.* Oral History Program, UCLA, 1987, p. 27 (transcript), tape III, side II, 1987.

15. Interview with Mel Weisburd, Los Angeles, 28 January 1997.

16. "Blunderbuss . . . what's going on around L.A.," *Coastlines* 3, no. 2 (spring/summer 1958): 53–54.

17. *Poetry Los Angeles: I* was edited by James Boyer May, Thomas McGrath, and Peter Yates. It was published in London by Villiers Publications, Ltd., in 1958.

18. Interview with Mel Weisburd, 28 January 1997.

19. "Blunderbuss . . . what's going on around L.A.," *Coastlines* 2, no. 1 (autumn 1957): 36–37.

20. Poems at this festival were printed as "Poetry Previews" and photocopied for the audience. The title given for Edwin Rolfe's final book was its working title, *Words and Ballads.* It was later published as *Permit Me Refuge.* Actors reading from the poems were Jeff Corey, Frank Greenwood, and Gale Sondergaard. These reprints can be found among the Ann Stanford Papers in the manuscript collection at the Huntington Library in San Marino, California.

21. The Writers' Workshops produced mimeographed programs of poets and poetry to be read. One on Sunday, April 27, 1958, titled itself "The Unconventional Muse." It included Thomas McGrath, Alvaro Cardona-Hine, Bert Meyers, and Ann

Stanford. Translations of Cesar Vallejo by Alvaro Cardona-Hine and translations of two Yiddish poets, Itzik Fefer, translated by Stanley Kurnik, and Nathan Alterman, translated by Marie Syrkin, were included in the readings. In one other workshop reading in the same year translations of Miguel Hernandez by Cardona-Hine and of Peretz Herschbein by Stanley Kurnik were included. These materials can be found among the Ann Stanford Papers in the manuscript collection at the Huntington Library in San Marino, California.

22. Mimeographed program for the San Francisco Museum of Art's Poetry Festival, June 21–June 24, 1962. This program can be found in Ann Stanford's Papers in the manuscript collection at the Huntington Library.

23. "Blunderbuss...what's going on around L.A.," *Coastlines* 2, no. 1 (autumn 1957): 37.

24. Gene Frumkin's account of that event at Bard Dahl's house in Los Angeles in "The Great Promotor," an article in *Coastlines*, differs from the accounts given by Lawrence Lipton in *The Holy Barbarians* and from the account given more recently by John Maynard in his book *Venice West* (New Brunswick, N.J.: Rutgers University Press, 1991). Passages from "The Great Promotor" can be found in these pages. Mel Weisburd, who was also present at the reading, has said that Frumkin's account is closer to what he remembers of that evening.

25. See Weisburd's "Lysergic Acid and the Creative Experience" reprinted in these pages. Mel Weisburd was subsequently referred to by Leonard Wolf in *Voices from the Love Generation* (Boston: Little, Brown, 1968) as one expressing an early version of the excitement about the drug and perhaps a more accurate one than those that were to come later. Weisburd's article was printed in *Coastlines* 3, no. 2 (spring/summer 1958).

26. The information about the CBS radio show comes from Mel Weisburd's own recollections. The two articles about Lipton, "Merchant of Venice" and "The Great Promotor," respectively by Mel Weisburd and Gene Frumkin, appeared in *Coastlines* 2, no. 3 (spring/summer 1957): 39–40, and *Coastlines* 4, no. 1 (autumn 1959): 3–10.

27. Gene Frumkin, "The Great Promotor," *Coastlines* 4, no. 1 (autumn 1959): 4.

28. Ibid., 5.

29. Writing in his 1965 dissertation "A History of the American Literary Avant-Garde Since World War II" (UCLA, 1965), Anthony Linnick says that *Coastlines* "consistently reflected an interest in social reconstruction. Because the *Coastlines* editors reflected the traditional liberal or leftist postures on social questions, a schism soon developed between them and the Venice Beat poets—who posited a more anarchic individual rebellion" (143).

30. "Blunderbuss...what's going on around L.A.," *Coastlines* 2, no. 4 (autumn 1957): 38. The information about Venice West was quoted by the *Coastlines* editors from the group's own literature. For more detailed information about the Venice West group see John Arthur Maynard's *Venice West: The Beat Generation in Southern California* (New Brunswick, N.J.: Rutgers University Press, 1991).

31. Lawrence Lipton, *Coastlines*, nos. 21 and 22 (1964): 4.

32. Once the musical evenings had ended, in the midfifties, Yates also organized poetry readings at his home. These evenings would also be called "Evenings on the Roof."

33. For more information on the musical scene surrounding "Evenings on the Roof" see Dorothy Lamb Crawford, *Evenings On and Off the Roof: Pioneering Concerts in Los Angeles 1939–1971* (Berkeley: University of California Press, 1995).

34. Interview with Mel Weisburd, 28 January 1997.

35. Thomas McGrath, "Poetry, Jazz, etc.," *Coastlines* 3, no. 1 (winter 1957–58): 39–41. See that review reprinted in these pages.

36. Peter Yates, "Reading Poetry Aloud," *Coastlines* 3, no. 1 (winter 1957–58): 36–39. See that article reprinted in these pages.

37. Selections from these artworks are reproduced throughout this anthology.

38. The editors of *Coastlines* noted its publication as "the first Eastern definitive publication of the Los Angeles Movement (*sic!*)." "East Coast Rendition of West Coast Division of the Muse," *Coastlines* 3, no. 2 (spring/summer 1958): 54.

39. *The California Quarterly* 2, no. 4 (summer 1953). The editors note, "In the case of *Salt of the Earth,* however, we have a prime example of what happens when hooligans have their torches of bigotry and demagogy. An unprecedented effort has been made to keep this work of art and product of free enterprise from reaching the screen. We consider this particular action to be a significant part of an expanding pattern of censorship" (32).

40. *Hollywood Quarterly* I, no. 4 (July 1946). Advisory committees are listed on the inside front cover of the journal.

41. "Editorial," *The California Quarterly* 2, no. 1 (autumn 1952).

42. "Regarding a Proposal to Merge *Coastlines* and *The California Quarterly* into one magazine," Alexandra Garrett Papers, Special Collections, UCLA. Part of this statement is reprinted in these pages.

43. The FBI file on Alice McGrath courtesy of Alice McGrath.

44. "The Editors," *Coastlines* 1, no. 1 (spring 1955): 1. This editorial is reprinted in these pages.

45. Barding Dahl, "Tijuana: a Profile," *Coastlines* 2, no. 2 (summer 1956): 19.

46. Gene Frumkin, "Editorial," Coastlines 4, nos. 2 and 3 (spring 1960): 87–88. A selection from this editorial is reprinted in these pages.

47. Erik Thyssen, ed., *San Francisco Renaissancen* (Copenhagen: Sirius Press, 1973). The Black Mountain group was centered at Black Mountain College in the rural mountains of North Carolina. It was represented by poets like Charles Olson, Robert Duncan, Denise Levertov, and Robert Creeley. Creeley edited the *Black Mountain Review* in 1955 and later moved to San Francisco.

48. The phrase "non-existent city" was widely used, sometimes negatively as Christopher Isherwood used it but mostly to describe the suburban nature of the Los Angeles experience, its lack of a city center.

49. William Pillin, "Statement," *Epos: Poetry Los Angeles, A Special Issue* 9, no. 4 (summer 1958): 4.

50. Ann Stanford did eventually publish such a collection of women poets and did her doctoral dissertation on an early American woman poet, Anne Bradstreet.

51. "Notes on Contributors," *Coastlines* 5, no. 2 (1962): 2.

52. After his death *The New York Times* had a favorable article about him.

53. FBI file of Alice McGrath courtesy of Alice McGrath.

54. Philip Levine, "Small Tribute to Tom McGrath," in *Triquarterly 70, Thomas McGrath: Life and the Poem* (fall 1987): 103.

55. Thomas McGrath, "Ode to the American Dead in Korea," in *New Poets of England and America,* eds. Donald Hall, Robert Pack, and Louis Simpson (New York: Meridian Books, 1957), 198–99.

56. Thomas McGrath, *Figures from a Double World* (Denver: Alan Swallow, 1955), 40–41.

57. Information on Thomas McGrath comes from both the *North Dakota Quarterly* of fall 1982, which was devoted to him, and from

Alice McGrath's memories and personal documents. Interview with Alice McGrath, Ventura, Calif., 16 November 1996.

58. Alice McGrath says that he wrote for the seaman's union newspaper.

59. Thomas McGrath, "Mr. and Mrs. Foxbright X. Muddlehead at Home," *The California Quarterly* 2, no. 1 (autumn 1952): 12–13.

60. Thomas McGrath, "All the Dead Poets," *The California Quarterly* 3, no. 4 (1955): 52.

61. Thomas McGrath, "Ambitions," *Triquarterly* 70, *Thomas McGrath: Life and the Poem* (fall 1987): 218.

62. Thomas McGrath, "Ode to the American Dead in Korea," in *New Poets of England and America*, eds. Donald Hall, Robert Pack, and Louis Simpson (New York: Meridian Books, 1957), 198–99.

63. Reginald Gibbons and Terence des Pres, "An Interview with Thomas McGrath, January 30–February 1, 1987," *Triquarterly* 70 (fall 1987): 99.

64. "McGrath on McGrath," *North Dakota Quarterly* (fall 1982): 25.

65. Thomas McGrath, "Letter to an Imaginary Friend," *Coastlines* 2, no. 3 (spring/summer 1957): 3.

66. Interview with Alice McGrath, Ventura, Calif., 16 November 1996.

67. Interviews with Stanley Schwartz and Martin Lubner. Martin Lubner says that Tom used to come to lunch at the studio he shared with Morton Dimondstein, Arnold Mesches, and Sam Pollack on Melrose Avenue during those years Tom was working at Stanley Schwartz's shop. Interview with Stanley Schwartz, Los Angeles, 10 April 1997. Interview with Martin Lubner, Los Angeles, 22 March 1997.

68. "Notes on Contributors," *Coastlines* 4, nos. 2 and 3 (spring 1960): 88.

69. Michael Bolter, interviewer, *The Education of Alice McGrath.* Oral History Program, UCLA, p. 301, tape number VII, side II, 1987.

70. Thomas McGrath, *Letter to an Imaginary Friend, I and II* (Denver: Alan Swallow, 1962), 111.

71. Ibid., 117.

72. Alice McGrath remembers that the "school" was founded by Janet Stevenson, Richard Slobodkin, and Tom. Alice herself acted as secretary. She remembers it as "like a university without walls." Interview with Alice McGrath, Ventura, Calif., 16 November 1996.

73. Thomas McGrath, "After the Beat Generation," in *The Movie at the End of the World: Collected Poems* (Chicago: Swallow Press, 1980), 162–63.

74. Thomas McGrath, preface to *Witness to the Times: Poems by Thomas McGrath* (Los Angeles: n.p., May 1953).

75. Complete information on Edwin Rolfe's life and poetry has been compiled by Cary Nelson and Jefferson Hendricks in their edition of his *Collected Poems* (Urbana-Champlain: University of Illinois Press, 1993).

76. For more analysis of and information about the Dynamo poets, see my article "The Dynamo School of Poets," *Contemporary Literature* (autumn 1970): 526–39.

77. Edwin Rolfe, "Season of Death," in *To My Contemporaries* (New York: Dynamo, 1936), 54.

78. Edwin Rolfe, "City of Anguish," in *First Love and Other Poems* (Los Angeles: Larry Edmunds Book Shop, 1951), 16, and "Elegia," ibid., 87, 90. Note that Cary Nelson and Jefferson Hendricks have published Rolfe's selected poems under the title *Trees Became Torches* (Urbana-Champaign: University of Illinois Press, 1995).

79. Note Nelson and Hendricks's point that *Masses and Mainstream* refused to publish the poem because of its biblical references. *Collected Poems*, 43.

80. Nelson and Hendricks make the point

that although Rolfe knew Chaplin personally, he chose to write about him as a public figure. Yet as they see clearly, the public was always personal to Rolfe and the personal public.

81. In the same issue the editors reprint quotations declaring the triumph of the film *Salt of the Earth,* which had been attacked by Donald L. Jackson, congressional representative from Los Angeles. Rolfe died against that backdrop.

82. See Nelson and Hendricks's edition of Rolfe's *Collected Poems* for a discussion of Rolfe's friends who were brought before the committee. Two that they don't mention are Thomas McGrath and Don Gordon, poets in this collection. Note that they argue that *The California Quarterly* would not publish Rolfe's "Little Ballad for Americans—1954" because it was too overtly about HUAC. It's hard to know how deep the paranoia went in those years, but it may be that the editors simply thought that poem less good as a poem than Rolfe's others. It is rather more like doggerel than the other poems they printed and certainly doesn't have the depth of "Ballad of Noble Intentions," equally as powerful a statement about HUAC and more personally engaged. As Nelson and Hendricks tell us, the poem was written in response to Clifford Odets's testimony before HUAC. Of course, Rolfe himself had notice to appear before the committee, although he did not actually do so. *Collected Poems,* 45, 54.

83. Donald Gordon, "The Middle Passage," in *Displaced Persons* (Denver: Alan Swallow, 1958), 41.

84. *The California Quarterly* 3, no. 3 (1954): 3.

85. Eugene Frumkin, "Elegy for a Soldier of the Spanish Civil War," *The California Quarterly* 3, no. 3 (1954): 4.

86. "Dedication," *Coastlines* 1, no. 1 (spring 1955): 4.

87. Edwin Rolfe, "Bon Voyage," in *Permit Me Refuge* (Los Angeles: *The California Quarterly,* 1955), 46.

88. Larry Ceplair, interviewer, *Hollywood Blacklist: Donald Gordon.* Oral History Program, UCLA, p. 58, tape II, 2 September 1988.

89. Ibid. All biographical information comes from the oral history cited above.

90. Ibid., p. 14, tape I.

91. Ibid., p. 20, tape I.

92. Ibid. The "stool pigeon" was most probably the writer, Ben Maddow.

93. Ibid., pp. 59–60, tape II.

94. Don Gordon, "Spain," in *Statement* (Boston: Bruce Humphries, 1943), 93.

95. Don Gordon, "Lenin," in *Statement* (Boston: Bruce Humphries, 1943), 74.

96. Don Gordon, "Unemployed," in *Statement* (Boston: Bruce Humphries, 1943), 32.

97. Don Gordon, "The investigation," in *The California Quarterly* 2, no. 1 (autumn 1952): 48–49.

98. Don Gordon, "The Kimono," in *Displaced Persons* (Denver: Alan Swallow, 1958), 12–13. The poem was also published in Thomas McGrath's journal, *Crazy Horse,* no. 2.

99. Don Gordon, "The Destroyers," in *Displaced Persons* (Denver: Alan Swallow, 1958), 37.

100. Don Gordon, "The Dissenter," in *Displaced Persons* (Denver: Alan Swallow, 1958), 23.

101. Don Gordon, "The Deportee," in *Displaced Persons* (Denver: Alan Swallow, 1958), 26.

102. Don Gordon, "The Silent Generation," in *Displaced Persons* (Denver: Alan Swallow, 1958), 30.

103. Don Gordon, "The Middle Passage," in *Displaced Persons* (Denver: Alan Swallow, 1958), 41.

104. Naomi Replansky, "Housing Shortage," *The California Quarterly* 1, no. 4 (summer 1952): 29.

105. Naomi Replansky, "Ring Song," in *A Dangerous World: New and Selected Poems, 1934–1994* (Chicago: Another Chicago Press, 1994), 38.

106. Letter from Naomi Replansky to Estelle Gershgoren Novak, 28 August 1996.

107. "Notes on Contributors," *Coastlines* 4, nos. 2 and 3 (spring 1960): 88.

108. For a discussion of this incident see Alvaro Cardona-Hine, "Poetry in Los Angeles 1945 to 1975: Part I," *Bachy* 12 (1978). A passage from this article is reprinted in these pages.

109. William Pillin, "Fugue," *Coastlines* 2, no. 1 (summer 1956): 21–22.

110. William Pillin, "Sabbath," *Coastlines* 3, no. 3 (autumn 1958): 6.

111. See *Coastlines* 4, nos. 2 and 3 (spring 1960): 44.

112. William Pillin, "Miserere," in *Epos: Poetry Los Angeles, A Special Issue,* 9, no. 4 (summer 1958): 11.

113. William Pillin, "Prelude and Dance on Quitting a Rotten Job," in *Pavanne for a Fading Memory* (Denver: Alan Swallow, 1963), 57.

114. Interview with Mel Weisburd.

115. Henri Coulette, "Migration," *The California Quarterly* 2, no. 2 (winter 1952): 31.

116. Ibid.

117. Mel Weisburd, *Coastlines* 6, nos. 21 and 22 (1964): 6.

118. Rexroth had published in the *New Masses* in the 1930s.

119. Bert Meyers spent a brief time taking undergraduate classes at UCLA.

120. Kenneth Funsten, "Bert Meyers (1938–1979)," *Bachy* (1979): 3.

121. Bert Meyers, "The Cougar Has Been Shot," *The California Quarterly* 3, no. 2 (1954): 15.

122. Bert Meyers, "Pity the Child," *The California Quarterly* 3, no. 3 (1954): 19.

123. Gene Frumkin, "The Daily Reality," review of Bert Meyers's *Early Rain,* in *Coastlines* 5, no. 2 (1962): 58. This review can be found reprinted in these pages.

124. Ibid.

125. Bert Meyers, "I Dreamed," *Coastlines* 5, no. 3 (1962): 12.

126. Denise Levertov, "Bert Meyers," in *Light Up the Cave* (New York: New Directions, 1981), 274.

127. Mel Weisburd, "My Father," *The California Quarterly* 3, no. 3 (1954): 19.

128. Mel Weisburd, "Descendent Robot," *Coastlines* 1, no. 1 (spring 1955): 26.

129. Mel Weisburd, "The American," *Coastlines* 1, no. 2 (summer 1955): 12–13.

130. Mel Weisburd, "The Sixth and Seventh Sense of Man," *Coastlines* 4, nos. 2 and 3 (spring 1960): 47.

131. Mel Weisburd, "Report from Evanston," *Coastlines* 6, nos. 1 and 2 (1964): 13.

132. Eugene Frumkin, "The Waiting Room in the County Hospital," *The California Quarterly* 3, no. 3 (1954): 16–17.

133. Eugene Frumkin, "Elegy for a Tailor," in *The California Quarterly* 3, no. 3 (1954): 17–18.

134. Gene Frumkin, "Men Fail in Communion," *Coastlines* 5, no. 3 (1962): 56.

135. Gene Frumkin, "Editorial: The Debt," *Coastlines* 4, no. 4 (autumn 1960): 48.

136. Ibid.

137. Gene Frumkin, "Speech to the Silent Generation," in *The Hawk and the Lizard* (Denver: Alan Swallow, 1963), 38–39.

138. Ibid., 41.

139. Ibid., 15.

140. Alvaro Cardona-Hine, "Doomsday and Components," *Coastlines* 5, no. 3 (1962): 38.

141. Alvaro Cardona-Hine, "Vindication," *Coastlines* 4, nos. 2 and 3 (spring 1960): 52.

142. *Pemmican* is now available on-line at www.pemmicanpress.com.

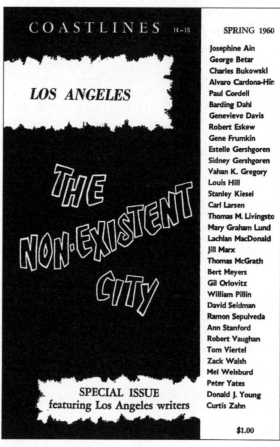

COASTLINES 14-15

SPRING 1960

LOS ANGELES

THE NON-EXISTENT CITY

SPECIAL ISSUE
featuring Los Angeles writers

Josephine Ain
George Betar
Charles Bukowski
Alvaro Cardona-Hir
Paul Cordell
Barding Dahl
Genevieve Davis
Robert Eskew
Gene Frumkin
Estelle Gershgoren
Sidney Gershgoren
Vahan K. Gregory
Louis Hill
Stanley Kiesel
Carl Larsen
Thomas M. Livingsto
Mary Graham Lund
Lachlan MacDonald
Jill Marx
Thomas McGrath
Bert Meyers
Gil Orlovitz
William Pillin
David Seidman
Ramon Sepulveda
Ann Stanford
Robert Vaughan
Tom Viertel
Zack Walsh
Mel Weisburd
Peter Yates
Donald J. Young
Curtis Zahn

$1.00

Milton Gershgoren, cover: *Coastlines* 4, nos. 2 and 3 (spring 1960).

# Poets of the Non-Existent City:

## Los Angeles Poets in the McCarthy Era

Thomas McGrath

Don Gordon

Naomi Replansky

William Pillin

Ann Stanford

Curtis Zahn

Edwin Rolfe

Sid Gershgoren

Charles Bukowski

Stanley Kiesel

Henri Coulette

Mel Weisburd

Gene Frumkin

Lawrence Spingarn

Alvaro Cardona-Hine

Bert Meyers

Josephine Ain

Estelle Gershgoren Novak

Lawrence Lipton

**Edited by Estelle Gershgoren Novak**

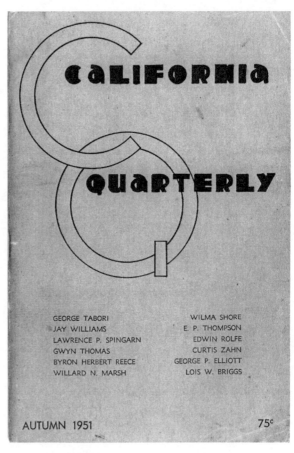

Cover: *The California Quarterly* 1, no. 1 (autumn 1951).

# YOU CAN START the POETRY now!!

—Thomas McGrath
"You Can Start the Poetry Now, Or: News from Crazy Horse"

*The California Quarterly* is founded
on the conviction that more good
writing will come out of the nineteen-fifties
than is likely to achieve publication. . . .
Contemporary writing is threatened equally
by censorship and by obscurantism. . . .
We hope to encourage writing that faces up
to its time—writers who recognize
their responsibility to deal with reality
in communicable terms. . . . If we have a claim
to newness, it is this moderate position
in an immoderate time.

Editorial Statement
*The California Quarterly*
Autumn 1951

# Thomas McGrath

Thomas McGrath. b. 1916–d. 1990. Thomas McGrath was born on a farm near Sheldon, North Dakota. He attended the University of North Dakota between 1935 and 1939, where he received a B.A. degree and was awarded a Rhodes scholarship. He was a graduate student at Louisiana State University between 1939 and 1940, receiving his M.A. Between 1940 and 1941 he taught at Colby College in Maine and in 1942 worked at a shipbuilding and dry-dock company in New Jersey. After serving in the Aleutian Islands during World War II, between 1942 and 1945, he took up his Rhodes scholarship and studied at New College, Oxford. Finishing everything but his thesis for the B.Litt. degree, he traveled to the south of France, where he wrote a novel he would later publish as *This Coffin Has No Handles,* then returned to the United States. He came to Los Angeles in 1950 with his first wife, Marian, divorced her, and married Alice Greenfield, then divorced Alice and married Eugenia Johnson before leaving Los Angeles in 1960. Between 1951 and 1954 he taught at Los Angeles State College and was on the editorial board of *The California Quarterly.* Brought before the House Un-American Activities Committee in 1953, he was subsequently fired from his teaching job. Thomas McGrath published numerous books of poetry and two novels. He was also a freelance worker in the television and film industry both in New York and in Hollywood. After he left Los Angeles, he taught at C. W. Post College, at North Dakota State University, and at Moorhead State University, Minnesota. He retired from teaching in 1982. McGrath was an Amy Lowell Traveling Fellow in Poetry, a Guggenheim Fellow, and a Bush Fellow. His books of poetry include *First Manifesto; To Walk a Crooked Mile; Long Shot O'Leary's Garland of Practical Poesy; Witness to the Times; Figures from a Double World; About Clouds; Letter to an Imaginary Friend, Parts I and II; Letter to an Imaginary Friend, Parts III and IV; New and Selected Poems; Movie at the End of the World: Collected Poems; Voices from Beyond the Wall; A Sound of One Hand; Letters to Tomasito; Open Songs: Sixty Short Poems; Trinc: Praises II; Writing for the Angel; Passages Toward the Dark; Longshot O'Leary Counsels Direct Action;* and *Echoes Inside the Labyrinth.* His two novels are *This Coffin Has No Handles* and *The Gates of Ivory, The Gates of Horn.*

"Yet McGrath's poetry will be remembered in one hundred years when many more fashionable voices have been forgotten. Here is a poet addressing not poets only but speaking in a public voice to a public which has not yet learned to listen to him."

E. P. Thompson

"Homage to Thomas McGrath"

*Triquarterly* 70 (fall 1987)


"Thirdly, as a poet I must refuse to cooperate with the committee on what I can only call esthetic grounds. The view of life which we receive through the great works of art is a privileged one—it is a view of life according to probability or necessity, not subject to the chance and accident of our real world and therefore in a sense truer than the life we see lived all around us. . . . Then, too, poets have been notorious non-cooperators where committees of this sort are concerned. As a traditionalist, I would prefer to take my stand with Marvell, Blake, Shelley and García Lorca rather than with innovators like Mr. Jackson. I do not wish to bring dishonor upon my tribe."

Thomas McGrath

Statement to the House Un-American Activities Committee, 1953

Reprinted in *North Dakota Quarterly* (fall 1982)

### Mr. and Mrs. Foxbright X. Muddlehead, At Home

Comes the murderer's evening, *ami du criminel,*
And Foxbright, Mr. Muddlehead—putting his X
On the dogchewed livingroom carpet, perplexed
By the activities of the love bird and the fish in the deep well.
Television turns wild horses loose in the hall,
And the radio laughs while supper and Vesuvius burn
And a three ring circus, with lepers, jumps out of the wall.

Meanwhile Mrs. Muddlehead, erotic in blue jeans
To Foxbright X, is answering three phones—
The Book Club, Christ Inc., Rebels Ltd. call while the bones
Of the wild goose flap in the pot and sail off the scene.
So, supper over, the Commanches enter, alas
As children, with axes, and proceed to chop down the lamps.
Mrs. M, lovely, smiles at the phones. All things will pass.

All things pass Foxbright. Comes another day
And the smile on the phones is the same. The children burn
His Sunday paintings while Mrs. M in turn
Queries one phone, then another. Hurried away
By destiny, and the need for the rent, Muddlehead keeps
The smile of his wife like an exile's memory of
Snow on the homeland, or love. And at last time creeps

Past smoky, incestuous noon with its straddling hands,
While the world and Foxbright wrestle. But on the clock
Of Mrs. M the whirling pointers mock
The busy degrees of her circle. Who understands
The world's needs but herself? And who will give
The Word? To her club? Or to God? The fish and the bird
Is each in his element happy. To serve is to live.

The children blast out a wall. Like a wolf from the hill,
The wind comes in with a rush. It is bad for the bird.
And the fish. And for Mrs. M, who does not know a word
Of the language the children have recently learned, and is ill
With the air, and the anguish of offspring asking for love,

And evening, and X coming home, and the three phones ringing,
And the rich demands of the world, which are never enough.

So Mrs. M takes her leave, as her surrogate spouse,
With his ex-life in his heart, like a dinosaur bone,
Returns from his dubious battle, mistaking as home
The place where he lives. O, ever the fish will browse,
Loved, in his glass room, and ever the love-bird cry
Secure on his perch. But will Foxbright X return
Always? The years pass. They go by

Foxbright like falling stars or Mrs. M, drawn
To PTA or a Black Mass: perilous, hurled
Like no known comet at the unwitting world
Elliptic. Cutting his orbit. Gone
To Duty. The goldfish swims. The moon
Provokes the bird. O lovers, pity, pity,
Pity them, who, in some lost summer, loved, were young.

■ **All the Dead Poets**

How vainly men themselves bestir
For Bollingen or Pulitzer,
To raise, through ritual and rhyme
Some Lazarus of an earlier time:
The thought that died upon the page;
The attitude stiffened with its age;
The feeling, once appropriate,
Now, like honesty, out of date;
The elegant tone elegiac
That embalms the venom of a hack—
All the outmoded consciousness
A timid reason can assess:
His sin that in the soul's dark night
Like an ancient Cod's head gives off light—

All of this some will sing or say
(As if God's death were but a play)—
All the dead poets of the day.

      I—Random Roderick
Here's one who sings (as he were wood)
The *angst* he has best understood:
What the Ash and Hickory
Feel toward Life and Poetry.
Of what the Willow should or shouldn't
He warbles his native wood-note prudent,
Proclaiming so everyone may know it
He's every ring the old oaken poet.
"Poems are made by fools like me
But only God can make a tree,"
Said Kilmer. Roderick proves the rule:
Too many trees may make a fool.
For there's a kind of Sallic law:
Such willowy whimsy is a bore.
Still, better his light than heavy work—
His agenbite's worse than his bark.

Earnest at his vatic trade,
He studies to be nobly mad;
Courts furor poeticus
(So long as it is decorous)
Thinking, when he has beguiled
The critic-beasts, to mount the wild
Pegasus of mantic verse—
If only someone holds the horse.
Yet to be "lyrically wild"
(And simple as a little child)
Is not enough. The art of sinking
Is not enough: he must be thinking—
Thinking, thinking all the while
(As a history doctor will)
Thinking, thinking all the day,
While the cute ideas play,

And when the hunting thoughts come home—
Lo! they've bagged another poem!
This philosophic poet's bold—
Proudly demands his right to hold
Such attitudes to church and state
As died in 1848.
Built from ruin and decay
His dome of many-colored clay
Arises—O Philosophy,
Can this jakes thy mansion be?
Wilt thou number in thy van
This shambling nineteenth century man?

Meanwhile our poet is romancing
And sets the small ideas dancing:
His poems would rather mean than be—
O Wouldsman, Wouldsman, spare that tree!


"In 1952 the House Un-American Activities Committee (HUAC) came to the City of Angels looking for devils, particularly in the motion picture industry and in education. Tom, who has been politically involved in the Left for longer than I've known him, was among those subpoenaed to appear before the committee. His responses to questions were as forthright as they customarily are; although they didn't get him thrown in jail for contempt of the committee, they did get him fired from his teaching post at LA State—this despite a strong student petition campaign urging his reinstatement."

Gene Frumkin

"A Note on Tom McGrath—the Early 50s"

*North Dakota Quarterly* (fall 1982)

## Escape

Hunting in the dark my father found me,
My mother claimed me, and led me into light
From my nine-month winter. In the herds of Right,
Branded and bawling, the christeners bound me.
God given, church shriven, hell washed away,
Adam purged, heaven urged, the dog would have his day.

Hell all about me with its infantry
Storming the fortress of my crying years
Could not get my notice. They had stopped my ears
With chrism of love in my infancy.
World poor, world pure, I kept my head level,
Unproud, but uncowed, shaming the devil.

And thus betrayed I fell into a world
Where love lives only in another name.
At eleven or twelve, when the kidnappers came,
I took the poisoned candy and off we whirled.
Innocence, nonsense, the seven priestly lies
Surrounded me, when, hands bound, I opened my eyes

Onto the bloody barnyard of my youth
Where the stuck pig wetly squealed against the wall,
And fell on the stone crop. False, rich, tall,
The elders judged me. The stone edge of truth,
Flint-sharp, heartless, stabbed my begging knee—
Harmed me but armed me: I cut my hands free.

## The Roads into the Country

Ran only in one direction, in childhood years—
Into mysterious counties, beyond the farm or the town,
Toward the parish of desire the roads led up or down
Past a thicket of charms, a river of wishing hours,

Till, wrapt in a plenum of undying sun
We heard the tick of air-guns on the hills.
The pheasant stalked by on his gilded heels,

The soft-eyed foxes from the woods looked on,

While hung upon the blue wall of the air
The hawk stared down into a sea of fire,
Where, salamanders in our element,
We ate the summer like a sacrament.

That was in memory's country, and is lost.
The roads lead nowhere. Aloof in his field of fire
The hawk wheels pitiless. Alone, afar,
The skirmishers of childhood hurry past,
Hunting a future that they cannot will.
Children of light, travelling our darkened years
We cannot warn them. Distant, they have no ears
For those they will become. Across a wall

Of terror and innocence we hear the voice,
The air-gun in the land of all mock-choice;
Around us not the game of fox and pheasant,
But the gunfire of the real and terrible present.

"She helped me, the Goddess of Poetry. I'll tell you how it started. Some of us used to go to each other's places. Don Gordon. Ed Rolfe. Naomi Replansky. We'd read poems to each other. They'd normally be torn to shreds. Don asked me, 'What are you doing now? Do you have any plans.' I told him, 'I have this notion for this poem. It's very long. As much as fifteen pages. I'm kind of worried about starting the poem.' He said, 'Go home and sit down and write the first line that comes into your head. And go on.' I did that. I didn't know what to write, so I wrote, 'I'm sitting here at 2716 Marsh Street Writing, turning east with the world. Dreaming of laughter and indifference.' 2716 Marsh Street is where I lived. Then I began to have these tremendous rushes, and I wrote the poem from morning until night, about fifty odd pages, then I stopped. I didn't know how long it was. I thought that was the end of it. It wasn't the end. . . ."

Thomas McGrath

On writing "Letter To An Imaginary Friend"

Interview with Julia Stein (1984)

Published posthumously in *Onthebus* (1991)

### Letter To An Imaginary Friend

1.

—"From here it is necessary to ship all bodies east."
I am in Los Angeles, at 2714 Marsh St.,
Writing, rolling east with the earth, drifting toward Scorpio,
        thinking,
Hoping toward laughter and indifference.
"They came through the passes,
        they crossed the dark mountains in a month
        of snow,
Finding the plain, the bitter water,
        the iron rivers of the black North.
Horsemen,
Hunters of the hornless deer in the high plateaus of that
        country,
They traveled the cold year, died in the stone desert."

    Aye, long ago. A long journey ago.
Most of it lost in the dark, in a ruck of tourists.
In the night of the compass, companioned by tame wolves, plagued
By theories, flies, visions, by the anthropophagi . . .

    I do not know what end that journey was toward.
—But I am its end. I am where I have been and where
I am going. The journeying destination—at least that . . .
But far from the laughter.
                  So, writing:
"The melt of the pig pointed to early spring.
The tossed bones augured an easy crossing.
North, said the mossy fur of the high pines.
West, said the colored stone at the sulphur pool."

2.

—And at the age of five ran away from home.
(I have never been back. Never left.) I was going perhaps
Toward the woods, toward a sound of water—called by what bird?—
Leaving the ark-tight farm in its blue and mortgaged weather
To sail the want-all seas of my five dead summers
Past the barn's ammonia-and-horse-piss-smelling dark
And the barnyard dust, adrift in the turkey wind
Or pocked with the guinea-print and staggering script
Of the drunken-sailor ducks, a secret language: leaving
Also my skippering Irish father, land-locked Sinbad,
With his singing head in a private cloud and his feet stuck solid
On the quack-grass-roofed and rusting poop-deck of the north forty
In the alien corn: the feathery, bearded, and all-fathering wheat.

Leaving my mother too, with her kindness and cookies,
The whispering, ginghamy, prayers—impossible pigeons—
Whickering into the camphor-and-cookie-crumb dark toward God.
    In the clothes closet.
Damp comforts. Tears harder than nails.
Summery. Loving. Laughter.

How could I leave them?
I took them with me, though I went alone
Into the christmas dark of the woods and down
The whistling slope of the coulee, past the Indian graves
Alive and flickering with the gopher light . . .

3.
—Dry runs and practice journeys through the earthquake weather
Of the interior summer . . .
                          the singing services
And ceremony cheerful as a harness bell . . .
—Bright flags and fictions of those hyacinthine hours
Stain and sustain me past the hell of this mumming time
Toward the high wake I would hold!
                                   No ghost, but O ill and older
Than other autumns when I ran the calico lanes
Past sleepy summer, gone, and the late west light
Downfallen. Lost. Autumn of distant voices, half heard,
Calling.
         Rain. Gunfire. Crows. Mist, far, woods.


Farther than winter birds in the most gaunt tree
Snapped in the frost, I was; or went. Was free, and haunted
By the reeling plunge of the high hawk down—down! O down
Where the curving rabbit lunged and was slapped with a sharp and killing
Heel.
         There, in the still post-solstice dark, among
Rococo snow, the harp-shaped drifts and the ghost-marked trees
                                             of the season
I went all ways . . .
—Spring came; the first cold rainstorms, dropping
Their electric hardware in the bright-work of the snow.
Then, the leather seasons by, and my bundling times,
My eye sustained the cow-bird and the crow
Their feather terms . . .
                    Then horny Summer come . . .
                                   —and Autumn growing
In the west steep wrestling light and the rain-wrung rheumy
                              wind in the rag-headed woods . . .


                •    •    •    •


Way stations on the underground journey; the boy running, running . . .
—Search for Lough Derg, or the holy waters of the Cheyenne,
Or the calf-deep Maple. Running away
I had the pleasure of their company . . .

4.

Took them? They came—
Past the Horn, Cape Wrath, Oxford and Fifth and Main
Laughing and mourning, snug in the two seater buggy,
Jouncing and bouncing on the gumbo roads
Or slogging loblolly in the bottom lands—
My seven-tongued family.
How could I escape? Strapped on the truckle bars
Of the bucking red-ball freight, or riding the blinds cold,
Or sick and sea-sawed on the seven seas,
Or in metal and altitude, drilling the high blue
I fled.
I heard them laughing at the oarsmen's bench.
Conched in cowcatchers, they rambled at my side.
The seat of the buggy was wider than Texas
And slung to the axles were my rowdy cousins;
Riding the whippletrees: aunts, uncles, brothers,
Second-cousins, great-aunts, friends and neighbors,
All holus-bolus, piss-proud, all sugar-and-shit
A goddamned gallimaufry of ancestors.
The high passes?
Hunters of the hornless deer?

5.
A flickering of gopher light . . .
The Indian graves . . .
And then the river.
Companioned, and alone,
Five, ten, or twenty, I followed the coulee hills
Into the dreaming green of the river shade,
The fish-stinking cow-dunged dark of the cattle-crossing,
The fox-barking, timber-wolf country, where . . .
The cicada was sawing down the afternoon/
Upstream a beaver was spanking Nature/
The cows were wilder/
Horses carnivorous . . .

The kittycorner river cut through the buggy,
Through Dachau and Thaelmann
Rolfe in Spain
Through the placid, woodchuck-coughing afternoon
Drifting
Past Grand Forks, Baton Rouge, Sheldon, Rome,
And past Red Hook and Mobile where the rivers mourn
Old Thames, Missouri, Rio Hondo.
Now
In far Los Angeles I hear
The Flying Dutchman in the dry river
Mourning. Mourning . . .
—Ancestral night . . .

Passages of the dark; streets with no known turning
Beyond the sleepy midnight and the metaphysical summer
Leading here. Here. Here, queerly here
To the east slant light of the underground moon, and the rusty garden
Empty.
                    Bounded by ghosts.
                              Empty except for footnotes
Of journeying far friends near.

Enter now,
O bird on the green branch of the dying tree, singing
Sing me toward home/
Toward the deep past and inalienable loss/
Toward the gone stranger carrying my name
In the possible future
                              —enter now:
Purlieus and stamping grounds of the hungering people
O enter

   "They died in the stone desert
They crossed the dark mountain in the month of snow.
Finding the plain, the bitter water, the iron rivers of the black North."
Horns on the freeway. Footsteps of strangers,
Angelinos: visitations in the metropolitan night.
"Hunters of the hornless deer."
Ancestral baggage . . .

*(The preceding is the first section of a book-length, narrative poem, quasi-auto-biographical in nature. The poem represents the journey of the poet in his search for individual and community identity. In its entirety, the poem alternates between lyrical and narrative forms.)*

**Letter to an Imaginary Friend**

1

Love and hunger!—the secret is all there somewhere—
And the fiery dance of the stars in their journeying for houses.
And if hunger ended in the cantrip circle.
In the union of hungry men, in the blue ice of the reefer
Where Cal traveled . . .

Jawsmiths
Commune of mystical sweat.
If it ended there.

It was she built the fire in the heart of the winter night
And rang all the bells in the stiff church of the ice.
Miners light/
Campfire/
Chipping hammer of purest flame, tunneling
The ultimate rock, the darkness that is as long as we are.
Seemed like no camp fire,
But the permanent warmth, the absolute seed of the sun
I could sow in my personal blood-ranch . . .
But I am a farmer of bones.

A season was ending.
                                White papers. Architectural changes.
In Whitey's Circular Bar, in East Grand Forks,
We stood like the signal figures under the legend tree,
Drinking. With Sam and Dee. Who were talking of marriage.
Stood in the rain of music and silver under the illegal machines,
Where Alton pursued the mechanical capitalist,
Jacking the slot machine's arm down again and again.

'Marriage is the continuation of sex by other means.'
Sam was going away to drive airplanes for the government.
Someone sang in Norwegian, under the metallic laughter
Of machines and money.

                          'Some people can be happy with a book by Donne
And a piece of Ass. It's lack of high thought keeps
My life poor.'
                         And went out in a chiming rain
Of jackpot silver.
And crossed the black river one instant before the breakup.
And turned dreamward.

                         One to the East and airplanes,
One, Marian, to the true North. One
To the West of Wish. Myself, South, toward speech.
And all to the wars and the whores and the wares and the ways of a rotten
                                            season.

And who could have guessed it?
The pole star stood to the North:
Fire was steady on the permanent sky.


2

Then South to the University with the 500,000 pianos.
Bought because Huey Long had written: 'Get rid of them nags!'
(Horses for the young ladies' riding stable)
Because one of 'em had broken the neck of a possible voter
To Baton Rouge, Louisiana, the University there.
Where they had bought football, pianos, horses and Donnish Oxonians
To start a culture farm, a little Athens-on-the-bayou.
And a good job too.

                         And they all put in together and they got up
A Tradition. They got hold of Donne, and before they had got done
They damn near had him.
                         And they got hold of Agrarianism—
Salvation—40 acres and a mule—the Protestant Heaven,
Free Enterprise. Kind of intellectual ribbon-development—
But I was Catholic, a peasant, from Sauvequipeuville—
I wanted the City of Man.

And Cleanth Brooks would talk, at the Roosevelt Tavern,
Where we went to drink beer. And Katherine Anne Porter sometimes.

(They've probably changed all the names now.)
And down the street Alan Swallow was handsetting books
In an old garage. A wild man from Wyoming,
With no tradition.

                                  But it came in handy, later
that tradition. The metaphysical poets
Of the Second Coming had it for God or Sense—
Had it in place of a backbone: and many's the scarecrow,
Many's the Raggedy Man it's propped up stiff as a corpse.

Then Asia Street, where I roomed at the family Peets.
A bug mine, a collapsible chamber of horrors
Held together by tarpaper and white chauvinism.
There was Peets with his gin, his nine foot wife, and his son
Who was big enough to be twins—the only man in the South
Who could play both guard and end with no tackle between—

And the daughter, big as all three, with a back-side for a face,
With a mouth of pure guttapercha, with a cast, with a fine
High shining of lunacy crossing her horsy eyes—
'Fuck or fight!' I can hear her yelling it now
And out of the room at the back the bed starts roaring.
The house is moaning and shaking, the dust snows down from the ceiling,
The old dog sneezes and pukes and Peets is cursing his wife:
'Teach your daughter some manners, you goddam cow!
Tell her to close her door, and come back to this goddam bed!'

And Crane comes in with his latest girl and *they* start
Kicking the gong around; and the whole place shaking and roaring,
Like a plane about to take off; and the gators awake
Bellowing, under the house, and flee for the bayous
While the old dog screams at the moon—
Order! Tradition and Order!
And all the beds in the joint a-flap at both ends!

Then I would get up, maybe, leaving that sex foundry
That stamping mill for the minting of unfixed forms,
And lug my chastity, my faithfulness, around the town.

Moon in the western dark and the blue permanent stars
Shifted a bit in the sky.
                        Toward music, toward speech, drifting
The night.
High noon of darkness now and the loud magnolias lifting
Their ten-thousand candle-power blooms.
                        Proud flesh, these flowers.
Earth offering, inescapable
Emblems.
Offering of night birds too, and the travelling far stars
And the round dance of the seasons: inviolate
Torment.

Open the night's cold book.
                        Salt for the quick.
Now from the farthest bar a music breaks and binds,
An icy necklace of bluest fire spills down the hour.
The river stirs and seethes, its steady working whispering
Into the ultimate South
                        Drifting
Toward Scorpio in the hangdog heat of the sullen season.
Toward the Gulf . . .
In the river-run hush and hurry of that great night water:
To the black lots and the god-mating beasts of the green man-farming sea.

"Tom McGrath is a nice fellow, and his wife is animated and attractive. He had a job, after his disemployment from State College due to the investigators, putting up numbers on a stock broker's board, but was displaced by a mechanical board. Now he helps polish the wood of objects d'arte manufactured hereabouts. His wife does weaving of material destroyed by moths, burns, etc. So the committee has really displaced him. Going home in the car we composed the following:

> First I lost my reputation.
> Then my job by automation.
> Now by way of consolation.
> I am on a long vacation.

It wasn't funny, though."

    Ann Stanford
    Diary entry
    Saturday, May 14, 1955

■ **Complaint**
The Queen
Of Accident
Shook a bloody fist at me.
Just about then
I realized
The hand she was brandishing at me
Was my own

O Reality
O great Queen
Where were you
When your sister, that bitch Illusion
Bit off my arm?

■ **Successions**
Whoever drives commands the speed that kills.
Loving cups, loves, sports cars, the heads of bears—
We show the trophies of our varied skills.

The fatal elegance that power distills
Unnerves the hunted, leads them into snares.
Whoever drives desires the speed that kills.

The Cross-cut slaves that stank on Roman hills
Invented godhead's posture unawares:
We show the trophies of our famous skills.

Let man be perfected of his ancient ills!
So say the Doctors and the doctrinaires.
(Whoever drives acquires the speed that kills.)

This dream comes down to purges and to pills:
The capitally sick are hanged in the squares—
We show the trophies of our cherished skills.

Neither papal successions nor Bolshevik wills
Insure old bones against heretic heirs.
Whoever drives deserves the speed that kills.
We show the trophies of our fatal skills.

■ **Longshot O'Leary Says It's Your Duty to be Full of Fury**
Sing a song for Thomas McGrath
Who rises splendidly in his wrath

To blaspheme the Pope and blaspheme his Leader
and takes no pity on Gentle Reader.

Distributing curses and kicks in the ass
Whenever he sees a Philistine pass.

*Longshot O'Leary Says a Square is a Person who Cannot Read Caudwell*

Thomas doubts and Thomas is wary
Of prigs with a leftist vocabulary.

Though full of praise for Mao and Marx
He'd throw Sam Sillen[1] to the sharks.

O Marx and Yeats and Sydney B.[2]
Are Thomas's Holy Trinity.

*Longshot O'Leary Says a Bad Poem is Sinful*

Swoon if you will at Percy B. Shelley
To Thomas he's a pain in the belly.

Whitman, he thinks, deserves to be sung
His imitators should all be hung.

*Longshot O'Leary Picks Sorcery over Physics—with Odds*

A mathematician looking sage
Drives McGrath to a high fine rage.

For science is drivel. The best it can do
Is manufacture a gadget or two.

What ails us all is plain to see
Be Saved! he cries, read Poetry!

    Alice McGrath (1952)
    *North Dakota Quarterly,* fall 1982
    1. Sam Sillen was the editor of *Masses and Mainstream*
    2. Sydney Bichet, the jazz musician.

## Alabanza Para Thomas McGrath
### Praises for Thomas McGrath

Perhaps I met Thomas McGrath somewhere in Nicaragua at a time when the blackbird's menacing thunder sounded over our heads. The blackbird flying invisible in the heavens, which alone guard our dreams and the dreams of men and women like him, on the other side of the trenches.

I don't recall his appearance, but I immediately recognized his essence as a poet, his true presence, one afternoon in September 1990 at Alice's house in Ventura—his *Selected Poems* shining like a blue jewel in the sunlit studio opening on the hills sloping down to California's serene sea.

That same night we flew from Santa Barbara to San Francisco. In the secluded Victorian house where we stayed (it was like a hide-out out of a novel by Dashiell Hammett) I began to enter the translucent waters of his poetry. I regretted the time I had lost for not having read him earlier.

*It is autumn but early*
*No crow cries from the dry woods . . .*

I thought of Thoreau in that enchanted forest which had not yet been troubled by the buffaloes with teeth of silver, as Rubén Darío described the empire builders.

*Where were these giants? The sea offered*

*A single clue, a symbol: no explanation . . .*

The echoes of Whitman—the grand old man with his beard full of butterflies, as Rubén Darío saw him—sounded in the poetry of Thomas McGrath, an American people's poet. It may sound over-simple, but that is my praise: *Lo más alto es lo popular.* One man, singing in the immense night, of the land of his dreams, literally, and to actual people, those who groan under the weight of the wheel of fortune in the carnival of consumerism.

I was beginning to translate Thomas McGrath's poetry—his praises for women and for vegetables—when Alice told me in Managua that he had died. I didn't know that. That there would be an event in Chicago to honor his memory. There, in the city of Carl Sandburg, it would be held in the Amalgamated Clothing and Textile Workers' Union Hall, as we might render homage in the Sandinista Workers' Center.

Alice asked me to write a few lines to be read at the celebration.

In answer to his question in *Echoes Inside the Labyrinth:*

*After a war, who has news for the poet?*

I reply: after the war, the revolution lives on. That is the news from Nicaragua for the poet who, from the other side of the trenches, was the guardian of our dreams.

Sergio Ramirez, novelist and vice president of Nicaragua
    under the Sandinista government
Managua, January 1991
Translated by Alice McGrath

Vol. 3 : No. 3 : 1954

75¢

The
California Quarterly

PABLO NERUDA
LES THOMPSON
TERESA MANN
DON GORDON
MILLEN BRAND
EDITH WITT
DAVID LEMON
BERT MEYERS
WALDEEN
RAY FABRIZIO
MELISSA BLAKE
EUGENE FRUMKIN
JEANNETTE MAINO
MELVIN WEISBURD
BERNARD RAYMUND
JOANNE DE LONGCHAMPS

EDWIN ROLFE: 1909-1954

Morton Dimondstein, cover: *The California Quarterly* 3, no. 3 (1954).

# Edwin Rolfe

Edwin Rolfe. b. 1909–d. 1954. Edwin Rolfe was born Solomon Fishman in New York City to Russian immigrant and radical parents. In his youth he joined the Young Communist League and the Communist Party. He published stories and poems in the *Daily Worker,* for which he would later become a feature editor. He attended the University of Wisconsin for a year and then left. In 1927 he used the pseudonym Edwin Rolfe for the first time, and in 1933 he was published in an anthology of radical poets titled *We Gather Strength. Dynamo* magazine published some of his poems; his first volume of poetry, *To My Contemporaries,* was published by Dynamo Press in 1936. In 1937 he joined the Abraham Lincoln Brigade in Spain to fight against Franco and fascism. He worked as editor of *Volunteer for Liberty* magazine and in 1938 was involved in the Loyalist military offensive at Ebro. When his wife, Mary, took a job in Los Angeles, he followed her there, publishing a novel, *The Glass Room,* and working off and on in Hollywood. When the House Un-American Activities Committee came to Los Angeles, Rolfe was blacklisted. His second book of poems, *First Love and Other Poems,* was published in Los Angeles in 1951, and his last book, *Permit Me Refuge,* was published posthumously by *The California Quarterly,* to which he had contributed toward the end of his life. He died in 1954 and was buried in Los Angeles. The first issue of *Coastlines* was dedicated to Rolfe. Forty years later his *Collected Poems* was brought out by the University of Illinois Press.

"He was a serious poet—that is to say, he did not believe that one could create a whole corpus of work out of little moral or mock-moral allegories concerning birds and animals, or out of the eccentric learning of pedantic uncles. He was always smelling the real sweat of the terrible Now, the terrible Always. Probably all really good poems have that smell. . . . At the end he was trying to write that not-quite-yet-written poem which is both lament and triumph. A hard work, and as good a signature as any."

Thomas McGrath

"Foreward"

*Permit Me Refuge*

### ■ Sentry

Asleep, breathing like an enormous child,
wounded, but soothed by the cool salve of night,
the army lies exhausted on its stony bed,
its lonely eyes clear on the outpost, envying the sleepers,
dreaming the special waking dream of solitary sentries,
but tense, fearing the naked knife in each blurred shadow.

Whether in Guinea or the Appenine hills,
during or after battle, or in maneuver,
each sleeping man is obsessed, weighted with anger,
uneasy at midnight against the mysterious mass,
asleep on the next ridge or beyond the ocean,
whose voice and touch are death, he knows as enemy.

The dreams are dinosaurs and moths, various
as ways of wounds and mutilation in battle;
and nightmare imaginings agitate the night
with wild and muted sound, while here and there a shriek
rises. But no one stirs except the outcast sentry
who envies the sleep that brings the dream and the shriek.

"On the eve of going to press we learned with sorrow of the sudden death of our friend and contributor, Edwin Rolfe. Our loss is an even heavier loss to American poetry. In a later issue we hope to present a generous portion of the unpublished poems of Edwin Rolfe as a memorial to a man of courage, talent and vision in an oppressive time."

The Editors

*The California Quarterly* 3, no. 2 (1954)

## ■ Bon Voyage

Permit me refuge in a region of your brain:
carry and resurrect me, whatever path you take,
as a ship creates its own unending wake
or as rails define direction in a train.

Permit my memory refuge: but not the recent years
when grains of dross obscured the bars of truth.
Delve deeper back in years to your first youth,
passionate, clean, untarnished by small fears.

And if your conscience truly bears my memory,
rekindle if you can the dying candle light:
let the wake not lose its contour, nor the bright
reflected sun waver as the rails glide by.

My wake and rail attend you, welded and wed,
through the blind tunnels of the years ahead.

### Edwin Rolfe: 1909–1954

The enduring strength of Edwin Rolfe was derived from and shared with the people. His best work speaks to us personally, helping us to remember not merely what we are but what we have yet to become.

His grievous death occurred as our last issue was going to press. There we announced that in our next we would present a selection from his unpublished poems.

We preface that selection with a tribute, by Eugene Frumkin, to Rolfe the man and the poet.

The Editors

EUGENE FRUMKIN

---

### Elegy for a Soldier of the Spanish Civil War

A gentle wind quiets his brow,
His star-crossed dreams, a man with Spain
In his blood, a sane Quixote—how
Bravely he charged the warmill in the days
Now bullet-fled and dead as bones!
And wisely charted were his ways,
Among the slings, among the stones,
As he walked the world against the grain.

His mind was always ripe with fields
Of stars and crosses, friends beneath
The Spanish earth, good seed to yield
A love of that ghostly nation, bled
To the wishing bone. He loved the leaves
Of long gone autumns and the dead
Flowers he saw where the sword cleaves,
And made of all a simple wreath

Of poems for cities dead and men
A tear's time seen, seen through the tears
In the eye of his blood-infused pen.
The gipsy wind has stolen him
And he too has lost the feral spin
Of mosquitoes in the mind, the grim
Scraping of files beneath the skin.
The wind is still. He nothing hears.

The sky is raw with reddish arcs
And yellow clouds hover, pretending
To the sun's dominion; no bird marks
The twilight slate with graceful curving
Nor abstracts of gyrating plumage.
Cold the forecast of the sky-serving
Mercury of our time; we rummage
Among the fallen stars, depending
On Christ who crossed to death ages

Ago and now, a lifelike waxen
Figure, is the prop of churchly stages.
We skim the ice, our words are smoke;
The skates of fear turn us to some last
Stroke of the sun, our passions cloak
Direction and we grope in vast
Meaningless figures, bungling oxen

Under a palsied yoke. However,
In the soft moments when the poet's lips
Opened his beliefs to me, never
Did that iron horseman of our hope
Ride more irresistibly through
The carnage of lost wars. What scope
His hunger had hunting the true
Flesh of love, wider than the worship

Of the rigid kneelers at the altars
Of artificial light! A man
Of balsa wood and crepe, whose fault or
Bane lay in the excess he willed
Of his too love-weak heart, he fought
More than dream battles, surely killed
More than tin soldiers. At times I caught
A glimpse in this tiny sparrow man

Of the goshawk straining in his eyes
To catch the wind, and yet this hawk
Too rarely rose in the clear skies
Of his poems. His voice is lost
Where Dylan and Yeats found words to boom,
Gold, rhythm-bobbing bells, across
The plains of our senses. But in the room
Where we, Phaedos to his talk,

Apprentices of the craft of words,
Listened, the moon-webbed seas enfolded
The living, dying men and birds

Of barb-wire beaches, and held the shore
In gentle sway until my heart
Could feel the world at ebb no more,
But all, all caught in his calm art,
The seas of peace coming on, moulded.

Each land is one now, Ed, and Spain
Is anywhere you lie, the part
Of you that would not sleep. The pain
You left behind took root in time,
Will blend with spring, survive the frost:
O such as you stay warm beneath the rime
Of years, and where your star crossed
A friend's, he marks the place in his heart.

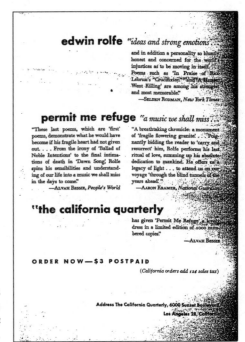

Advertisement for Edwin
Rolfe's *Permit Me Refuge,*
from *The California
Quarterly* 4, no. 1 (1956).

"Edwin Rolfe, one of the contributors to this issue, died before the magazine was completed. He was a poet and a writer of fiction and reportage; he was a member of the Lincoln Battalion which fought in the Spanish Civil War, and much of his work deals with experiences resulting from that war; above all, Edwin Rolfe was a man whose friends and even brief acquaintances can find satisfaction in remembering. His extreme gentleness, combined with the strength to act, to kill or die if necessary in defense of the value of the human being, made him unique among his contemporaries. Because many of the other writers represented here knew and admired Edwin Rolfe and his works, and because he is a man who ought to be honored, we dedicate this issue of *Coastlines* to him."

The Editors

"Dedication"

*Coastlines* (spring 1955)


Except for light or comic verse, Pulitzer-prizewinning volumes, and the highly select list of Alan Swallow, commercial publishers hardly dare touch poetry any more. Not even the university presses—though one should except Yale with its series of Younger Poets—have given asylum to poetry; at best their explication-stuffy quarterlies use a little verse as filler.

As an independent publisher, THE CALIFORNIA QUARTERLY from its inception has given generous space and attention to poetry—particularly to the poem of major dimensions and significance. So it is fitting that as its first venture in book publishing it now offers a distinguished volume of verse, Edwin Rolfe's posthumous *Permit Me Refuge*.

We invite those of our readers who do not yet possess Edwin Rolfe's *Permit Me Refuge* to inspect our back cover and act appropriately. Publishers can be only as independent as their patrons are discerning.

The Editors

*The California Quarterly*

1956

### ■ Poem

Many an outcast calls me friend
    and with that word compels
my pity to embrace his loneliness,
my meagre share of goodness to expand
till friendship and intense
    compassion warm us both.

Many a weakling thinks me strong
    and with his thought endows
my weakness with an unsuspected power,
unearths within my heart a fire
and in my mind an iron
    that was not there before.

Many a fool has called me wise
    and, doing so, has forced
the little sense I had to rise
up from its deep morass of ignorance
clear to the surface, there to solve
    his problem and my own.

And loveless girls have called me *love.*
    These do I most enshrine
because their simple longing builds
love amid lovelessness, and gilds
even the tarnished feelings till they shine—
    yes, theirs and mine.

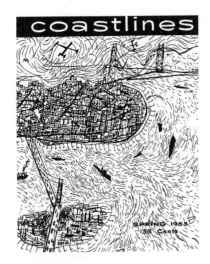

David Lemon, cover:
*Coastlines* 1, no. 1
(spring 1955).

■ **Idiot Joe Prays in Pershing Square**
**And Gets Hauled in for Vagrancy**
Let us praise,
while time to praise remains,
the simple bullet,
the antique ambuscade
and the fanatic justice-crazed assassin—
we who have made
and fired napalm
and casually—
alone among all men—
dropped on Man
the only atom bomb.

Morton Dimondstein,
cover: *The California
Quarterly* 3, no. 1,
(autumn 1953).

Autumn 1953
75¢

ESTHER McCOY
*The Pepper Tree*

FRANK SCULLY
*Portrait of an
Undesirable Alien*

JAMES WYCKOFF
*The Homesteader*

Poems by Randall
Swingler, G. W. Brandt,
Ewart Milne, Montagu
Slater, Norman Buller,
Jack Beeching, Roy
Fuller, W. V. Evans,
Sydney Tremayne

Drawings & Engravings
by Arnold Mesches,
Morton Dimondstein,
Marion Campbell

The
**California Quarterly**

"Publishing a magazine in the humanist tradition is scarcely less of a struggle in Los Angeles. However, *The California Quarterly* is determined to remain alive and kicking in the community that has blacklisted so many of its most talented craftsmen."

The Editors
*The California Quarterly* 3, no. 2 (1954)

# Don Gordon

Don Gordon. b. 1902–d. 1989. Don Gordon was born in Bridgeport, Connecticut, to an American mother with English parents, Sadie Levy, and a father Morris J. Gordon, who had immigrated as a boy from Lithuania. In 1912 he moved with his family to Los Angeles. He was part of the first class of what was to become the University of California at Los Angeles, then called The Southern Campus. He received his B.A. from Pomona College and spent a year at the University of Southern California (USC) law school. He married Henriette Goldfinger in 1931. During World War II Gordon was a corporal in the California National Guard. He then found various kinds of employment and ended up as first a law clerk and then a reader of books on which scripts for movies might be based, working for Republic Pictures, Universal, RKO, Paramount, and Metro-Goldwyn-Mayer. He lived in Los Angeles except for one year in the late twenties that he spent in New York. In 1953 he was brought before the House Un-American Activities Committee and lost his job as a reader for the studios. Eventually he worked in community homes for the mentally disturbed. Gordon published several books of poetry: *Statement* (1943), *Civilian Poems* (1946), *Displaced Persons* (1958), *On the Ward* (1977), *Excavations* (1979), and *Sea of Tranquility.* Gordon's *Collected Poems* will be published soon by the University of Illinois Press.

### The Dissenter

People will turn the middens we bequeath:
>the hunters
>or the hunted
>express the age.

The facts go with the cities into the rock strata:
>someone is not to be spoken to
>someone is not to occupy the house
>>in the sacred wood
>dangerous thoughts are exported
>>on the outgoing tide
>it is verboten to play with the
>>dissenter's child.

The tributaries feed into the sea
>of violence.
The iron cells multiply like the amoeba;
>the nucleus
In each is a man who does not agree
>with the warden.

They nail in the hands and feet
>the bill of attainder,
They display in the German silence
>the broken mirror,
The image of forbidden people.

They need an enemy to tear apart
>in the mad season
When the air is burning and the cloud
>signals unbearable change.
The dissenter is born alive on the edges
>of the weather.

### The Travelers

The endurable voyages are those I do not take.
The gulls drop like summer on the nervous heads
    in transit;
The iron statesmen receive them with grins
    in the foreign parks.

The sun is a gold branch of my tree
    as they meet themselves
At the tombs of leathery kings, the moon
    over the house
When they leave the Gothic block on the spine
    of the natives.

The birds move in their southern arrows.
    The travelers return,
The snapshot of the overfed shrewd pigeon
    on their fingers,
Always out of focus in the corner the same
    opaque eye:
      to whom does it belong?
      to whom is it visible?

I have wondered if they know
the name of the child with glaucoma,
As I wonder how they sleep
with their eyes full of bones.

### the investigation

Somewhere in his mind,
Like a lost toy in the attic
    of his childhood,
There must be an absolute, the secret
    that will rescue them.

The man and the girl were seen in the doorway:
He must have said something to her
    and she to him.
If they knew what it meant, they would
    all be saved.

Someone besides the police must have been
    at the scene of the crime.
He was on another continent at the time:
    in uniform, a gun in his hand.
What were his intentions?

When the special and sacred explosive
    was dropped,
The cabinet explained: it was to save
    the city.
They have saved the city, he said,
    but the people are dead.

On a morning of sun and birds he was heard
    whistling in his house.
A whistle can be dangerous: it could lead
    to singing.
The budget unbalanced        the deficit mounting
    what if they danced in the streets?

Yesterday he talked of the sail on the azure line
    after the hull vanished.
The day before: of the sun like a flower, the earth
    as circling insect;
Or later in the stone room the men hooded, sandals
    on their feet,
The book open at the fatal page; or in the village
    on a rockbound coast
When a child was sick or the corn failed
    there were evil eyes.

The bailiff in his gray corner,
the gendarme at the door like a public statue,
cowled or bare, the committee is always in session:
    tell
    tell the secret
    tell us before we go.

### At the Station

Which way do the trains run?
Traveler, lost under the station lamp,
I am farther from home than you.

Nothing is familiar except the damp memory
    of childhood:
The inhabitants are woven in their cocoons;
    each recalls,
Long since dismantled by the wrecking crew,
    his house and his beliefs.

The landscape has been subtly shifted, it is
    out of focus or we are:
Yesterday, manacled to the marshal, I saw the boy
    I knew at school;
There were trees where we stand, then the sound
    of hammers,
In the morning you will see the scaffolds
    with their solid arms.

Who has displaced a nation? The people
    arrive and depart
On their laughter-ridden tragic errands
    shot with music.
Nearly midnight in the station and they sleep
    like plants.

The military train has always the same destination;
    the circus train ends
In a dream of carousels; the quieter cars
    head for the resurrection
In the shelter; the scientists are borne on the
    Special to their last grave convention.

Which way does the big train go?
Traveler, lost under the station lamp,
I'm a stranger here myself.

### Consider the Meaning of Love

Consider the meaning of love in the time
    of the murderers;
Examine the heart as the brain goes blind
    with fear;
Observe the flower in particular when the house
    is burning.

They blew up the island like a fish in a hole
    in the killer Pacific:
That was the day the world embraced itself,
That was the day for lovers under the sign
    of the active cloud.

When in the hour of night the windows are lit
    in the famous buildings,
A cold wave crosses the frontier of a generation
    in its sleep,
The coyote howls, the vulture comes down
    from the sky.
It is the hour of fever, the hour to study
    the nature of love.

Everything is lost to the dead, they are
    not continuous,
The generals are not continuous nor the diplomats.
    Fired on
Or flattened or strangled by vines, the cities
    are restored
By love in the living, the continuity of healing
    and remorse.

Remember the flower in particular when the house
    is burning;
Revive the heart as the brain goes blind
    with fear;
Dare to announce the meaning of love in the time
    of the destroyers.

### The Middle Passage

I think of the young, of their disbelief in dying:
Someone who is not there is at once a stranger;
It happens to another generation—always, fortunately.
Willing to slide off the ant-ridden globe.

My mother and father went too often to funerals;
Their lives seemed bleak to be so fond of ceremony.
Later I knew they simply went to say goodbye:
When they were old I saw they had no friends.

The landmarks, at the middle passage, began to go:
First the physician, my friend back from war
With the unexploded mine in his breast:
Next the architect, his spine temporal,
Malignant, his houses lighted and enduring:
Then the poet, his sun blackened in Spain.
Who lived among us by reflection for a time:
Now the great artery closed by questions.
The refugee stays as long as we remember.

Loss is unendurable until it becomes a fact.
There is an insight to be sought at noon
At the intersection of the busiest streets
Where only commonplace objects converge.

Here in the inescapable sunlight, discover
You are not the axle on which the world turns.
Abstract yourself like a number from the scene.

The landscape with its motions will not quiver:
The cars will roll on, the people buy and sell.
The officer will stand like a statesman.
The signals will stop and go, stop and go, stop and go.

Intolerable the pain until you surround it:
Neither happy nor unhappy, return,
Relieved of the weight of the axle
And armed for once with a fact.

There are no new words or ways to live with death.
The old ones keep their secret like a cabal.
The ego comes lonely, a recruit to his first battle;
It is not cowardice, it is ignorance about to be shot.

Morton Dimondstein,
cover: *The California
Quarterly* 4, no. 1 (1956).

# Naomi Replansky

Naomi Replansky b. 1918—Naomi Replansky was born in the Bronx, New York, the daughter of Sol Replansky and Fannie Ginsberg. She started writing poetry at the age of ten, and a group of her poems was published in Harriet Monroe's *Poetry* when she was sixteen. Replansky was educated in New York public schools and graduated high school in the middle of the Depression. Much later, in 1956, and after publication of her first book, she attended UCLA and graduated with a degree in geography. Her first book, *Ring Song,* was published in 1952 by Scribner's and was nominated for the National Book Award in poetry. In the 1980s her translation of Bertolt Brecht's *St. Joan of the Stockyards* was performed in New York. She has contributed poems and translations to both American and European magazines and anthologies. She published a chapbook, *Twenty-One Poems: Old and New,* in 1988 and in 1994 published *The Dangerous World: New and Selected Poems, 1934–1994.* She has had such varied jobs as office worker, factory worker, computer programmer, and teacher—to mention only the longer-lasting jobs. She now lives and writes in New York City.

Mario Casetta, Woodcut: "Car Barn" in *The California Quarterly* 4, no. 1 (1956).

### ■ Ring Song

. . . When that joy is gone for good
I move the arms beneath the blood.

When my blood is running wild
I sew the clothing of a child.

When that child is never born
I lean my breast against a thorn.

When the thorn brings no reprieve
I rise and live, I rise and live.

When I live from hand to hand
Nude in the marketplace I stand.

When I stand and am not sold
I build a fire against the cold.

When the cold does not destroy
I leap from ambush on my joy . . .

Mario Casetta, Woodcut: "War Orphan" in
*The California Quarterly* 4, no. 1 (1956).

---

**Naomi Replansky**

## Housing Shortage

I tried to live small.
I took a narrow bed.
I held my elbows to my sides.
I tried to step carefully
And to think softly
And to breathe shallowly
In my portion of air
And to disturb no one.

Yet see how I spread out and I cannot help it.
I take to myself more and more, and I take nothing
That I do not need, but my needs grow like weeds.
All over and invading; I clutter this place
With all the apparatus of living.
You stumble over it daily.

And then my lungs take their fill.
And then you gasp for air.

Excuse me for living,
But, since I am living,
Given inches, I take yards,
Taking yards, dream of miles,
And a landscape, unbounded
And vast in abandon.

And you dreaming the same.

Mario Casetta, Woodcut: "Deportation Hearing"
in *The California Quarterly* 4, no. 1 (1956).

"The editors of *The California Quarterly* admired the artwork and felt
it improved the magazine after continuous questioning of the cost."
  Mort Dimondstein, art editor, *The California Quarterly*
  Interview with Estelle Gershgoren Novak, November 1996

### Night Prayer for Various Trades

Machinist in the pillow's grip,
Be clumsy and be blind
And let the gears spin free, and turn
No metal in your mind.

Long, long may the actress lie
In slumber like a stone,
The helpless words that rise from sleep
Be no words but her own.

Laborer, drift through a dark
Remote from clay and lime.
O do not tunnel through the night
In unpaid overtime.

You out-of-work, walk into sleep.
It will not ask to see
Your proof of skill or strength or youth
And shows its movies free.

And may the streetcleaner float down
A spotless avenue.
*Who red-eyed wake at morning break
All have enough to do.*

*Enough to do. Now let the day
Its own accountings keep.
But may our dreams keep other time
Throughout our sprawling sleep.*

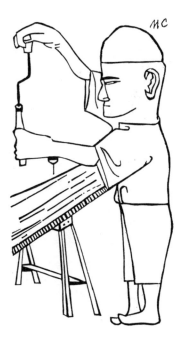

Mario Casetta, Woodcut: "Apprentice," in
*The California Quarterly* 4, no. 1 (1956).

---

**N a o m i   R e p l a n s k y**

### ■ You Walked a Crooked Mile

You walked a crooked mile
you smiled a crooked smile
you dropped a wandering tear
all in a crooked year.

When there was one kiss
against ten curses
and one loaf
against ten hungry
and one hello
against ten goodbyes
the odds stalked
your crooked steps.

And you turned no corner
without heart-tightening
and against ten cannon
you had one fist
and against ten winters
you had one fire.

This page and facing page:
Martin Lubner, Four Drawings,
*The California Quarterly* 3,
no. 4 (1955).

[ 45 ]

### ■ Epitaph: 1945

My spoon was lifted when the bomb came down
That left no face, no hand, no spoon to hold.
One hundred thousand died in my hometown.
This came to pass before my soup was cold.

**Naomi Replansky**

# William Pillin

William Pillin, b. 1910–d. 1985. William Pillin was born in Alexandrowsk, the Ukraine. The son of Elconon Pillin and Anna Naiditch, he came to the United States at the age of fourteen. He spent six years in Chicago, where his father was a pharmacist, and there met Richard Wright and Nelson Algren. In 1934, when he was nineteen, Pillin married his wife, Polia, a milliner who was studying painting and sculpture. He attended Lewis Institute of Chicago, Northwestern University, and the University of Chicago. William Pillin worked in Los Angeles in front of his wife's studio, where he fired the pots she made and wrote poetry. They raised a son, Boris, who became a musician and composer. Pillin published numerous books of poetry: *Poems, Theory of Silence, Dance Without Shoes, Passage After Midnight, Pavanne for a Fading Memory, Everything Falling,* and *To the End of Time.*

"We want to point to tangible evidence that poems are being written in the southern part of this State.

Actually the number of poets in Los Angeles area is as great or greater than in the northern city. . . .

The poets of Los Angeles are moved by the same psychic motivations as the poets of San Francisco, but perhaps in a manner less calculated to provoke a journalistic sensation. We all experience the tensions and anxieties of our uncertain era; the alienation of man from the main sources of his being; of man from man, of man from Nature, of man from the very means of his livelihood. And these motivations are as likely to prevail in Berlin and Rome as in Los Angeles and San Francisco."

William Pillin

"Statement"

*Epos: Poetry Los Angeles: A Special Issue* (summer 1958)

Polia Pillin, linoleum block cut:
*Epos* 9, no. 4 (summer 1958).

"I have mentioned William Pillin, a retiring and lyrical poet. More should be said about him. I believe I met him through Bert Meyers or through Gene Frumkin. He had a book out and his home was a nice, warm place to be in. However, one night we were invited there to meet James Dickey. Gene was there, Stanley Kiesel and his wife, Ann Stanford and her husband, Pillin's brother-in-law and his wife, the Dickeys, and, of course, Polia, Pillin's pottery-making wife. Everything went well, small talk about poetry during the first part of the evening, but after dinner the conversation veered to the Israeli-Arab conflict, where it was obvious that the fiercely partisan viewpoint of part of the Pillin clan did not meet with Dickey's approval. Slowly but surely, the verbal conflict was enlarged to include racial overtones and Dickey dropped the word *nigger* as a matter of course (it must be noted that he and his wife were—or are—Southerners). Things came pretty close to the physical and we all took our leave through separate doors, cursing in different languages. An absolutely memorable evening."

Alvaro Cardona-Hine, "Poetry in Los Angeles 1945 to 1975: Part I"
*Bachy* 12 (1978)

## ■ Sabbath

Not the prescribed movement of hands,
not the ritual whispers
out of antique books with broken bindings,
not these you left me
people of blessed candles,
but a certain music, a secret between us,
so that even I, a pagan in Babylon,
celebrate the Creation's completion.

I can spare but a few hours
for this evening's silence
as I can't afford a whole day without labor;
and the hymns I sing are
alas, not Zemirot, the Sabbath hymns,
but snatches from Handel, an Anglican rabbi;
but I will praise the Indwelling Glory,
putting, however briefly, my trials behind me,
putting, however briefly, Egypt behind me.

I will not stint, I will provide of the finest.
The floors will be scrubbed, the furniture polished.
With choice meat and hallot I will praise Thee,
aye, with a double portion of manna,
with broiled fish, with a goblet of brandy.

Overlook therefore the profane, the informal.
Send Shabbat Shalom, the peace of the evening,
to us who are doing their ignorant best at this altar;
son, wife and husband
basking at twilight
in the tender effulgence of grandmother's candles.

## Aubade

Life, be fresh with daybreak!
Though papers print death
            by wind, by fire,
and wolf teeth are bared
at curving hollows
where little homes sleep,
may I wake, my storms scattered
on lovely landscape of her body,
and wonder at life's small matters
that continue forever.
                  Light jostles
sea-waves, ghosts cough
in trees, the twig
drunk with raindrops
            snaps, falls
to junkyard of dead leaves;

all these will last
beyond the moment of being
as the wind of flutes persists
past the bright hoard of sound.

## ■ Two Jewish Poems

1.

The rabbi noted: it is worse to violate
your neighbor's place beneath the blue
than to sin against the Holy One. For God
is where you are, in field or home.
His address known
your moral litigation can be solved
by a contrite and an absolving sigh.
But if your neighbor move away
how will you find him? To what teeming street,
what far-away and unfamiliar shore
will you address regrets?
And you will carry all your years
the memory of someone's downcast eyes
and grievance unredeemed. Somewhere will walk
a murdered man, your knife between his ribs.

2.
Take what is at hand
as sparrows take to doorways
when rain whips oak-leaves.
Take to the lonely hills
to gather silences
when wolf-eyes gleam
in the green valley.

Better, though the work is beneath you,
to sell your muscles to a mason
than to ask favors from God.
Take what is at hand
to look freely
in God's blue eye.

You, rider of clouds, wake up!
You can starve waiting
for singing tomorrows.
Black bread freely eaten
makes a calm melodious Sabbath.
Wait no longer for tinselled
mitsvas from heaven
but light your candles
to bless what is at hand.

### ■ Ocean Park

I confront the star-spell of the esplanade!
I walk as jaunty as a sailor
among fortune-tellers, dancers, gymnasts,
among girls that stroll like swaying flowers,
among gamblers, among all sorts of gypsies.

Necromantic presences mingle among us:
this cute whore is Phryne, sister of moonlights,
that old Jew under a streetlight is Merlin;
Shahrazad serves coffee and pancakes
and Sindbad lures the unwary with trinkets.

I have an illusion of freedom
and it well may be a prelude to trouble.
Who cares? This is a magical evening!
All things assume a novel succulence; clusters
of black grapes, sausages, pastries. I am hungry!
And avid too, like a cat in the jungle
seduced by a scent of musk or civet.

In blue-bright air flares are falling
to dissolve on restaurants, wineshops,
dance-halls and dimly lighted interiors
from one of which (an obscure shrine of Pan?)
we hear a bacchic wail of clarinets.
Here is a café where Lesbians gather
and here is a place where, they tell me,
anything can happen. The unpredictable
lures like an unwritten poem. All else failing
one could shoot down a bomber or witness
a piquant disrobing in a penny arcade.

I turn sadly back to my curfewed suburb
of discreet doorways and subdued lamplights.
What is lacking there, what tang, what tonic?
Nocturnal laughters and musical whispers
have been exiled to this sea-edge
by the police and the jeering merchants.
Held by a dangerous moonlight
between cold stone and colder waters
life's subtle djinns clamor for release.

Morton Dimondstein, cover: *The California Quarterly* 3, no. 4 (1955).

■ **That which is good is simply done**
That which is good is simply done
without the manifesto's noise
as Francis talking to the birds
    or Leo to the peasant boys.

The socialism of the heart
is not in schedules, is in man
and what is generous on earth
    is generous without a plan.

As when creative fingers roam
anarchic space in hit or miss
and suddenly discover there
    a luminous caprice.

So musical this silence is!
so natural the heart's technique
like sunlight glittering in trees:
    the rest is rhetoric.

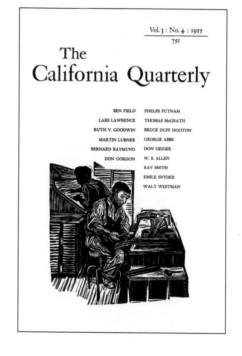

Vol. 3 : No. 4 : 1955
75¢

The
California Quarterly

BEN FIELD    PHELPS PUTNAM
LARS LAWRENCE    THOMAS McGRATH
RUTH V. GOODWIN    BRUCE DUFF HOOTON
MARTIN LUBNER    GEORGE ABBE
BERNARD RAYMUND    DON GEIGER
DON GORDON    W. S. ALLEN
RAY SMITH
EMILE SNYDER
WALT WHITMAN

## Miserere

I will not endow you with a false glow
ghetto
or say that only poets and seers
died in your ashes.

Many mourn the scholars and dreamers,
the beautiful, innocent, talented victims.

I will spare my tears for the
loudmouthed, unhappy, conniving
jews
the usurious lenders

tuberculous, hunchbacked,
scum of the ghettos (the sweepings of Europe).
For them I will weep,
                 for the whores
pale in the doorways, for the spiderous tradesman
with his false measures
            and for all the grey sparrows
hopping about the winters of Poland
               the grief of whose eyes
went up in thin smoke like a final prayer.

For them I weep, I want them returned,
the dwellers of dives, brothels and taverns.
I want them
back as they were, piteous, ignoble,
instead of these grey ashes
that like a winding sheet settles on
                shivering Europe.

# Henri Coulette

Henri Coulette, b. 1927–d. 1988. Henri Coulette was born in Los Angeles, the son of Robert Roger Coulette and Genevieve O'Reilly. He served in the U.S. Army between 1945 and 1946 and received his B.A. from Los Angeles State College (now California State University, Los Angeles) in 1952. Afterward Coulette studied at the University of Iowa and received an M.F.A. in 1954 and a Ph.D. in 1959. He married Jacqueline Meredith in 1950. From 1957 through 1959 he taught English in high school and was an instructor at writers' workshops at the University of Iowa. In 1959 Coulette began teaching at California State University, Los Angeles, and taught there until his death in 1988. He contributed to the Donald Hall, Robert Pack, and Louis Simpson collection, *New Poets of England and America,* in 1957, and to other anthologies. His published volumes of poetry include *The War of the Secret Agents and Other Poems, The Family Goldschmitt,* and *The Attic.*

## Migration

Autumn, and migratory birds begin
Their long passage south, following the river,
Their sword's shadow sheathed in the black night
Of the fixed globe, of the factory towns.

Fatigued, the workers lie in coffin rooms
And listen while the birds parade the streets
Of the midnight sky, and mingle sweat
And grief with contemplation of time.

Not time of poverty: meticulous
Timeclocks that regulate the common sun;
Not time that mocks the pulse it binds; nor psalmed
Hour of the church, or bankers' fiscal year.

But time as movement measured by its goal:
Holding the turning seed, the womb holds time;
And calloused hands holding products of their
Labor are movement's valued calendars.

And measured, too, these dreams, for they will end
With poor men rising, leaving poverty
Wrapped in the wilted winding sheet of their
Long suffered innocence, and, rising, they

Will walk, communing in the warm spring nights,
The avenues of purpose, and, walking, learn
The revolutions no clock ever knew,
Leaving the birds poised like an arch of stars.

### The Head's Dark House

It is childhood's haunted house
That shapes the rapt mind in its warp;
Warp of the fabled house of winter nights
Where choirs of cold wind troop through empty rooms,
Wail in a multitude of tombs.

Dust on the spiraled stair records
Your step and comments on your search;
And ritual of seeking hands that find
In secret places childhood's fading letters
Whose rumors tenant egregious manors.

It is the labyrinthine house
On the legendary midnight hill.
Antique its corridors, those catacombs
Where memory hears the gothic heart
That hallows you always through the caroling dark.

Morton Dimondstein, Engraving:
"Gerry," *The California Quarterly* 3,
no. 2 (1954), also the cover for: *The
California Quarterly* 3, no. 4 (1955).

**Henri Coulette**

### The Problem of Creation

For Thomas McGrath

Noting here the lean burro leaning against
The dry wind, the tourist cars with insects
Smeared across windshields like emblems
Of escape, the corn and the Corn God dying,
I note, too, that the river moves south,
Raising mesas, confirming these reflections.

And south the Gulf, where Crane's bones,
Washed by salt water, stain that sea
And take it, for have we not words where
Others have marrow, or is bone
Obedient to wild genesis, the source, the sea?

In Mexico, where lakes are metaphors
For later myths, the eagle remembers
The serpent dead beneath the thrust
Of talons; his sharp, enameled eye will watch
While images become bread in the oven
Of your words. His scream is your reward.

Morton Dimondstein, Engraving: "View from Toluca," *The California Quarterly* 3, no. 2 (1954).

# Curtis Zahn

Curtis Zahn, b. 1912–d. 1990. Curtis Zahn was born in 1912 in Detroit, Michigan, to Oswald Francis Zahn and Edith Langalier. His grandfather had founded the first German Lutheran church in Los Angeles. He attended the University of California, Berkeley, between 1936 and 1937, San Francisco State College in 1937, and Williams Institute and School of Authorship, Berkeley, in 1938. He worked as a freelance newspaper writer, a lifeguard, and a secretary for the San Diego County Fish and Game Association. He was employed by the *San Diego Tribune* as outdoor editor and worked as a seaman on the Scripps Expedition of Oceanography. An artist, Zahn painted in oils between 1957 and 1963. In these years he organized the poetry readings that were broadcast on Pacifica Foundation's radio station in Los Angeles. During World War II he was a conscientious objector and served a year in a federal penitentiary. Between 1942 and 1945 he was associate editor of *The Compass,* a Public Service Camp magazine. He won the Dylan Thomas Award in 1960 for a poem and the Old Globe Theater Award for the best one-act play in 1963. His books include *American Contemporary,* a collection of stories, and *One Extraordinary a.m.,* a collection of poems.

### ■ The People's Choice

Destined to be born and born to lead,
He was raised to be born, to be led
To be destined. And here,
In this greatest of cities
In the best of counties; in the
Finest of States in a
Nation among nations over
This largest of worlds, he was
First to oppose war, the
First to fight.
The last to be first, yet, first
to be last. No one
Was more in favor
of fewer people; for less
Time than most citizens.
Nor gave more for less
While doing less for more, than
The Honorable Candidate.

Morton Dimondstein, Engraving: ""Musicians,"
*The California Quarterly* 3, no. 2 (1954).

### Unposed Photograph of I. I. Freitag, Esq.

They say he could blow life into the F-holes
Of waxed, waning, leatherstained old violins
And smash corporations
While owls in the eaves laid cross eyed eggs
And build universes on a cost-plus basis
As termites bit on the buyer's market

Venerable old I. I. Freitag
Muttering, charging, retreating
And caning the cameras
And benevolently dictating to a small rubber dog
Gone suddenly crazy with trees and hydrants

Surprised at his birdcalling and whistling
To the mighty wheelbase of his limousine
Though informed by his Hamilton
That John with his Princeton diploma
Shall not glide comfortingly to the curb
For exactly 43 seconds yet, then
Mother his master into the grey-gloved
unrecognizable face of plateglass anonymity

Gentlemen, you come upon him as do ferrets
Whose teeth persecute the blue, frantic old eyes
Ordained to gnaw away at the Great Man
Worrying and always scurrying
For deadlines and flashbulbs
And he has no statement to make today.

"I used to go to see Curtis [Zahn] in Malibu when he had his meetings. . . . It wasn't just poetry, also stories. . . . Curtis would make spaghetti. . . . Then he moved to a place on Miller Drive and had poetry and story readings. . . . He willed it to the Pacifica Foundation."

Josephine Ain

Interview with Estelle Gershgoren Novak, October 1996

Morton Dimondstein, Engraving: "Street Musicians," *The California Quarterly* 3, no. 2 (1954).

### Officers, Gentlemen, Reluctant Violence

Colonels Oddbold & Fieldglove, and the
Tall, charitable stance of Major Brassblower
Were the men
Behind the men
Behind the 8-ball, sir,
And well—it's a living.

Who in
Hellever
saw such a sight
As manmight, cannonshot and Jeepropelled,
And a folding steel umbrella
Across the sky? No,
And whamming whole armies with riding crops.
Drinking airfarce toasts
In gentlemanic haberdashery so inscrutably allied
To women's fashion journals,
And the good life of glamorfaked backgrounds,
Soft to the touché,
The smoothquip
And fine young U.S. couples

Reluctantly engaged in the awful practice
Of blowing up the entire frigging universe.

Fellows,
The brains that frapped today's anyhow
Hatched foulducks and money-chicks, yes,
and a majority citizenry idolmugging might—
Or anything,
Except ice cold charity
Or themselves . . .

## ■ Tijuana

In all that thin, squalid, exploited valley
There exists no security, only the stoic
Freedom of the economically damned, and
Everywhere hangs listlessly the olive-eyed
Color of greasewood's smoke. Here, crab-grass
Rebounds under the lifted hooves of melancholy
cattle, but it's crew-cut, it's sparse, dry
And creamed with dust. And manzanita thinks
adolescent thoughts about willow, knowing, too
the peculiarized smell of corrugated tin
roofs that defend from rare rain, the radios
Which talk all day long of things
Nobody will be able to buy.
Here they grow soft, small, men with musical hearts
And wives gone fat with poverty's diet, and absurd
Dogs that caricature a civilization
Ground thin between two restless nations, and
Slowly pulverized by shock of opposed ideologies.

A wire fence makes it Mexico, but God
Has never been asked. And the vegetation
Does not change its citizenship overnight, nor do
The Animals, and even the river
In its winter plumage, traffics casually
Across the International Line, bringing home
The raw sewage deposited there when
Good Neighbors built the fence
And created an incident, and
Caused a City, a roadside beggar whose hat had
Better stay away from his head.
But no, the birds need no passports
And coyotes can cross and re-cross; the
Tourists too. Only the residents are immobilized;
Frozen to the north by
The sprawling verbage of passport wordage
And turned back south and east by centuries
Of sterile desert, and held to the western

Beaches by the Pacific's relentless combers.
Tijuana? One can get into but not out of it
And into it from the whole world
Have come seekers, drifters, escapes;
Wanted men and unwanted women, come here
For the final stalemate. Their shoes—
Their city shoes frozen by dust, and
Stomachs bleached by begged Tacos shot with horsemeat.
Here to dry up while drinking and stealing
And waiting. Converting their German, French,
English, Chinese into the oiled, grey
Pidgin Spanish of bordertown; to wait
beside the flagrant streets for new faces
Come to be horrified by sin, and to
Grovel in the spectacle
of abortion and absorption. And to hear
Lame, warped, U.S. made guitars, chord-wreaked
by Indians too poor to fatten
Their dogs for the eating.

### One Star for "P.R."

In church, from between artificial shoulders
(squired by khaki's brilliant epaulets;
pantsed by reverent, highvoiced tailors)
His head dignified a Captain's rank

Stimulated maidens, though unhappily his sex
was ordained to make old women naughty
Now kneeling in prayer, meditating his mission
He was grateful to God for his reflected features
In the capitulating faces of religious teenagers

The campaign on that innocuous morning
In this odd, undeclared war of Public Relations
Had brought surrender from the entire choir,
A Rotarian, two bobbysoxers and the Preacher's wife
Plus the voluntary enlistment
Of a Prep-school sophomore
Who kept white mice
Well done, sir! The Army—
Had held the line against Christian wisdom
Assassinated logic; exploded history
He'd captured a date for the cocktail party
(all in the line of duty of course)
While learning Bibles frontwards, backwards
At $485 per month, plus incidentals
Men, it wasn't any Sunday School picnic

And now, dignifying shaded sidewalks
He moved swiftly, guiltily toward Headquarters
Hating the eyes that loved his back
Aware of the prisoner by his side—
A mother of three who promised surrender
All in the line of duty, lady,
And that line forms to the right, lady—
I'll make a man out of your boy
A corpse out of the man
A memorial out of the corpse

A moral out of the Memorial
They'll call it Army Day
There will be flowers
Sad, sympathetic upper-brass
will hold hands with sexless mothers

—He gave his life to the country
Gave his country to the military
Gave the military to God
Gave God to the devil
And lady,
He gave the devil a Captain's rank.

### Southern California as the State of the Union

Southwesterners
Who'd avoid clobbering doves on Sundays
Must forget remembering East
When an afternoon's wry glean was crossfiled with
Neo
Geo—
Political webbery; their humbled sky sucks
From exhausted Buicks
Some mysterious chemistry. And sad old steel towers
Have their backs to the wall
Heads in the clouds; it is
Time for Life
And ultrasimplification.
To reduce thought down to its lower common denominator
The highest brains draw tall salaries.
The months pass through
Whistling sternly.
A splendid year for removing old promises
For exorcising promiscuity from the premises.
And ashore, in the absolute west
Birds on spindles
With sticks for beaks bleat
For tidal deposits of paper milk cartons.
Exclamatory gulls commute to work
In the city's playingrounds
And the tested Coast comes a land of e-flat alto saxes.
Still a great Cadillac country
Reverberating its echoes to the forgotten east
Where remain
Secret wetnesses
On posteriors and exteriors.
And there exist acrid stratas, and ochre afternoons
In Pasadena's washes,
And high tension wires, and Ford-owners
Who perforate beercans with .22's
Their radios running full volume, unattended
And falling onto the Sunday side of it all. Sunday?

The children nagging donkey-rides; the parents
Hurrying home for factory-fresh cliches
And all
Promised always
The classified superiority of practically everything.

Friday
March 28, 1958
8:30 P.M.
THOMAS MCGRATH
JAMES BOYER-MAY
Municipal Gallery
Barnsdall Park
Sunset and Vermont
Friday
April 26, 1958
8:30 P.M.
LAWRENCE SPINGARN
JOSEPHINE AIN
CURTIS ZAHN

## the california quarterly

Ira Wallach
William Norton

Richard Nickson
Bruce McM. Wright
Herbert J. Biberman
John Greenleaf Whittier
Leslie Woolf Hedley
Jack Beeching
Curtis Zahn
Norman Rosten
Naomi Replansky

LeGarde S. Doughty
Harold V. Witt
Edwin Rolfe
Lee Jenson
Carl Selph
George Abbe
August Kadow
Tiba G. Willner
David Cornel DeJong

### summer 1952
SEVENTY-FIVE CENTS

Cover: *The California Quarterly* 4
(summer 1952).

# Lawrence Spingarn

Lawrence Spingarn, b. 1917—Lawrence Spingarn was born in Jersey City, New Jersey, the son of Joseph Spingarn and Ann Birnbaum. He received his Bachelor of Science degree in 1940 from Bowdoin College and in 1948 took an M.A. at the University of Michigan. Marrying Sylvia Wainhouse in 1949, he did graduate work at UCLA and taught for many years at Los Angeles Valley College. Earlier he had worked as a librarian at the Library of Congress and at freelance writing. From 1968 on he founded and edited the Perivale Press. Spingarn received Bread Loaf Fellowships in 1941 and 1942, the McDowell resident fellowship in 1946, and the Huntington Hartford Foundation Award in 1950, 1955, and 1956. He was a Yaddo resident in 1958 and won the Poetry Society of America prize in 1975. His published books of poems include *Rococo Summer* (1947), *The Lost River* (1951), *Letters from Exile* (1961), *Madame Bidet and Other Fixtures* (1969), and *The Dark Playground* (1979). He worked as one of the founding editors of *The California Quarterly* and as a subsidiary editors for *Trace*, an important source for listings of little magazines on the West Coast.

## Night in the Funeral Range

Night where the Greyhound never stops, lizard's night;
Cold blood like a river underground, the stab of stars;
High wind, neighing of a wild horse, whips of sand;
Promises whined by a loose board in an empty house—
Is it the house of the harlot dance-hall girl
Who stored in garters the careless green of men's eyes?
House of a pledge, a draught, the greasy but unrubbed lamp
Shining through curtains out on the busy sand
Where the centipede counts drops from a broken bottle,
Drops that work through rock to the drifts and slopes,
Dram for the thirsty veins that boast and roar?

Feet stamped on the planks, the fiddles squeaked.
Careless, O careless green, with bullet and blade
Wore boots to bed, and wide, and handsome high
In the shale of time, shaken and hurtling down
With a stockinged kick and ten-dollar kisses
Spun from a wheel: charity, all was charity!
Now, where the Greyhound never stops, lizard's night;
A dry mouth gasping out its angry death,
Rouged lips like a crater in the void.

### ■ The Ship of Fools

The ship of fools moves down the burning world
Into the shadows of nocturnal fire
Between the gulfs of stars, the capes of fear,
Bearing the Babel-tongued, those innocents,
The foster-darlings of a vast neglect
In idle postures of obeisance.

While in the tender zone so suddenly seared,
So treacherously assailed by China gongs
Of clamor, and by monkeys with stopped ears
Howling the words rehearsed by supple priests,
The wise stand under palm trees in the rain
Beating their chests in featureless regret
For sending out a ship of fools to chart
The journey of their need, such arrant need!

### ■ an imperial fragment

We speak again to all in the city built on a swamp:
To priests, money-lenders, brigands, the horde of women
Who suck on the corpse of love before the god of flies
Where the wind perishes in little mounds of sandalwood.
We have gathered from many lands these jars of myrrh,
These pots of basil, and ambergris shaking like pampered flesh,
The virgins, and the carpets that plead quiet,
Clocks that run through the drunken days and night
Winding themselves, and silks that polish the skin.
It was the rare brain in the lonely skull
That looked from the Great Wall and dreamed of this city:
Each man could name his price, each woman her hour or place.
The scrolls would be read backward. Nobody would heed them,
Shrined in the Porcelain Tower by the Peacock Pool forever,
And the feeble king, fanned by the desirous eunuchs,
Would sleep in the tub of his fat till gongs sound alarm.

Now, at the frontier, a tiger rages. Flames mow the grass.
Barbarians peer from the bamboos at the rich caravans,

Guarded by janizaries, that fetch us this tribute.
And in the padded towns a red dawn belches its fear.
We must arise from the easy couches, the pliant bodies;
Sons of the ribboning lights, daughters of success, we go
For the spear again, the just bow, and the blazing stick—

Superior weapon that beats foes back over the hills
And out of the mines and markets where our treasure lies.
We have squatted on crossed feet long enough, to the lute
And the jugular wine, where the maidens bathe at dusk.
There are deeds, and the deed, and the furled banners
Of that ancient chief who will lead us across the line . . .
Then, back to our own surrender, to the terms of night,
To the couch again, and the sleek days as before.

Spare sons for the final battles. Our uneasy allies
Must pass first from the hoarded island to that coast
Where children spit on the ruins of our brothels,
Where temples are inns, and the godowns dormitories.
It is said that evil breeds like mice. Know by these signs
The enemy, or who moves with him: darker skin,
Small eyes, a hair queue not his own. Words
Sound like snarling on that mainland, and betray
The baser origin, notorious lies, a poor diet.
Brother against brother, coin for bribing—use them all
And spare no one. Delay! Defend! And then, attack!

If you go to the mountain, the tombs may remind you
(Priest, merchant, woman of the tinkling fountain laughter)
That the ancestors sleep in the percentage of shadows
Where the sun will last for a thousand years.
There, when the pines moan at the dieting wind
And the melon-ripe moon sweats pallidly, and dies,
Rejoice, for the convinced slaves with their broken bodies
Can block the passes at the north against all harm;
The blazing stick works well, and the toadstool forming
Makes life of our death, and death of their life.

**Lawrence Springarn**

### Rococo Summer

After split skies and tardy thunder, rain
Recalled the children in their pinafores
To porches tense with sportsmen. Bores
Peddled the myth of Vicksburg once again.
Grant himself, bribed with a fine cigar,
Sinister, taciturn, sick with his cancer,
Snatched from a silver tray the cabled answer,
Read he would die, smiled, headed for the bar.
The sky protested. Mallets clicked dismay.
Beneath wet elms the darkey waiters served
Tall, minted juleps. Sudden horsemen swerved,
Missing a child, reining another way.
The sun returned . . . Oh, what is left to tell?
No pen stabs reputation. From the lawn,
Duly escorted, not without a yawn,
Women moved gravely toward the dinner bell.

Morton Dimondstein, cover: *The California Quarterly* 3, no. 2 (1954).

## Jack of Diamonds

Be nimble, Jill. The legends in your purse
Drug me for slumber like the autumn rose
That stings and pricks us both while budding out.
Each boy invades your cavern with a shout:
Each fails, but still assumes the martial pose
When garments scatter and your guardians curse.

A subtle moth predicted such pale freight.
Paired silver wings abetted me, then fled
Beneath a fog of blankets. Your harsh lips
Urged greater speed, more pain than comes from whips.
Clouds festered in the weird glow from your bed.
Mist soiled the windows. Storms unlocked the gates.

We drowned in satin, favored by no star.
The captious waves that groomed me for your stud
Must steer you landward in a greener smock
And wind be quick to bind you on this rock
Before the dragon that will suck your blood
Consumes at last the kindling that you are.

### The Grammarian: Parts of Speech

'Professor, what are we doing in this institution?'

He started from the nouns, the feeble names
For creatures of the swamp that eat and sleep
In corsets, smocks, or planetary frames.
And when the sick moon bleached his face.
Pale 'he' and 'she' converged to 'it'
As tricksy delegates in silk and lace.
While action limped and thinking lacked a curb
The fangs of progress and the claws of time
Retreated to moist jungles with the verb.
Ah, beauty was a bubble in his blood:
Like *easily, slowly, patiently,* it grew
Slack and adverbial before the flood.
And next the prepositions dinged him down:
He tottered through a sacerdotal maze
To whip these drunks and harlots out of town.
But in the yard no priest would give him unction.
The bones he loathed were rattling in their shrouds
Until he joined them to a fat conjunction.
A heavy corpse, he answered very well
The interjection that resounds each night
Across the precincts and the wards of hell.

# Bert Meyers

Bert Meyers, b. 1928–d. 1979. Bert Meyers was born and grew up in Los Angeles. He was mostly self-educated. Although he did not graduate from Marshall High School in Los Angeles or ever receive a bachelor's degree, he nevertheless completed all the requirements but the dissertation for a Ph.D. in English and taught at Pitzer College in Claremont for the last eleven years of his life. Before teaching, he worked with his hands as a housepainter, printer, ditchdigger, janitor, warehouseman, and sheet metal worker and became a skilled picture framer and gilder. Meyers began writing poetry while hanging around Thomas McGrath near Los Angeles State College and became a member of Tom's "Marsh Street Irregulars." In 1957 he married Odette Miller, and in 1960 Alan Swallow published his first book, *Early Rain*. He had published early on in the *California Quarterly* and in *Coastlines* and in 1964 and 1967 was given an Ingrim Merrill Foundation award. Other books by Meyers include *The Dark Birds, The Wild Olive Tree,* and a translation of poems by French poet François Dodat with his wife, Odette. His *Collected Poems* will soon be published by Creative Arts Books.

"The inner life of man, it seems,
grows toward society as surely as the sparks fly up."
—Letter, Bert Meyers to John Haines, February 17, 1967

### In the Alley

At noon an airplane,
a hard drop of sweat,
rolls down the sky's
huge forehead.

The dry alley
dreams of water—
trampled root.
Fenced-off the housewife trees
multiply their fruit.

Later, a man,
grey as gravel,
comes up the alley.
In a garbage can
an alarm of flies
goes off in his face.
The passing dogs
wouldn't even piss
on such disgrace.

Scared by a wind
that walks through gates,
among the leaves
the fallen man
curls like smoke around
a wall, disappears.

In the yards the trees
drop loquats, and yellow
ripe round pears.

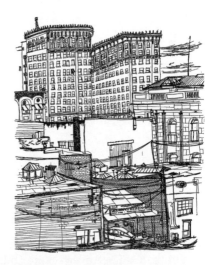

This page and facing page: Arnold Mesches,
Four Drawings: "Seamy Side," "The Boners,"
"Coronation," "Vernon Trucks," in
*The California Quarterly* 3, no. 1 (1953).

### The Daily Reality

EARLY RAIN, *by Bert Meyers; Poets in Swallow Paperbooks, 75c.*

Bert Meyers's poetry is founded on the daily reality and makes no effort to soften the grimness. If these poems are often sad, often ironic, sometimes even bitter, it would have been dreamy to have made them otherwise. They are true to themselves. But, at the same time, it must be noted that when they celebrate, they don't go halfway. Listen to 'Picture Framing':

My fingers feed in the field of wood.

I sand pine, walnut, bass,
and sweat to raise their grain.

Paints, powder and brush
are the seasons of my trade.

At the end of the day
I drive home
the proud cattle of my hands.

Meyers speaks to us about the things we usually pass by without knowing what they are: the minute satisfactions and disappointments that, added up, give our lives their community essence. It is because we don't look carefully enough that the world of the outside appears unrelated to us, as well as dull and meaninglessly repetitious. While a poem like 'In the Alley' is hardly joyous, it won't let us go, its bitter meaning impinges on us, the violence of the calm, hot scene strikes at us:

At noon an airplane,
a hard drop of sweat,
rolls down the sky's
big forehead.

The dry alley
dreams of water—
trampled root.
Fenced-off the housewife trees
multiply their fruit.

Later, a man,
grey as gravel,
comes up the alley.

At a garbage can
an alarm of flies
goes off in his face.

Scared by a wind
that walks through gates,
among the leaves
the fallen man
curls around a wall
like smoke, and disappears . . .

In the yards, the trees
drop loquats, and yellow
ripe round pears.

This is a social poem in the best sense, one that pays heed to the sound and language of the 'content.' It is a poem of surprises, the kind that stun us with their truth. There are a number of others of like quality in the book.

As the final two poems, Meyers offers translations from the work of Louis Aragon. These have a different sort of power from his own: a longer line, a more rolling cadence, a larger arena of space and time. It would be interesting to see Meyers himself explore a method of this kind.

—Gene Frumkin

## I Dreamed

I dreamed of a light that kills:
there wasn't a sound from man.
A clinic of clouds appeared
and the moon dressed as a nurse.

Then, khaki colored leaves
fell from the public trees.
I saw that we'd all come
to the corner to say: *Peace.*

At last the generals
were beaten with ploughshares
and you and I became
two hammers with one blow that builds.

## Picture Framing

My fingers feed in the fields of wood.

I sand pine, walnut, bass,
and sweat to raise their grain.

Paints, powder and brush
are the seasons of my trade.

At the end of the day
I drive home
the proud cattle of my hands.

The Editorial Board of Coastlines

expresses its regrets at the loss of

# The California Quarterly

from the Little Magazine field.

End of publication of so high calibre a magazine

will be deeply felt by the literary community.

Obituary for *The California Quarterly,*
in *Coastlines* 2, no. 2 (winter 1956).

### ■ Because There's So Much Speed

Because there's so much speed
without any place to go,
and naked, blind as light,
we rush from stone to stone
and bump against the world,

I like the silly snail:
wrapped in its wooden fog
it crawls across my yard;
and where it goes, it paints
the ground with useless roads.

Day and night, in its world,
leaves fall without a sound;
and flowers become suns
that bugs like little planets
in a green astronomy
go round and round and round.

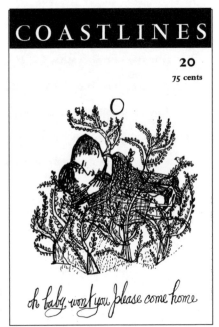

David Lemon, cover:
*Coastlines* 5, no. 4 (1963).

# Mel Weisburd

Mel Weisburd, b. 1927—Mel Weisburd, the first editor of *Coastlines,* was born in St. Paul, Minnesota, in 1927. He moved to Los Angeles in 1942. Growing up in Los Angeles, he attended UCLA and received a B.A. in English in 1950. After his studies at UCLA, he attended classes with Thomas McGrath at Los Angeles State College and was editor of the student literary journal, *Statement.* In that journal he published his first essay on Los Angeles and its air quality, titled "The City that Outgrew its Air." Between 1952 and 1962, he edited *Coastlines* in various capacities, as editor in chief and as managing editor. A first fund-raising party raised $60 to launch the magazine. Weisburd worked at the Los Angeles County Air Pollution Control District (APCD) from 1951 to 1962, then he went briefly to Evanston, Illinois, returning to Los Angeles in 1966. On his return he worked for Systems Development Corporation, where he worked on projects having to do with air pollution, and remained there from 1966 to 1971. In 1971 he was the principal founder of the company Pacific Environmental Services; in 1985 he sold his interest in the company and retired. From his very early years working with the environment, Weisburd's work was groundbreaking. He wrote a manual on air pollution enforcement that was a cornerstone for all environmental enforcement agencies. He was hired by the American Medical Association (AMA) in their newly created Environmental Health Department, where he wrote articles for the AMA's journal and organized conferences. Weisburd wrote articles, poetry, and fiction. His article from *Coastlines* on lysergic acid was reprinted in *Best Articles and Stories* in 1958. Weisburd published no full-length collections of poetry but was included in Walter Lowenfels's collection *Poets of Today,* published in 1964, and in *The California Quarterly, Coastlines, Midwest, Poet Lore, Transatlantic Review, Epos,* and *Statement.* He continues to write and live in Los Angeles. At present he is writing a memoir as a participant in and witness to the culture clashes, both literary and nonliterary, that took place in Los Angeles during the 1950s.

**Editorial**

The poems in this first issue of *Coastlines* represent the work of many individuals in finding, encouraging, collecting, and writing. The magazine itself is actually the result of a fortunate meeting between these workers, who, having on their hands a collection of poems, had no magazine, and the editors, who, attempting to found a magazine, had no material. Such a meeting, of course, is more than an accident, since the founding represents no more whimsy, but an actual need for a magazine. The need for *Coastlines* became quite obvious when it is realized that Los Angeles is undergoing a vast social revolution whose shape, although sometimes causing despair, is not yet altogether clear.

There is no necessity, then, to build an editorial policy on the delicate superstructures of other little magazines, but rather, simply, to continue discovering the source of writing here. In so doing, we are particularly interested in the new writer, the promising writer who has already had his start, and the writer who is maturing, or is discovering for himself new directions. We are interested in works which define the cultural problems of our world and era, as well as those of this region. We are interested in the lyric poem, in the poem which binds, resolves, and clarifies; in works with strong centers, as opposed to the sheerly allusive, formless and peripheral. In criticism we shall not be concerned with the apologetic, or defensive, but again with the affirmative, the fearless, and the clear thinking. At another time, these attitudes may have reflected a mere wise eclecticism. In these times, however, the advocate of taste and reason must of needs take on a vigorous partisan character.

The Editors

*Coastlines* 1, no. 1 (spring 1955)

Chris Jenkyns, cover:
*Coastlines* 1, no. 4
(spring 1956).

### My Father

My father, a laborer, forty eight, divorced three times, timid
And always tired, comes home with the furnace blast in his ears
And speaks in an empty egoless voice. His grey stubble is dry
And electric, and his eyes, reverberatories of fire. Thin
And hollow, he burned the core out of himself until his marrow
Flowed, flipped his cigarettes away, half smoked, lifted castings
Above purple fumes, almost above his head from a strength
Of not believing in doctors. His passion was fire, and his love
Was his death. Now against the remaining womanless days
He walked abroad the earth in robes of heat waves,
Diaphanous excrements of hell and this world.

Tired and timid, alone in the corner of his kitchen
Until the cool shadows formed in the summer, at 7:30,
He finished his coffee and his papers, and
Cool, clean, and in pain, rises and sends
Two clocks, two clocks,
Ahead of him
Into the night.

### A Crow Black With Purpose

A crow,
Black with purpose, shifts from one to the other
Of the holly boughs
On my disheveled lawn. Suddenly a hundred-thousand pig-weed
Moths rise
From the Hollywood Hills. The blackbird darks about to do his work.
These thoughts come to me:
Did many poet-moths die propagating that will? Did one give the signal
To rise? Perhaps
That is unimportant. Like a snapping sheet on Monday's wash they
Rise and flow down
Beachwood Drive across fifty miles of L.A. asphalt.

The black crow forages
Among necessities. I sit here thickening with abstractions
Darting among the limbs
Of confusion. I think: it is refreshing to my eyes
To cavil with distance,
Instead of illusion. I should exercise the seat of my vision

More often, I mean
Actual physical exercise, instead of propounding myself
To a tasteless oblivion.
I dream here in the green shade of how poetry should
Retaliate from my pen,
Like white ski-soldiers camouflaged on a white field of snow—
Except by the tracks,
I see how poetry wanders afield and loses the argument.

The black crow has what
He wants and flies half way up the variegated ivy of these hills.
With little thought
He manipulates the precise equations of his will, and leaves aliquots
Of air to forgetfulness.

Poets—whether they admit it or not—articulate by trial
And comparison, with little
Statistical significance. Their art, they confess, is an artificial
Physics, a Heisenberg .
Insouciance of we-measure-what-we-measure. Or else, they drink
Poetry
Like the dark wine of unconsciousness, and
Never get drunk.
Such self-expression seals the fate of poetry.

My neighbors,
Whose names I forget, are full of immense empirical secrets.
The way they vote
Often comes as a shock to me. They do not see me here excavating
In a public quarry.
They think I vote like them. Actually, I am playing on
The stops of reality,
A querulous old flute. If it is not poetry then let it be oratory.
The opinion of
Imagination, consuming what is publicly unsaid.

I do not have
An inkling of what my fellows are writing
At the moment,
Or when they shall rise to the light like these moths.
They are just as
Preposterous as myself, sitting and thinking and writing.
A time will come though
When my neighbors must think. It will be either too late,
Or just a little
Before it is too late—in time, when thought will
Set the thinking
Mass ablaze, and we will break our appetite with our will.

"I guess what I am saying is that *Coastlines* was more than a literary magazine and that, in my view, some of the greatest things happened around *Coastlines;* it was a 'context,' a culture of its own and, as far as I know, before Venice West came along, the only literary culture in LA at the time. I include in these the numerous parties and the events. . . . Perhaps the great valuable things that were lost and nobody captured were the intellectual and political discussions going on at the time."

Mel Weisburd

Interview with Estelle Gershgoren Novak, September 1996

■ **When I Go Down to That Sleep**

When I go down to that sleep
It is to the marrowed villages that I go
Where the tail-bone sinks in the bush
And the marsh is shallow with fish.

I am hung like a possum from a limb
And nothing will harm me now,
The hunters are flat on the meadow
As they go down to their sleep.

My wife has moved a face-length
And has fallen from my arms
Into the bottom of her gravity
When she turns down to sleep.

Our baby drops deeper than us all,
To the bed of nutrient visions
And the simple remembrance of creation,
Where sleep first began.

Outside of houses like ours,
Power is wide awake,
Or the guards are playing cards.
Somewhere as the sun breaks

Pilots rub the sleep from their eyes
And fly above the darkened earth
In Alaskan and Siberian skies
And drop the bombs of nightmare.

And we are sound asleep
Drifting on the earth like wreckage,
As if our parts were laid on tables
Like books with open pages.

Let power read through the night,
Before they turn the light out:
Let them read our sleep,
Then turn down into their own.

Now you stir the lovely waves
That split the sun on me.
We lug ourselves from sleep
And love and fly away.

### ■ Dreamsong

a sirvente for Mel Weisburd from Thomas McGrath

When I go down to that sleep
It is to the willowy marrow that I'll go,
Where the yarrow colors the heat
And the shallows are hollow with fish.

What ghosts would harrow my sleep
May burn in the yellowy hush
Of mallows and sulphur bush
As I burrow into that deep.

But through the narrows flash,
Like cloudy arrows of flesh,
Or shrouded unhallowed wish,
The bite-shaped bones of Night

And all the marsh goes wild
As the cold dead arise.
—When I go down to that sleep
I would be covered deep

To shelter against surprise
From the hollow Fish of the Breath,
From the cawing circle of death,
From the dead with their colorless eyes.

**Mel Weisburd**

## ■ Editorial

With much laughter at ourselves,
Enough ignorance to pretend a reality
Of our choice; with much fear and fever,
We have assembled here to argue art's illusion.

"But why?" you ask. "The risk is not worth it.
There is too much to lose, giving up the art
Yourself, for instance. There is not much
To be gained from waylaying honesty;
Honesty, after all, is dirt cheap. If you must,
Interpret for us, or give us a summary,
Or a handy index. There is nothing,
Nothing new under the sun."

Well, we feel that because there is nothing
New under the sun, much has been written into a kind
Of darkness. Fortunately, imitation
And advertising perpetually cancel that
Darkness, just as the corporation of ideas
Is self-liquidating, expendable, or bankrupt.
Waste paper, indeed, has given rise to a
Tremendous rubbish industry. Nevertheless,
The sun, we note, is still on fire,
And much creation is yet to be done.

We know that even poetry has an economics,
And Time is money. And since poetry is poverty,
We have no 8 page signature, coated stock,
Bulmer, Baskerville, or Bodini types—we have here
Only the rich but unemployed aesthetic of free speech

The truth is our hands are perpetually unemployed,
And since we have nothing better to do, and
Since there is not much better to be done,
Be calm and a little curious, reader; pretend
That we are the angry or loving relations
We really are. Consider a little our
Crudeness, and be amused or shocked
As you will at our attempt to sing the
First song again.

David Lemon, cover: *Coastlines* 3, no. 2 (spring–summer 1958).

## "Lysergic Acid and the Creative Experience"
### Mel Weisburd

*Lysergic Acid Diethylamide, a synthetic ergot alkaloid, is one of the several types of hallucinogenic drugs that have been coming into experimental use in the study of schizophrenia and mystical and creative experiences. Some experts believe that Lysergic Acid differs from such drugs as mescalin in that the experience it induces is primarily 'schizophrenic' whereas mescalin is primarily 'hallucinogenic.' As a subject of an experiment here in Los Angeles I seemed to have experienced both. Actually, I first went through a period of anesthesia, withdrawal, 'schizophrenia,' hallucination and euphoria, and in the day following, severe depression. The effects of the drug were accompanied by a slight difficulty in coordination which lasted for six hours. Although my normal senses returned to me in the two days following, I still retained a sort of cineramic vision. At least for me, this experience, which was the happiest day in my life, seemed to reveal the following:*

1. *LSD demonstrates beyond a doubt the true realisms of the sense perceptions and the renewed possibilities of both the child-like imagination and mature wisdom.*
2. *Experience is born from a common source, and all significance is simultaneous and equal.*
3. *Human values are primarily aesthetic.*
4. *The values of human existence are not abstractions, but are direct reactions to the basic experiences of our sense-perceptions. These sense perceptions can only lead to moral precepts based on an affirmation of life.*
5. *The drug only brought out my truthful self. For someone else, these truisms might not apply, and for still others, the direct opposite might obtain.*

\* \* \*

Six tiny spheres of lysergic acid diethylamide—150 micrograms—so tiny that they lodged in my teeth before I could swallow them. Dr. Irving commented that he thought I was resisting the experiment. I explained that as a child I swallowed pills only with great difficulty. He said he thought that was significant.

At this early in the morning I couldn't have been more indifferent to the thread of analysis. As a matter of fact, I had never been to his office at this early in the morning, and I was already taken by the unfamiliar aspect of these familiar surroundings. The office was damp and had the dusty smell of carpets. The lounges were cold and clammy. His desk was unarranged, as if there had been a seminar here the night before, followed by coffee. There was already a little touch of conspiracy here, perhaps, because, just off the foyer another analyst and patient were in session. At any rate, despite my fears, I felt as if I were in competent hands: incisive competence in the book shelves, emergency competence in the recovery rooms, unabashed competence in the ugly morning light of his fashionable waiting room.

Dr. Irving seemed impatient. I was perhaps his one-hundredth subject. He himself, had fumbled with the pills, they were so small. 'Do whatever you feel like doing,' he said, 'walk around the room, read, write. Do whatever you like.' And he sat down to read. He looked up every now and then to ask whether I felt anything. I said I felt nothing.

After about 50 minutes the chill intensified. It was in my veins now, cold and viscous. I began to feel as if I were being prepared for surgery. There was, for instance, that peculiar salt-like, blood-tasting nausea produced when one takes a barium salt injection for an X-ray. My gums and teeth also became anesthetized as if from novocaine. My jaw and bridge-work enlarged, and I felt embarrassed by a decided feeling of prognathism. I had neanderthal features. Then my lower jaw seemed to disconnect from my skull as if it could be mechanically detached and manipulated, like the head-piece of a knight's armor.

It seemed as if I could have sat for hours, weary, but sleepless as well, watching the Venetian blind and Dr. Irving glancing up at me from time to time as if to make sure that I was not yet a hazard to myself. The room was dark and the sunlight cluttered through the Venetian blinds on the window. Dr. Irving was seated at his desk, but on the dark-side of the room. I had to observe him through the stream of morning light. Nothing was changing—except I seemed to capitulate to something—I was staring without thinking, as if what I saw went through me like X-rays, or better yet, that I had two retinas in each eye: one which registered and the other which photographed. Or that I saw a sort of variegated ivy of shadow images, like the double exposures of three dimensional movies, before you use the 3-D glasses. Except, that I saw the room and Dr. Irving and the street outside the window in their single outlines.

I was annoyed at Dr. Irving's suggestion that we go and have some tea at a coffee shop down Wilshire Boulevard. Going out was like diving into an ice-cold pool. I would never have made the decision, if it weren't for Dr. Irving. Nevertheless, we went. Outside the sun was shining, and Wilshire Blvd. was merry with all colors and styles of automobiles. There was a smog nesting in Wilshire Blvd.

At the counter I noticed that the ceiling of the coffee shop rose to cathedral heights and that I had the feeling of being squashed. The Negro waitress who came to take our order rose above me, gigantically beautiful. Her eyes were large and swollen, brilliantly enlarged. The blood vessels in the corners of her eyes were a deep coral red. There seemed to be an almost intolerable pressure behind those eyes. There was a dexterity in her pupils, a dexterity that came from terrible experience, terrible fear. Otherwise, she had a lean and documentary look.

She was waiting for my order, but I could not gather myself. Impatience seemed to flare at her nostrils. I felt like backing away, but I could not move. I managed, however, to give her my order for tea and toast—or rather it was my habit speaking as if through centuries. 'Don't worry how you look,' Dr. Irving assured me, 'you look quite normal to others.' But this was no assurance, certainly everyone in the coffee shop must be aware that I had a bird's-eye view of him. There was not an attitude or mood of the waitress that I could not avoid observing with great detail and with much embarrassment, as if she had disrobed before me in public. And not only was I confronted with the magnificent detail of all the faces in the coffee shop, but with their strange language. Nuances which were ordinarily subtle and discrete leaped out of their contexts, as if I had overheard conspiracies. A phrase, a word would amplify itself into a major theme, just as background music in a movie anticipates impending disaster. I became a most daring accessory to everyone's crime. One was in great danger to be so close to the innermost jungles of people in that well populated coffee shop.

Outside, the sun filtered through the smog, but I was still cold. My clothes hung on me like coarse damp muslin sheets. My body now as quite petrified, I seemed to have lost sensation, especially the sensation of a filled stomach. Yet, I felt preserved and protected. When we reached Dr. Irving's office, I saw the sunlight flooded in the leaves of grass. It was like a photo-reconnaissance flight from which

I mapped the rugged insect terrain. Each blade of grass was a flashing green followed by a yellow pantomime of a blade, as yellow as Van Gogh's cornfields. It seemed now that anything that grew possessed a surplus of life, that it overflowed to fill a complementary portion of the spectrum with its image. At this point I was suddenly aware that while the grass drew my attention I had somehow lost Dr. Irving. That I was distracted and that it would take centuries before I could speak to him. I was aware, though I could not resist it, that experience was discontinuous, and yet simultaneous. Dr. Irving was now sitting close to me with his feet crossed just next door in another world.

Just then a women came up the walk. I do not remember what Dr. Irving said to her, but he seemed to speak to her personally. His familiarity with her seemed almost adulterous, and all of the sexual implications of what he said were articulated simultaneously. As if all double meanings were now in the public domain. She smiled and laughed at what Dr. Irving said. I began to giggle convulsively, tickled by the distortions in the conversation. Somehow, we were all three communicating in short wave. Dr. Irving was the signal, and it made no difference what he said. And whatever the signal, I would receive it on whatever gorgeous frequencies vibrated through me. Still there was the devastating undertone that I was the butt of a private joke hidden in the hibiscus; the secret of my whole experience, laughed at, with no one in all of the wide world to let me in on it.

After she disappeared into the building, I attempted to organize my experiences so I could talk to Dr. Irving, but without success. I seemed to have a minute memory. Dr. Irving asked me what I had been observing. I said the 'grass.' But I could not explain anything more. He said then, as if showing off his grasp of both unity and discontinuity, that a new biochemical theory holds no distinction between animal and vegetable matter and that all forms of life are vegetable, and that the earth itself was the common environment of what we think of as a dichotomy. Another socialist exercise, I thought. But the theory was truth at the moment. It seemed as if the deepest intelligence of my mind wanted to synthesize, to unify cats, dogs and onions. I was in the center of the godhead like a plane in a thunderhead.

I finally asked Dr. Irving what would in all normal reality be a trite and embarrassing question, 'What is reality?' It was not, however, a philosophical question. I simply wanted to be oriented to get my bearings. And yet the question was philosophical in the sense that I did not *need* the directions, I was not going any place. Not requiring the direction, I only desired with curiosity the experience of orientation for whatever it was worth. 'Why, this is reality,' he replied. 'Yes, yes, I know *this* is reality,' I replied, 'but I mean before, was that reality?' 'Yes,' he replied, 'but now only more so.' I couldn't keep up with it any longer. 'Signal Blinkers.' I replied, as if I were telling him to go to heaven in one of those automobiles. 'Oh, you get a kick out of the blinkers,' he replied.

We then went into his office and I reclined in a lounge chair. Dr. Irving then moved off to talk to a colleague somewhere in the suite of rooms. Now my body was really numb, as before, but with some difference. My insides were not quite focused in my skeletal cavity. It felt, almost, as if I were being manipulated electromagnetically. The effort required to move my body whispered through invisible muscles over great relay systems. Silent digestive processes telegraphed phenomena in my vision. I closed my eyes and saw a sailor waving his semaphores from a yawing ship at a great distance away. I saw blasts of light reverberating purplish clouds and plumes of smoke; red lightning, as if traced from the blood vessels in my eyes. Line drawings: white, red, and purple faces and eyes upon velveteen black. Gigantic proletarian murals. Often I would see a pillar of light against a blackened horizon, like an atomic blast. And this, the world of light and dark, I viewed with my hands cupped to my closed eyes as if through the eyepiece of a cinemascope.

To open my eyes, as to change any state I might happen to find myself, required a major revolution of will. The thought to do so came half-formed, only to be immediately forgotten, then thought of again. And then there was a time interval between the thought and the action permitting an onrush of new distractions.

With my eyes open again, it was like looking through a new and special eye piece. It might have been a telephoto lens, with its peculiar distortion of depth of field, flattening the background, or a powerful pair of binoculars, with a slight quality of astigmatism. Or it might have been a microscope through which I observed the rock-like strata, in a sliver of wood. Or it might have been polaroid glasses diffracting blue and green light. It was through this latter instrument that I sometimes observed a pastel green halo forming in the shade around Dr. Irving's features. Each of these 'visions' comprised a complete and distinctive reality, holding to its own requirements of natural law. In this way, the four walls of the room would be dissociated into corollary dimensions. Thus the Venetian blinds streaming sunlight were governed by the slats of solar fire and the moon-dark bars, an imposing penology. The opposite wall, on the other hand, with its framed medical and university degrees, dissolved in a kind of cool tubercular light; a divine illness that the medical world would never diagnose.

And if distraction held me inert, so did activity. It seemed as if I would run forever across tremendous units of time and space, farther and farther into interiors, into basements and closets, into private therapy rooms, recovery rooms, crashing outwards into the curving yields of the outdoors. Restlessly on my feet, I would sometimes be sidetracked into special channels of time and space. The change in sensation produced in each room by its light, texture and size, existed for its own sake. It was sometimes as if I were in a tesseract, as if I were in a supremely designed building whose entire plan I would never comprehend or whose rooms I would never completely see.

After a while—I cannot say 'a while' either, time was not recognizable—the immediate past did not disappear from forgetfulness, but was something seen, heard or felt that withered physically away from the new impression. It was not the past of memory, but the echo, the halation of a current effect: the doubling, tripling images seen; I felt as if I were being pushed out from the head of a mushroom; the fading experiences squashing and dropping away with the driving effect of music. The future did not exist, except in an inexplicable yearning.

After a while, Dr. Irving returned with the woman. We sat around and talked. There were some jokes made at my expense and some comments about my 'pro-dromal' symptoms. I criticized them for wasting their time structuring, since the whole business had been planned. Why all of this sophistry? Dr. Irving ignored me and continued to tell some professional jokes which illuminated the difference between psychiatrists and psychologists, as if to mediate the scene with levity. Had I been able to retain the levity, before he ran amok in burlesque, comedy and deep philosophical introspection, I might have explored it like a dark continent. Even a flat statement would send me into uproarious laughter, as when later during the course of the 'experiment' I sat morosely in a chair contemplating the effects of the drug as they wore off, he dialed the phone, and after one and a half centuries said rather urgently, 'Hello, hello, Encyclopedia Britannica? No, well I'll call back later.' I died with laughter, and it seemed as if there was a tremendous audience laughing with me. Couldn't he see that we were already here in the deepest, darkest Africa, here in the superabundance of life, of knowledge, catalogued and indexed by its own laws, here where everything is at the rock-bottom of arbitrariness—here even in his own biochemical unity of animal and vegetable. 'The Encyclopedia Britannica,' indeed!

I was dizzy now, with the three of us, from moving through rapidly changing topographies of conversation, dizzy from free-falling like Botticellian angels into spirit atmospheres.

Dr. Irving suggested that we leave, take off in his sports car and head for a park. This time I did not feel confined to my own inertia. I was eager for experience.

If the first three hours were a taste of the power of consciousness, the second three were to bring me in touch with its living secret. Outside, the vicissitudes of my experiences died down, and in the sunlight I began to explore the nature of existence itself. In the alley, I heard two kids yelling in a room on the second story of a building. The voices grew sharply in volume until I heard an entire gym echoing with scores of children's voices. Suddenly there was a pool there among the kids, and they were splashing, laughing, talking, screaming. I felt the father and the son of the germ plasm brewing in the warmth of the sun on the ocean and the amniotic fluid of the great mother of morning in the sky! Now, I could almost touch and speak to my own childhood, heal it, and kiss myself.

Then we climbed in the sports car and rode off like itinerant angels. At first, I held on for my dear life, for it seemed as if we were flying. I turned to Dr. Irving to warn him that he was going much too fast and noticed that his face had been streamlined. As he shifted gears, the motor roared and stampeded like a hundred unharnessed stallions. We seemed to flash by cars like mammoth whales. Dr. Irving's determined 'drag-race' look aroused in me the literal feeling that he was straining at a gnat. 'Don't worry,' he said. 'I'm not going as fast as you think I am. We're only doing around 30.' 'Really?' I said, holding tight to my hand grip, unsure of my invulnerability. 'Well, how do you like this, isn't it wonderful?' Dr. Irving barked. 'Yes, yes, it's fine,' I said still worried by the pavement which rushed at us like a tidal wave. 'This is it, you have it now!' he said. 'What?' 'The common pathways of all human experience. This is where we all came from.' 'Yes,' I replied. I could not make sentences, but I was deliriously happy to know that my suspicions were correct. As we stopped for a light, I reached over the door of the sports car and pounded my pipe on the asphalt. 'Knock on wood?' he asked smiling. 'No, no,' I replied, 'knock on earth!' 'That's right,' he replied. I might have said then, 'How are things on earth these days?' for despite my knowledge and intimacy with many planets, I had an extremely warm regard for the earth. It was like being back to your hometown and standing on the precise spot where you were born.

We were on Olympic Boulevard which, like all six-lane boulevards in Los Angeles, was sick with nervous stop-and-go traffic. But now Olympic Boulevard was Olympia, a great Sunday-drive pageant moving in vehicular streams to and from the cities and beaches of beautification. And suddenly, with the logic of a heavenly-wise wish, who should appear but a guardian angel formed in the likeness of an old girl friend, high on a motor scooter. Her fresh windblown face radiated the quintessence of the power of recognition, the sublimest nostalgia imaginable. In our matter-of-fact glance, there was not only the recognition of a friend, but the pure principle of kindredness. I had an overpowering warmth for everyone I knew and with everything that lived.

When we arrived at the park, we began walking towards it. 'Yup, this is it!' I remarked as if marking the place of my ecstasy. The air was unbelievably fresh. 'Wonderful,' Dr. Irving answered, 'You're supernormal now, supersane.' He patted me on the back. 'Just breathe this air. Isn't it wonderful? Here, look at this tree. What do you think of it?' 'Supernatural,' I said and savored the word as if I understood it for the first time. The lawns, the wide sidewalks, the rows of leafless, sinewy sycamore trees, all of these underscored with living emphasis, the word. 'Supernatural,' no division in nature, no separation of myself from anything, everything whole, everything integral. And in this fulfillment of existence, all desire was lost. Imagination transparency of my vision. No living thing was obscured or darkened by civilized opinions or by overshadowing institutions. Wordsworth and Vaughan and Traherne and Blake and Coleridge, they had it, and even Dylan Thomas, who drunkenly had it, but never understood it.

'It's like an orgasm,' Dr. Irving suggested, 'like an eternal orgasm.' And yes, yes, he was right, by everything that is holy and sexual. That constant feeling of abandon, of giving oneself up to a driving force that exuberantly fructifies in every living thing; that selfless exhilarating releasing flight; that cool, damp breast-milk feeling of satisfaction in my throat and lungs.

And here, in complete innocence, I was in the garden again, and I would never leave, hobbling with Dr. Irving across the broad glittering silk bottoms of La Cienega and Wilshire Boulevards, helpless and idiot-like in the teaming parades and pageants of the world.

"When we are asked to applaud and reward Lipton's literary underground, to blow the 'whistle on the social lie'—well, we would let it blow just for the 'hell of it' for we are just about ready for anything to happen—anything at all to move the present generation to some kind of action since creeping conservatism has so stultified the literary landscape that good poets, docile and broken by the times, permit their reputations to be taken away from them.

But, as editors of *Coastlines*, undertaking to represent as we can at least the writers of the Los Angeles area, we cannot help but to signal the alarm when writers in this area are grossly misrepresented . . .

We must ask Mr. Lipton, what of those silent and steady writers in Los Angeles such as Don Gordon and Ben Maddow, who are light-years ahead of Perkoff and Newman? What of Naomi Replansky, who in a couplet can say memorably all that Ginsberg attempts to hysterically catalog? How about William Pillin whose lyricism is both realistically positive and yet closer to a meaningful attitude of dissent than Creeley will ever get? And what about Thomas McGrath who, in the literary tyrannies of the time, himself waged the staunchest underground struggle with greater overground results than any of the fake publicity that Mr. Lipton has generated."

Mel Weisburd

From "The Merchant of Venice," *Coastlines* (spring–summer 1957)

■ **Between Chicago and St. Paul**
I had expected something quite different.
But this almost forgotten, familiar country
Sours with the headlines of the day's news:
The neutron bomb. Another incident . . .

---

Like a smooth war-machine, the torque
of the earthy turns the dark over
My clattering, yellow-streaked passage. From
The train, the peace is glaring and inconsolable.

The trees are gangrene with throttled sun.
The farms are galvanized for war.
The moon, melancholy, and out of mind,
Hurls a charge down the missile slopes.

But past the hostages, whose yellow lights
Cling like willows to the darkness,
And the metric of the neutral Mississippi
I return to make peace with my father,

To settle with my mother, mother of fact
In whose counties the leaves drop with dispossession,
Who complains from the crippled distance to her Poland,
How all America stings in crabby rooms.

The Germans shot her in the head. I
Remember now that wound that never stood the heal,
Suppurating an unforgotten war. I suppose
That tinny conflagration of 1914.

Because she is certified psychotic
I must make a compensation; I have learned,
Alone, to make my way in the unknown, to accept
How God chokes Minnesota into beauty.

Still I configure my malaise on the window glass.
My breath stains the world as it passes.
In the dark, the human is a catastrophe,
The minute an unexploded moment.

It is not that I am afraid to die
With distance and escaping time,
But that we should die at once,
Sends me slowly home.

### Report From Evanston

Somehow under the stagnant air,
By the polluted lake,
Ambushed by people on three sides,
It got trapped between Chicago
And old money and old grass.

You'd think it would be overrun
The way continents of students and air
And many an alcoholic from N.U.
Despite W.C.T.U. roll through.
Yet local rule and a civil tongue
Hold the line across
A corridor of liquor stores.

Or you'd think it would collapse
The way it accumulates, but commutes away.
Even as the old guard makes its stand
The schools integrate the children away.

Cities are rarely made from joy
And nothing lasts.
Yet in the winter, when you come home,
Ten thousand men scrape their walks at once.
And in the Spring, the elms open like parachutes.
On quite an ordinary day
The Mayor lights a candle for peace
And nobody resists.

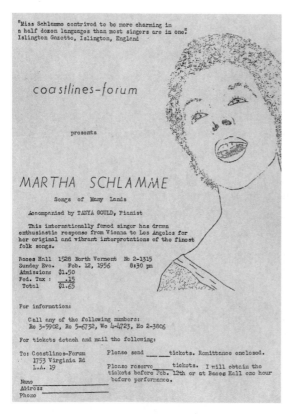

"Miss Schlamme contrived to be more charming in
a half dozen languages than most singers are in one."
Islington Gazette, Islington, England

coastlines-forum

presents

MARTHA  SCHLAMME

Songs of Many Lands

Accompanied by TANYA GOULD, Pianist

This internationally famed singer has drawn
enthusiastic response from Vienna to Los Angeles for
her original and vibrant interpretations of the finest
folk songs.

Bases Hall  1528 North Vermont  No 2-1315
Sunday Eve.    Feb. 12, 1956      8:30 pm
Admission: $1.50
Fed. Tax :   .15
Total      $1.65

For information:

Call any of the following numbers:
Ro 3-5902, Ro 5-6732, We 4-4723, Ho 2-3806

For tickets detach and mail the following:

To: Coastlines-Forum    Please send ____ tickets. Remittance enclosed.
    1753 Virginia Rd
    L.A. 19             Please reserve____ tickets.  I will obtain the
                        tickets before Feb. 12th or at Bases Hall one hour
Name _____       before performance.
Address _____
Phone _____

Announcements of *Coastlines*-Forum concert.

Friday
May 16, 1958
8:30 P.M.
GEORGE ABBE
Municipal Gallery
Barnsdall Park
Sunset and Vermont
Friday
June 28, 1958
8:30 P.M.
ANN STANFORD
LAWRENCE LIPTON

It's kind of silly soliciting poems for a dead issue. Who wants to see their poems in a dead magazine. And no hope!

Really, this is a terrible thing. I'm beginning to realize it. Here there is a poet explosion riding with the population, the end of *Coastlines* is like the end of California. I send my poems out and all the mags announce they're filled up until 1978. Ye Gods. Genocide, Infanticide! You should be ashamed of yourself. Honestly people out this way are horrified.

What the hell? Perhaps it's just as well. I'm the last person to say anything about. Your note gave me a twinge. Naturally. But, perhaps, like a lame horse it should be killed dead!

Brave soul!

Why couldn't the god damn thing ever have an issue or a point of view, now with a revolution on our hands. The problem is jobs. We're scared as hell at publishing our real feelings, our real beliefs. That's the real problem. *Coastlines* has always wanted to, but was never willing to truly represent itself.

Love,

Mel

Letter, Mel Weisburd to *Coastlines*

*Coastlines* 6, nos. 21–22, final issue

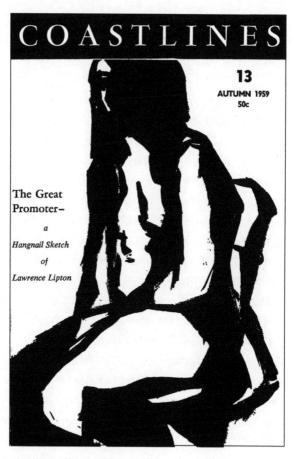

Manuel Santana, cover: *Coastlines* 4, no. 1 (autumn 1959).

# Eugene Frumkin

Eugene (Gene) Frumkin, b. 1928—Gene Frumkin was born in New York City, the son of Samuel Frumkin and Sarah Blackman. He came to Los Angeles in 1938, attended UCLA, and received his B.A. in English in 1950. In 1955 he married Lydia Samuels, an artist, and they divorced in 1971. As a student he was alternately sports editor, city editor, managing editor, and editor in chief of the UCLA student newspaper, *The Daily Bruin.* He was executive editor of *California Apparel News,* a trade newspaper, between 1952 and 1966. In 1966 he became a lecturer in English at the University of New Mexico. Between 1967 and 1971 he became an assistant professor, in 1971 an associate professor, and finally in the 1980s a full professor of English at the University of New Mexico. In 1994 he retired as professor emeritus and lives in Albuquerque, New Mexico. Gene Frumkin's first book of poems was *The Hawk and the Lizard,* in 1963. Other books of poems are *The Orange Tree* (a long poem) (1964), *The Rainbow Walker* (1971), *Dostoevsky and Other Nature Poems* (1972), *Locust Cry,* (1973), *The Mystic Writing Pad* (1977), *Loops* (1982), *Clouds and Red Earth* (1982), *A Lover's Quarrel with America* and *A Sweetness in the Air* (1986), *Comma in the Ear* (1991), *Saturn is Mostly Weather: Selected and Uncollected Poems* (1992), and, most recently, *The Old Man Who Swam Away and Left Only His Wet Feet* (1998) and a chapbook, *Falling Into Meditation* (1999). Frumkin's poetry has appeared in several anthologies and has been published widely in literary quarterlies across the United States. He was the cofounder of *Coastlines* with Mel Weisburd in 1955 and poetry editor between 1955 and 1958; guest editor of *The New Mexico Quarterly: A Double Issue of the Contemporary American Imagination* (1968–69); coeditor with David Johnson of the *San Marcos Review* in 1977; served on the founding editorial board of *The Blue Mesa Review;* and was coeditor of an anthology titled *The Indian Rio-Grande: Recent Poems from Three Cultures* (1977).

"Those days were for us like the primal academe of Plato. We didn't walk and talk among the trees, but we didn't confine ourselves to the classroom either. We were friends, of Tom and of each other. Frequently, Tom and his wife Alice asked us over to share a meal and try out ideas into some part of the night. The McGraths lived on Marsh Street in Los Angeles and we—Stanley Kiesel, Mel Weisburd, Alvaro Cardona-Hine, Carol Zimmerman, the late Bert Meyers, Tom Viertel, Rita Mosher, Sid and Estelle Gershgoren, myself, and a couple of others— came to be called the Marsh Street Irregulars. In *Letter to an Imaginary Friend,* McGrath's long 'pseudo autobiography' still in progress, we the Marsh Street Irregulars have our 'pseudo' place. It was all a Socratic banquet and the savor of it still remains alive in the buds."

Gene Frumkin

"A Note on Tom McGrath—the Early '50s," *North Dakota Territory*
Festschrift for Thomas McGrath (fall 1982)

## Elegy for a Tailor

Myopic old tailor, you poked at life
As at the eye of a needle. The bird-dreams
Skimmed through your mind with their falcon screams
And vanished. Stiff eyelids blackballed your wife,

While your face hung limp in Cyclopean sleep.
The twelve lizard hours you daily pursued
In sewing circles tired you. You suffered, slued
Around the master axis, but wouldn't weep.

You lived beneath the humid clouds of press
Machines and walked on grass of wool and cotton,
And in spring breathed the sweat of walls hot in
Golden fur. Lost, to you, life's summer dress.

But the Talmud, father, was prophet still of pleasure—
Antique made richer by teachers' voices, old
Silver tucked away deep in beards, and sold
To you before you dozed in bankrupt leisure.

While the tombs of viciously mounting skulls
Made marmoreal the fields, you quietly waned
To the grave; museum of Jehovah you gained,
Until Messiah's rod startles your pulse.

O tailor, muted totem-head in state,
How mourn your sterile decades? Yet in this place
Where I, you loved too little, scan your face,
You are the chalk that scrapes my mind's grey slate.

## The Waiting Room in the County Hospital

(For Dr. Marvin Marsh)

Gangrenous day! Caries
Of the old Hebrew, once
Marcher in the torah pageant,
Moaning to the sweet of his God
On the stretcher of his last belief,
Wheeled through the gauntlet of eyes
To the rubble room, to wait

In the pile of people. The choir
Of calypso-hearted quiet;
The young mulatto taped
To the spirit of the mummy room,

Hearing the names unwind
To a vault-gapped cadence,
Waiting in the masked and cryptic

Light. Aztec hearts,
Scalpeled out, bled
For their gods on the teocalli
Altar—the señoras here,
Amid a rosary of thoughts,
Feel, too, an obsidian
Presence in their temples, waiting.

No microscope sees
These poor shuttling in the culture
Of the charity-raw room,
Nor stethoscope hears
The cyclone of hearts in the silence,
Nor fluoroscope reveals
This anatomy's hidden lung.

Then, doctor, do as you must.
Your love, not in teaspoons
At appointed hours, but always,
By the whole bottle, must tonic
All these patient, who wait
In the chemical air for the day
When a better solution prospers.

"Regarding a Proposal to Merge *Coastlines* and *The California Quarterly* into One Magazine"

"There should be no attempt to integrate a political base to the magazine. The humanistic philosophies of both magazines are, apparently, compatible. It is hoped that the magazine, however, will be individualistic in its approach, that it will not echo party lines. In regard to this *Coastlines* has felt it necessary to criticize the left-wing press, or to advocate social conscious works which exhibit none of the typical faults of left-wing writing. This attitude is aimed to improve the left-wing press, and the right-wing press for that matter, in order for literature to reassert its leadership for the society as a whole. It is our aim to write what is appropriate for the '50s, not for the '30s and '40s."

*Coastlines* editors' unsigned memo,
c. 1956

### ▪ Iowa, Kansas, Nebraska

Iowa, Kansas, Nebraska,
all combustible country
under a tortured sky.
Nothing ever happens here
except loneliness;
wheatfields squirming in the sun,
the plains dry as biscuits.

Yet the people grow.

In the Oklahoma air
oil is prince of blossoms;
Texas is the Kingdom.

*Fortune's* richest man
plays croquet in Dallas.
He is seventy,
afraid of centipedes,
hesitates at watery places,
for a gypsy slipped him once
the dark blue ace of drowning,
never kissed a woman

(nor a man either),
likes to ride his zebra
several times each morning
round his private race-track,
bought the Lone Star his third
year collecting our planet,
later added forty-
seven others: stars, white,
plays croquet in Dallas
at four o'clock in starlight.

Yet, somehow, the people grow.

## The Clue

#### DETECTIVE

Bring me the evidence of the dead man.
Let me see his shoes, for the agglutinations
of the soles may show me his mysterious way . . .
 Ah, you see? A stamp of dirty gum.
  Across it, like a postmark,
   some needles of hay.
Significant. Is there a farm nearby?

#### CORONER

Yes. Many horses grazing on the sea,
glaring furrows of sun with fish implanted,
the hands, lovely boys, with moccasinned glee
 hauling in the red and purple clouds,
  the rainbow of bugs and feathers
   in the struggling net
—or flying off, like boys, with the morning crop.

#### DETECTIVE

A dazzle for tourists, sounds like, but we'll go
whatever my suspicion of artifice.
Death is so uncomfortable, always old-fashioned:
 a Pony Express sort of country
  whose mischievous Indians twang
   false directions.
Here we are. Sir, are you this farm's butler?

#### FARMER

Indeed. But won't you step out of your past,
your puddle, so we can dissect our commerce
in a huskdry attitude of head and heart?

#### DETECTIVE

No commerce, my friend. I want the facts.
 The dead man's an anagram,
  the letter by letter
rebuttal of life's laws and lexicons.
I must solve him: the taxpayers demand it.

---

Eugene Frumkin

Where is your hay? I'll have to test your stack
by microscope against my sticky clue.

                    FARMER

        O he was here, why trouble the hay?
                Your lens would magnify
                        its own myopia.

                    DETECTIVE

Then I have traced him to a hopeful report.

                    FARMER

Indeed. Hope is our staple industry,
manufactured by the signs of the Zodiac
and packaged for promotion in department stores.

                    DETECTIVE

        But the dead man, you saw him last . . . ?

                    FARMER

        On stilts, learning the water
                like his first skates.

                    CORONER

Winter must be the season of greatest joy

for then the gods come rushing down in snowflakes
to sweeten the birds and lay their swift saddles
on backs of horses. The heavens get white and hard;
        the weightless boys slide up the mountains,
                Aladdins on the sleds
                        of their smoking breath . . .

                    FARMER

Well, this place is almost Hollywood

but we are nature's costume turned inside out,
not a man-made duck betraying its true feathers.

                    DETECTIVE

I must talk to the dead man. Where is he now,
        this chief witness against himself?
                His story is awaited
                        like a Hitchcock shock.

BOY

He's a watermelon climbing a lemon tree.

FARMER

Be quiet, fool. Ah, sir, there is no science
in such talk for it would be a dialogue
with a snowman whose words would melt before your eyes.

BOY

With only the smoke of his cigar
souvenir in your nostrils.

DETECTIVE

At least that's something
to show them back home: a ten-cent smell of death.

FARMER

You amuse me. Come to that house floating in the sea.
Walk there: the path of roses through the water
will buoy your step to the dead man's hideaway.

CORONER

Friend, do not go unless you would make
foolscap for the sharks that wait
beneath the floor
—sharp black pencils—to write obituaries

for the morning news. My knife has long dissevered
the many disguises of death, one time a woman
with frank blue eyes and charming Oxford lips
who spoke of Bach in trapezoids,
who met Apollinaire
in a metaphor,
who was the dream *behind* the dream of Freud;

another time a man with a hero's flag
who marched from town to town inciting violence
against the local Attila and his militia
—all of them masks, all mere symbols.
Death itself is a child's face
open as the sky . . .
but cunning as a bomb. Beware the Farmer.

---

DETECTIVE

Ah, Coroner, you have a firmer vocation,
you probe deeper than clues: to the pearl of meaning
But I am not an artist. I stop at the oyster
    for that is all I can plainly see.
       I have a job to do,
         a living to make.
Come, Farmer, I'll follow you along the flowers.

BOY

Oho, what a fool! He'll walk forever
behind the Farmer, trampling the fake roses,
getting no nearer the lazy denouement,
    the house a horizon holding its place
      in the distance, its vacancy.
      Look at that dunce:
the Master'll make him stand in the corner forever.

CORONER

Goodbye, friend. May you find better reason
for being brave than your paycheck's gun in your back.
May you imagine the ocean's Fourth of July,
    I pray it, as once in a child's brain
      I followed a string of flame
        so close to the sun
that still the flaring hawk holds fast my eyes.

"As a literary magazine, our first duty is toward the things of the world, for without these there is no literature, no art—just desolation. Among these things are the timeless human problems, public and private. We must try to see them honestly, from the inside, in the material we publish and in our own commentaries. We must try to see them freshly, too, for otherwise we cannot see them honestly. But originality should not be our only value; it dare not be accepted as an abstract value cut off from the world's images."

Gene Frumkin

"A Birthday Editorial," *Coastlines* (spring 1960)

Editorial

## The Debt

When I read of worms slipping
through the skin of children's feet,
swimming in their blood with open mouths,
damning the currents of their lives,
my muscles thunder and my eyes
become the bells of a burning city.

When I read of peasants' hands,
sweet for a sugarfield month
and dust for three in the desert,
my hand is an arrow quivering
in the white mango of this paper.

When I read of the grey canvases
in their brains, and read
how the shells have grown around their eyes
—in a land whose mountains are a rainbow—
the falcons and peacocks of my library
ascend from my house and migrate to Cuba.

People, ploughed like the soil.
Because they are the hands of my clock
I must wear their clothes,
eat their food, think their thoughts
or I will forget
—forget I owe them doeskin slippers,
grapes and apples, cigars, wine, poems.

This poem of mine is an attempt to make an important event of our time a personal matter. The problem of the poem is to get beyond Premier Castro's beleaguered truculence and the ignorant floundering of the U.S. Government vis-à-vis Cuba to a relationship with a long-victimized people. The point to be made is that poets with a social and political conscience may find this method useful and possibly more fruitful than submergence of the personality within the objective limits of the particular event itself. What it comes to, simply, is the *gathering in* of the towering, multi-faced and, in the end, ephemeral occurrence rather than the *going out* to meet the occurrence on its own plane—an effort by the poet to find what his involvement *is* with the factual transformations the world is undergoing.

### ■ Men Fail in Communion

They fail in communion, a surplus of failure
stored in grief, and the birdwrist
lying open to the razor. Who knows what hand
passes through the wind? Perhaps it's ours,
a peninsula clutching at the savage emptiness.

A man starves within sight of flowers.
A king lies drunk on the mountain. The black man,
darkest leaf on Alabama's autumn tree.
Whisper it: Men fail in communion.

And they arrive at the temple of ruins.
Footsteps on the polished floor
of a thousandmile corridor.
Far from the beginning.
Each man alone, each waiting for night
to dream the old wishes.
But flies are dancing
to the music of dust.

Men fail in communion, being greater than beasts.
Men possess circles and numbers and death.
Their fictions are lions. Men are caught
in their stealth, caged by their own treachery.
Their grasshopping fingers
infest the earth, fingers which unite
in prayer . . . and in fists.
Even man's innocence deserves prison.

Still, the heroic wrist,
graceful as a seed in the sowing.
What huge blood does it channel?

Listen, the surf erodes men's sleep.
They awake . . . and vanish in the glare.
The morning cannot hold them.
The earth cannot hold them.
Only the sea contains their echoes.
Only a man's wrist contains the sea.

## "The Great Promotor"
## A Hangnail Sketch of Lawrence Lipton
### Gene Frumkin

Two thousand years ago Lawrence Lipton could have found employment (otherwise known as 'voluntary poverty') as a gospelmonger for the new religious sect that was beginning around that time. Earlier, he might have made the Bible scene as a minor prophet. But today, so debased and business-conscious have our attitudes become that, in his recently-published book, *The Holy Barbarians*, his hosannas for the beat way of life are like unto the sounds of a pitch-man. Mr. Lipton, to use the vocabulary of our day, is nothing more nor less than a promoter— a kind of encyclopedia salesman (he is crammed with knowledge) with a quick Madison Avenue flow to his prose style. Except, of course, he observes 'Ezra Pound's advice to poets: Make it NEW!' (*The Holy Barbarians*, p. 72). Mr. Lipton makes it NEW! by doing the same things the grey flannel suit crowd does, only he does them counter-clockwise. Somebody who read this book with a careful eye and ear could doubtless deduce this for himself; however, it does help to have known Mr. Lipton personally, even if briefly, as I have. That clears up any doubts.

A most important weapon in the promoter's arsenal is distortion: making his own product seem splendid and the competition's seem awful when really they are exactly the same. If a bit of the truth does ooze in between the lines, that's okay, provided it's on his side. But beware of treading on the corns of the promoter, for he will tread back on yours—with a steamroller. He will smear you. He will do or say anything to put you out of business. Such is the position in which *Coastlines*, for example, finds itself in relation to Mr. Lipton. We have questioned and criticized his tactics as a spokesman for the beats. Here, at some length, because the matter is important to us, is how Mr. Lipton retaliates:

I was not unprepared for Allen Ginsberg's visit to Los Angeles, since he had written me from San Francisco, but when he got to town Nettie and I were so exhausted from all the poetry-reading parties we had been throwing for visiting poets that I was relieved when the editors of *Coastlines,* the L.A. quarterly, offered to sponsor the reading. I know they had no use for the sort of thing Ginsberg was writing or what we were doing in Venice West (in fact, much of their magazine is devoted to attacking it), but now that it looked like it might be attracting wide public attention they wanted to get into the act.

DISTORTION No. 1: *Coastlines* has devoted a very small number of its published pages to the beat-anti-beat controversy. Most criticisms therein were directed at Mr. Lipton himself rather than the beat environment. On the other side, Mr. Lipton neglects to mention our publication of an article by himself with a pro-beat slant, a poem of his which one could call beat if one wanted to (though Mr. Lipton's poetry in general has seemed to us away from the mainstream of beat literature), as well as poems by Ginsberg, Rexroth, Corso and Philip Whalen.

DISTORTION No. 2: The reading referred to by Mr. Lipton happened around the middle of 1956 just after the first edition of Howl was published, before it ran into customs trouble in San Francisco and began making the news headlines. Ginsberg and Howl were hardly known then. We didn't know there was an 'act' to get into. We agreed to host the reading because Mr. Lipton (whom we had known just a little too briefly at that time) asked us to and because one of our editors knew Ginsberg. Also, it has been part of our self-conceived function to serve as a sponsor or co-sponsor of poetry readings and cultural events of various kinds in Los Angeles.

Mr. Lipton continues:

The reading was to be held in a big old-fashioned house that was occupied by two or three of the *Coastlines* editors, living in a kind of Left Wing bohemian collective household, furnished—what there was of furniture, which wasn't much—in atrociously bad taste, nothing like the imaginative and original décor of the beat generation pad, even the most poverty-stricken.

DISTORTION No. 3: 'Left Wing . . . bohemian . . . collective household.' How does one tell a Left Wing from a Right Wing household? By the proprietor, I suppose. But Mr. Lipton didn't and still doesn't know the proprietor (one of our editors). Bohemian? Does a bachelor boarding house have to be bohemian? Neither of the other two editors who lived there (and paid rent to the proprietor) pretended to such a distinction. They were simply living as cheaply as they could. This boarding house also served as *Coastlines* headquarters and as a place where an actors' group met. But Mr. Lipton is right about one thing: the furniture *was* atrocious. It came with the house and nobody bothered to remove it.

> I consented at their request to conduct the reading, 'chair the meeting,' as these people are in the habit of saying. To them everything is a meeting. . . .

DISTORTION No. 4: As far as we were concerned, the 'meeting' was Mr. Lipton's from beginning to end. Our then-editor said a few words to those present as a matter of welcome. We considered Mr. Lipton part of the show and our own responsibility merely to provide the stage.

DISTORTION No. 5: We are not 'these people.'

> The audience, except for Anais [Nin] and the people we had brought with us from Venice West, was a square audience, the sort of an audience you would find at any liberal or 'progressive'—how the word lingers on even though the song is over—fund-raising affair of the faithful who are still waiting for the Second Coming. Few of them had come knowing what to expect. They never read anything but the party and cryptoparty press. The avant-garde quarterlies are so much Greek to them. Most of them don't even know such magazines exist any more. They associate that sort of thing with the little magazines of the twenties which were swallowed up with the advent of *the* Movement, the *real* Movement (capital *M*), in the thirties and transformed into weapons in the class struggle. The few who *had* heard rumors of what was going on in San Francisco and Venice West were there as slummers might go to a Negro whorehouse in New Orleans, to be *with*, briefly, but not *of*. . . .

DISTORTIONS No. 6 through No. 79: I don't know if Mr. Lipton was really *there* (italics mine) that night or if he has a weak memory for details (but, no, he remembered the furniture) or is pushing the truth too hard. Only because it suits

Mr. Lipton's purpose can the Movement (capital M), the thirties, the class struggle, progressive (in quotes), etc. possibly enter the reportage of that evening. I would estimate that more than half of the audience consisted of the Venice West group. The remainder comprised people invited by the editor who was a friend of Ginsberg, plus the editors, their wives and a very few close friends of *Coastlines*. *Coastlines* did not advertise the event. If anybody present that night was waiting for a Second Coming, it was in the sexual sense, not the political. The audience Mr. Lipton describes did not exist, except perhaps in his own rejected past.

It is one thing to criticize Marx, Khrushchev, the Communists and the Left in general, but quite another to Red-bait an individual or individuals by name or group association as Mr. Lipton has done. In the context of our place and time, to do so is to commit a moral outrage, and it is equivalent to becoming an ally of the committees and one of those 'hunters' (Lipton's word) who do the Social Lying. A queer position for a man who wrote a satiric poem called 'I was a Poet for the FBI.' (The thought occurs that maybe he really *was*.) Mr. Lipton's action demonstrates the (involuntary) poverty of his personality, his cliché thinking. This man who says 'make it new' has not approached the progressive in that spirit, has accepted in toto Mr. Luce's thinking on the subject, while at the same time offering to the public in *The Holy Barbarians* a grotesque stereotype of certain human beings known as beatniks. When there is no ready-made cliché available, Mr. Lipton has the gift of being able to invent one.

As it happened, Allen and Gregory [Corso] were not the only ones in the place who had been drinking [Mr. Lipton had noted they had been drinking before their arrival]. There was one other—in the audience. He was someone who had drifted in, having somewhere picked up one of the pluggers advertising the reading.

DISTORTION A: I can't say whether or not the gentleman was drunk, but I do know he did not drift in. He was invited by our editor friend of Ginsberg. He could not have picked up one of the ad pluggers because there weren't any.

At first he applauded Allen's reading—at all the wrong places and too loudly. Then he took to cheering, the kind of cheers that are more like the jeers they are intended to be. . . . He began to heckle. Allen ignored him and, at one point, interrupted the reading to ask the heckler . . . to hear him out. . . .

Then several paragraphs later:

The drunk was indignant. He was outraged. When he heard snickering in the audience he started toward the front of the room, menacingly, repeating his challenge to step outside and settle this thing—'You're yella, that's what. Like all you wise guys. You're yella—'

Ginsberg got up and went forward to meet the drunk.

'All right,' he said, 'all right. You want to do something big, don't you? Something brave. Well, go on, do something *really* brave. *Take off your clothes!*'

That stopped the drunk dead in his tracks.

Ginsberg moved a step toward him. 'Go on, let everybody see how brave you are. Take your clothes off!'

The drunk was stunned speechless. He fell back a step and Allen moved toward him, tearing off his own shirt and undershirt and flinging them at the heckler's feet. 'You're scared, aren't you?' he taunted him. 'You're afraid.' He unbuckled his belt, unzipped his fly and started kicking off his trousers. 'Look,' he cried. 'I'm not afraid. Go on, take *your* clothes off. Let's see how brave *you* are,' he challenged him. He flung his pants down at the champ's feet and then his shorts, shoes and socks, with a curious little hopping dance as he did so. He was stark naked now. The drunk had retired to the back of the room. Nobody laughed. Nobody said a word. . . .

DISTORTION B: Besides the styleless dialogue, this bit also presents a fictionalized version of the affair. I can speak first-hand on this since I am the one who gathered up Ginsberg's clothes, stitch by golden stitch. The way it sounded to me, the heckler did not challenge Ginsberg until after the latter yelled, 'Take off your clothes.' The heckler thought Ginsberg meant jacket so, thinking *he* had been challenged, suggested they go outside. It was only when Ginsberg began stripping that the other first realized when Ginsberg said clothes, he meant clothes.

---

. . . Then the room was suddenly filled with an explosion of nervous applause, cheers, jeers, noisy argument. Our hosts, the editors of *Coastlines,* had been having a huddle on the sidelines. Now one of them, Mel Weisburd, dashed up front and stood over Allen menacingly.

'All right,' he shouted, 'put your clothes on and get out! You're not up in San Francisco now. This is a private house . . . you're in someone else's *living* room . . . you've violated our hospitality. . . .'

DISTORTION C: Though he is adept at a few swift jabs and an uppercut or two in writing when these are called for, Mel Weisburd is incapable of standing over anybody 'menacingly.' He asked Ginsberg to restore his clothes alright, but rather with the idea of getting the show back into orbit. Besides, Weisburd thought as I did that the strip was irrelevant to the argument and a meaningless act of exhibitionism. Had it happened as Mr. Lipton relates it, there would have been some justification for the act, for then it would have amounted to a unique and effective response to a challenge.

Mr. Lipton again, just once more:

. . . Corso was all for leaving at once. 'We'll go somewhere where we can get good and drunk. . . .' But Allen shook his head and quietly put his clothes on, one piece at a time [how the hell else *could* he put them on?], in slow motion, smiling to himself with half-closed eyes. A sly, mysterious, inner-directed Buddha smile.

While the outer-directed Buddha slyly and mysteriously writhed on his pedestal.

2

Although the incident I have dealt with above at some length occupies only a few pages in Mr. Lipton's book, it is of prime importance in estimating the value of the work as a commentary on the beat generation. *Coastlines* and its former editor, Mel Weisburd, were among several who got the knife in this book, but what about its much wider application as a credo for the beatniks? As such, it seems to me, a grave mistake. I think Mr. Lipton has been a mistake for the beatniks all the way, for as a spokesman for them in life and letters he has been a cold, dogmatic wind blowing in from the past. In contrast to the more original influences of other key figures in the rise of the beatniks (mainly Miller, Rexroth, Ferlinghetti), Mr. Lipton has spent some years codifying the beat mores into what he would like to think of as the beat 'ritual,' harking back to the orgiastic rites of the Greeks and of primitive peoples. By doing this, he believes that he has given this movement sanction as a force for a new birth, bringing back the spontaneous life flow of the ancients, the primitives. By repeated use of the word 'holy,' he feels he bestows on beatism a religious base.

On the surface it might appear that such a framework is precisely what the beatniks need. But I think that surface is an illusion. What Mr. Lipton's book—his Napoleonic codification—does is to petrify individuals, turning them into moulds which future beatniks must emulate. He casts in bronze those stereotypes of the beatnik which have already emerged in the wake of *Time, Life, Mademoiselle,* et al, publicity. Instead of the people the beatniks really are, Mr. Lipton has done much to advance a few caricatures which are not at all likely to frighten the middle class and, more significantly, may serve to rigidify the beatniks to suit the caricatures. This process, if we are to take Mr. Lipton's commentary at face worth, has already begun.

In *Liberation* (June 1959), Curtis Zahn puts the situation this way, ' . . . by having been made into colorful clowns by the slick magazines they [the beatniks] have been rendered socially obnoxious and ridiculous . . . the slicks have given the innocent reader the illusion that a real Underground is being given an ear. It isn't. Only a harmless, crackpot, soapbox kind of character is being plugged. They know that these kids aren't going to do or say anything important—and if they did, they are already disqualified by being passed off as freaks. . . .'

A department store in San Diego recently advertised 'Beachnik' swimsuits. Several fashion houses have beatnik ensembles or items in their collections. A San Francisco merchant recently referred to North Beach as an amusing part of town. I suppose next they'll be manufacturing beatnik beards and sandals for the kiddies or setting up a miniature beatnik lemonade house in Disneyland.

'Well,' the beatnik mutters, 'we'll show them. Let them be amused now. Later we'll show them just how funny we are . . . when we tip over their quaint old society and the bottom falls out.'

But, no, that won't happen. Once a fashion dies it stays dead . . . for a decade, anyhow. What's the market for coonskin caps these days? Much as they may dislike the thought, the life of beatdom—by that name—will continue only as long as the beatniks remain interesting to the rest of society. That may not be much longer.

What will be left then? By Mr. Lipton's process—though he is trying to accomplish exactly the opposite—nothing but figures for somebody's wax museum. Rexroth has indicated a slackening enthusiasm for the beat path; Patchen says he was never on this path in the first place. Only Mr. Lipton doggedly rides his horse, whipping it to its last breath of promotional impact. But, lo, the other horses have gone home.

At all costs, and though it makes Mr. Lipton angry, the beatniks have to retain their humanity, their separate individualities. They have to break away from the pattern that has been charted for them.

THERE IS NO SUCH THING AS BEAT VS. SQUARE.

That, I think, is the first break that has to be made. What Mr. Lipton preaches is the isolation of the beatniks within the structure of their own society. He preaches not love but a mild form of hate, a contemptuous sneer, for everybody who has a regular job and doesn't live in a pad. This is no way toward peace with one's soul, no way to enlightenment. Standing between the power-politicians of the Soviet Union and United States there is only the human power of love. Not beat versus square, but only as much love as we—all of us, people—can hoard against our own follies, neuroses and corruptions. If, as its adherents claim, the beat way of life is an expression of love, then it must begin to formulate this expression more clearly.

The beat literature, I expect, is not yet adequately formed, not yet capable of presenting the full case. It is too shrill, in large part, for it still has itself to prove. It is not yet formed because most of the people writing it are either not talented enough or not themselves sufficiently formed. But there is much that deserves to survive. There is Ginsberg—maybe not the poem 'Howl' itself but rather 'Sunflower Sutra,' his poems in the *Evergreen Review,* and work he is doing now or has still to do. Corso, yes; a talent that seems to be developing, maturing, still distracted by a need to explode in shapeless protests—but he's a poet. Gary Snyder, Michael McClure, they've done noteworthy work and promise more. In the end, it may be Ferlinghetti who becomes the freshest poetic talent to come out of this milieu. Burroughs's *Naked Lunch* is a hopped-up Rabelaisian picture of our drugged time and as apropos a way to look at it as any other. (The Chicago University administration is to be censured for blocking its publication in the *Chicago Review,* while the *Review's* walkout staff that launched *Big Table* and published it deserves the praise and support of the literary world for its action.) And Kerouac—he too may discover that talent should be harvested, not tortured.

As for a way of life, the beat way—here Mr. Lipton is most intransigent. Salvation—indeed we are already saved if we but knew it, he says (Zen is part of the big package promotion)—is through disaffiliation from society, refuting the Social Lie, taking pot, living in a pad, voluntary poverty (in which Mr. Lipton is able to indulge despite what seems to be a well-stocked refrigerator). This beat identification may be useful and liberating for some who may have had just such a revolt smoldering in their bones for many years. It is good that this revolt manifests itself, provided it becomes a channel to a creative something. Too often it doesn't; it turns into the ultimate out, the complete disengagement from reality. In any case, this way toward liberation, salvation, need not be the style (as Dostoyevsky would put it) of every man who desires the same end. One man's freedom may be another's dungeon though both men are brothers of the heart. One can go the high road and one the low road and get to heaven at the same time. The true wise man knows there is no chosen people and no chosen way. Only the struggle and the mystery, and those infrequent moments of felicity. Mr. Lipton, however, gives us generalities about what the beats do and don't, which through his acerbic pen grow into dogmas. For instance, on page 165:

> . . . The beats are not to be found in the baseball stands or tuning in on the play-by-play on radio or television. They never know who's ahead in the pennant race. The World's Series, which one of our new theologians analyzed, in a liberal weekly, as something culturally homologous to the tribal religious celebrations of the fall equinox, leaves the beat spiritually unmoved and unregenerate. They are likely to take their theology in matters of church and sports from *Mad* magazine rather than *The Christian Century* or *Sports Illustrated.*

He might had added *Escapade,* one of the *Playboy* ilk of magazine which in Mr. Lipton's lexicon is square in Beatville (see p. 126). For in the August 1959 issue of *Escapade,* on the last page, is an article by none less than Jack Kerouac

---

on—of all things—baseball. And he even sounds as if he knows somewhat whereof he speaks. There is comment on the change in Willie Mays's batting stance, on Karl Spooner's operation (you have to know something about the game to have heard of Karl Spooner or that he had an operation), on Early Wynn, on Bob Feller, etc. The way Kerouac writes about the sport indicates some feeling of his that there is something holy or spiritual about it; and he concludes the piece with the phrase, '. . . when Babe Ruth . . . boomed homeruns to the glory of God.' I guess he feels that way about everything. Sure, he wrote the thing for money, but if nothing else, the article demonstrates the beats have minds of their own and if there is money to be gotten by writing about baseball, they will do it. I think the article—cornball though it is—is no black mark against Kerouac except as an inflated bit of writing, for if a few pieces of this kind can sustain him sufficiently to enable him to get *new* serious writing done, then the taint is worth it. If he gets bogged in this trash, well, god save his beatdown soul. . . .

My own article, this one, is getting itself written not for money but to cast doubt, to the fullest extent I am able, on Mr. Lipton as an authoritative spokesman for beat literature. He is rather their unsolicited advertising agent, (believe, a man who is using all the tricks of the trade—including the hatchet and TV appearances—to sell a product, a way of life). His own success, his own fame, are embodied in the fortunes of the beats. I do not intend to question his sincere concern with jazz, the spoken poetry, what he calls Jazz Canto and the other things he has hammered at for the past few years and consolidates in *The Holy Barbarians*. I do question his calling the beats, who are neither holy nor barbarians, by that sales-stimulating juxtaposition. That is a gimmick, and Mr. Lipton is full of them. I do protest 309 pages (and pictures, notes and glossary) by a man who knows all the answers except the vital ones. It makes for boring reading, because all sense of inquiry, of concern about the terrestrial dilemma and the meaning of human existence, has been forsaken in documentation and dogma.

It is astounding to me that those, like Mr. Lipton, who profess their retirement from business as far as society is concerned are so intent on publicizing his retirement. It is a basic contradiction inherent in Mr. Lipton's entire effort. If the beats really want to disaffiliate, why do they not do so quietly, since that would do the most to insure a successful disaffiliation, whereas publicity in the major slicks cannot help but prolong the connection? A look at the record, however, will disclose that they—through their literary representatives—have never parted company from the 'others'; they have always cared. The work of Ginsberg, of Kerouac and Corso is not cool: it cares and shows that it cares. This means that they are not really beat (and a strong case has been made for that view by Herbert Gold) and/or that the beats are people with special egos who have to create their own particular place *within* the social structure.

But Mr. Lipton concludes his book this way:

> The editorials and the ads and the speech makers keep telling youth that the world is his, the future is his, and in the next breath cries out with alarm that 'the other side' is plotting to blow up the world with hydrogen bombs. The holy barbarian's answer to all this can be summed up in the remark of Itchy Dave Gelden when he dropped in one day with an evangelist leaflet that some 'christer' had shoved into his hand, announcing that the world was coming to an end—
>
> 'Whose world is coming to an end?'
> Not the holy barbarian's.

I suspect that Itchy Dave Gelden, whoever he is, knows, even if Mr. Lipton doesn't, that if the world does explode, the 'holy barbarian's' will explode with it.

The answer then to Gelden's question is maybe *our* world. Everybody's. The bomb will not ask who is disaffiliated and who isn't.

*What is the sound of one hand clapping?* asks the Zen master.
*Two hands clasping.*

Yes, too rational an answer. I realize I have flunked the exercise.

But dig?

## SNORT-RIPPIN' COASTLINES PARTY

ooze, irls & oys!

Saturday night, May 2, 9 p.m. to the wee hours
471 Sycamore Rd., Santa Monica Canyon

### NO POETRY
### NO JAZZ
### NO TALK
Just a good simple homespun orgy
Also quiet accomodations for quiet people

We will have beer for sale,
but if your taste runs to other potations,
do not hesitate to bring your own.

DIRECTIONS: Take the Pacific Coast Hwy. (101) to W. Channel Rd.(the only signal between the Wilshire Ramp and Sunset Blvd. ) and turn east (the other way is the ocean).Go slowly up Channel to the first left turn which is E. Rustic(sign on the corner building reads "Edmundson Real Estate"). Take E. Rustic to the first right turn. That's Sycamore. If you get lost, call GL 4-5783.

Donation – ONE DOLLAR

For further information call HO 4-6070 or WE 4-8441.

Coastlines is a very non-profit organization. Subscriptions ($2.00 for 4 issues) may be obtained at the party from one of the lovely dancing girls.

## COASTLINES LITERARY MAGAZINE
presents
**"Three Faces of Literature"**

a panel discussion of literature today and
perhaps tomorrow
Friday night, April 3, 1959, 8:15 p.m. at
Silver Lake Playground
1850 Silver Lake Drive, Los Angeles

Speakers:
**Lachlan MacDonald,** non-fiction editor of COASTLINES and former editor of the CHICAGO REVIEW, who will take the "little magazine" viewpoint.
**Myron Roberts,** editor and publisher of L.A. MAGAZINE, speaking from the standpoint of the larger circulation magazines.
**Peter Yates,** well-known poet and critic, who will look at the situation with the critic's eye.
Moderator:
**Thomas McGrath,** poet and novelist, winner of the 1954 Alan Swallow Poetry Prize.

This is the first in a projected series of cultural programs, under the auspices of COASTLINES, intended as investigations of many aspects of literary life today.

Proceeds from all programs will be used to finance publication of COASTLINES MAGAZINE, published by California Quarterly, Inc., a non-profit corporation.

Donation – ONE DOLLAR

For further information call HOllywood 46070

---

## HIGH FLYING COASTLINES PARTY
*U-2 Are Invited*

SATURDAY EVENING, JUNE 18TH, 9 P.M.
471 Sycamore Road, Santa Monica Canyon

### DANCING

in the house, patio and streets (if they'll let us).
Conversations and provocations until the wee hours.

BRING ALONG

more *uu*inhabitants to help us launch our Los Angeles "Non-Existent City" issue.

Beer on hand or B.Y.O.L.

---

NAVIGATING INSTRUCTIONS:

Take the Pacific Coast Hwy. (101) to W. Channel Rd. (the only signal between the Wilshire Ramp and Sunset Blvd.) and turn east (the other way is the ocean). Go slowly up Channel to the first left turn which is E. Rustic (sign on the corner building reads "Edmundson Real Estate"). Take E. Rustic to the first right turn. That's Sycamore. If you get lost, call GL 4-5783.

---

Donation—ONE DOLLAR

For further information call HO 4-6070 or WE 4-8441.

## Coastlines
### INVITES YOU TO DIG ITS BIG
### POEMS AND (not with) MUSIC PARTY

Saturday night, August 8, 9 p.m. and onward
(possibly upward, too)
471 Sycamore Rd., Santa Monica Canyon

Poems will be read by
**William Pillin**
and
**Judson Jerome**

Music in the Starlight Room by
**Robert Eskew ◆ Bill Bailey ◆ Dan Clements**

Beer for sale (or bring your own jug)

DIRECTIONS: Take the Pacific Coast Hwy. (101) to W. Channel Rd. (the only signal between the Wilshire Ramp and Sunset Blvd.) and turn east (do not turn west into the ocean). ◆ Go slowly up Channel to the first left turn which is E. Rustic (sign on the corner building reads "Edmundson Real Estate"). ◆ Take E. Rustic to the first right turn. ◆ That's Sycamore. ◆ If you get lost, call GL 4-5783. ◆

Donation ◆ ONE DOLLAR
For further information call HO 4-6070 or WE 4-8441

Subscriptions to Coastlines
(a non-profit literary magazine)
will be available at the party at $2.00 for 4 issues.
Also single copies for 50 cents.

# Alvaro Cardona-Hine

Alvaro Cardona-Hine, b. 1926—Alvaro Cardona-Hine was born in San Jose, Costa Rica, to Jorge Cardona Jiminez and Alice Hine. Cardona-Hine came to Los Angeles in 1939 as a boy and has lived most of his life in the United States. In 1945 he entered Los Angeles City College, where he intended to study science, but after meeting Bert Meyers and Stanley Kurnik, he began writing. He married Orpha Willis in 1950, and the couple had four children; they divorced in 1967. Cardona-Hine is a self-taught artist working in three disciplines: musical composition, writing, and painting. His music has been performed at the Pasadena Museum of Art; The Bakken Library in Minneapolis; the Organization of American States in Washington, D.C.; the Minneapolis Institute of the Arts; Trinity Church in Brooklyn, New York; Greenwich House, New York; Santuario de Guadalupe, Santa Fe, New Mexico; and most recently at the St. Francis Auditorium in Santa Fe. His poetry has appeared in over sixty literary and national journals like *The Nation, Coastlines, Prairie Schooner, Ironwood, Chelsea, Poetry Northwest, New Mexico Quarterly,* and *San Francisco Quarterly.* His publications include *Romance de Agapito Cascante* (1955); *The Gathering Wave* (1961); *The Flesh of Utopia* (1966); *Menashtash* (in English and Spanish) (1969); *Agapito* (1969); *Words on Paper* (1973); a translation of Cesar Vallejo's *Spain, Let This Cup Pass from Me* (1974); *Two Elegies,* with Alfredo Cardona-Pena (1977); *The Half-Eaten Angel* (1981); *When I Was a Father* (1982); *Miss O'Keeffe,* a collaboration with one of O'Keeffe's nurses (1992); four poems about sparrows; *A Garden of Sound* (1996); and his latest book, *Spring Has Come.* Cardona-Hine has been awarded fellowships from the National Endowment for the Arts, the Bush Foundation, and the Minnesota State Arts Board. He has exhibited in one-man shows at various venues, including Chatterton Gallery in Los Angeles, the School of Associated Arts in St. Paul, Minnesota, and the Bixter Gallery in Pennsylvania, among others. His work is also included in the collection of the University of Minnesota in Minneapolis and in various business and private collections.

Facing page: Announcements of *Coastlines'* parties.

### Three Personal Poems of Grandeur and Magniloquence

I

when lemons bloom
when lemons flower
when in the sound of more sound's birth
two deltas summon riches upward and the sunshine down
to one accord of acid as quietly and green
as any look that love's between
and when the seas
flooding a brook of lightning
lodge their plaint
in flimsy girlish scarf-like valleys
there'll be no other man
calls earth the bluest orange
after me

oh damage done after the flash
and long before the peal of thunder
damage done the season of a leave and absence and returning
when all his former stays dissolved the pending stranger into encounter
with shapes of life that have a star for seizure
since time availed itself of always and of dawn

to youth to the clamor of youth a magic labyrinth of force and splendor
in all its ways most strange most baffling and appealing
and fifteen or as you are and lost in a branch of nectar
to come at all to come on shoulders of the crowd of one
it'll cause you to walk alone
hearing the lonely echoes
brief and suddenly brief and sudden

one may survive the skin-permitting limelight of the years to come
unaware the weight of ghosts or trapped
in the backwoods of the first cruel questions
one can and does survive slide through the speechless grammar of a piano
scamper over scaffoldings of odd leaves sighted once
past the verboten dogs engrossed upon their plots of sex
and never hear the nervous laughter spilling on the paper waters
as life wraps up its yield of welcome to the fish

unaware of death and in the whirlwind of a trigger at man's height
one can invest the harmful doom of an ancient axis
or wed a golden step on its two handsome roots
deep in the grottoes of its lovely shame
till tenderness and horror come leaping out of caves
out of the breast of tide at bleak day's rise
scattering an ash of sweat upon the roar of sleep

our eyes then fall upon the cold grey nest
upon the sticky mask that gloves the world and foxes
and knives into subservience
knives to limbo through its amber suede
our use of words slips the tongue of rulers
our match of lovers in the park begins to blaze
we walk the madness of this glad surfeit amazed at poverty and at friends
amazed at trees familiar with the nomad skies
and tender faults of the cage and custom of the hawk
we nurse an ache for a shack of gales
where men man replicas of women over billowing beds of foam

the enigmas of oneself made possible before
no longer carry you past doors of actual toil
but frame all of a day's sweet miser wake of night
to burst in human limbs that wander and go lame

everywhere the same sad miracle of agony on sight
the street a narrow margin burrowing in the tight mortal length of its fine coffin
a windlass stream in ignorance of how and when its finest gown
is apron to an alley when the hollyhock dons light

and endlessly this way we grow or simply walk
and come and go with ink or voice upon the path of sun

one goes away only from those already away
the no-one that nobody can rule

remembrance calls and all reward scorches the sycamore with frost

---

II
today a leaf and yes
today
a leaf again
a leaf
and the wind
today
and the wind how slowly
the sun how slowly
and the sun and leaf and windy leaf and wind
at the language of a leaf

tonight the moon a moon
and brief in nothing
and again themselves how slowly but themselves
the moon where the moon is
where the moon has gone
itself a tame unutterableness
the wind harass

tonight an ache and trembling and a leaf
in bent reply all bent all day with rain
till daily dawn its sunlight breathes
and glad thin sunlight breathes of steam
the green leaves all assuming
till down again to dusk again against

with darkness before dark allotting
its plural twig in drowsy thunder
to the same long tendency the saplings hoist and light
the slow night darkens
and a wind of miles in a mild bend buds and bursts
unwinding nothing but a touch

the killing scherzo
believing zero one the fuzzy pollen and a wing
two little pedal insects trust the bluejay
such saintly-paralleling worlds
no longer silent

and no longer silent the loud hill
its bell of apex and of pap
a flesh now shed of its sore silk
for gently skin and gently core and seed
descend or rise unto themselves
expand and curve their wound

allowing half a day a half itself
one green half raw the red half yellow
both sagging fruit and earth diurnal
sending a sun in solace upward
and a boiling root in search of foothold rivers

humdrum and windless the wind hums dry
past grass-punctured dung and sod
its milk perplexed through webs
that yo-yo with a spider
in its round of knees
windless the heat of trunk and middle leaf
propels its burgeoning disciples
through blue-maturing husk of timeless hush
and pensive night
and pennywise moon
and cool deep gulf and leaf by leaf set free
while birch-held leaf holds lightly
in bend of water of itself
and stillness on all sides

themselves
the stringless kite
the wooden child
goodbye above called autumn and the cold

III

this has happened lately
that I've sensed my release
through rain that fell in childhood
rain with no meaning
but for a dog a block from home
which would wake from its nap
as I went by each afternoon
and chase me on to school

unlikely
most unlikely
you will say
bound as he was
to a comfortable round
of rosaries and dinners
blessing him backwards
but then again

why that seamstress remembered from childhood onwards
why that sunlit colonnade in Panama
on a day of tremendously solemn clouds as lonely as

no
my friend
I come with stones
as intimate as a cry for help
with seedlings
performing their lovely handsprings in silence
and grandmothers to remind me
of eggs and eucalyptus

these things come up at will
the pictures of those saints avoided later
but at that time
dripping benevolently down the walls
and onto the concave boards
on the floor of the servants' room
the marvelous pool silenced by swans
in a cove of cypress and moonlight

not five blocks from home
but of course
you don't know the pink berries
that overlooked the town
you simply ignore
the armpit smell of flowers I've played by
because
naturally
you had your own siege to contend with
your own streetcars to flatten nails
and crush all other hubbub into burly halves for you

it is precisely by that token
by this our common ground of separate delight
that I am allowed to utter my salvation
state great things of my volition
how eating that second luminous and most clairvoyant pear
I lapse into the grit
        tremor
        football
        dung
        spike
        bloom
        and game of grass
between father and his loneliness arriving
while each reserves a single point of reference
to hang his freedom and agreement on
(and this
that varnish argues with recollection
        mattress
        bullet
        gum
        geranium
        or whatever
that varnish argues in English
or grows quiet at the silver
that some garlic is a nickel's worth of
will do well for a start)

I am ready for some peace
for profound understanding
in connection with balloons and noodles
drunkards or seashores politic in girls
with long canonic legs
ready for that pain of paper
in two lines

crazed elegy
those who knew you
say goodbye to themselves


■ **Vindication**

(For A.C.T. on her sudden death)
Upwards now
into nest and entrail
I send my hands to pluck
I send my tongue my sorrow

and my tenderness
and forget the annoyance
and death reminds me to forget
and these returning
justify
in utterance and dignity
all of the grey vulgarity
you may have shown
or betrayed

betrayed
where death never does
but rather
when purpose turns to flotsam
that was childhood once and a cluster
and proves that laughter can die
and go rotten
it comes to make it into brightness again

proof is my compassion
and the way that corpses laugh
or smile
or look
in the cleaner fabric of remembrance

don't trample on it oh brother
or stranger
let it go whole
for the living to forget the dead
not speaking ill of their flesh
verging into spirit
or oblivion
faults
errors
let them go
and not recall whether virgin or whore
whether it's I go first or you
for death is a kingdom in reverse

or a mirror where you part your hair to the right
or a lake where you breathe in the depths
and always a dignity recurring
or a vagabond
and in his dirty pockets
this apple whose cheek burned to the sun.

"Friendship, youth, poetry and the immensity and heat of Los Angeles: not a bad thing to have lived through; a local phenomenon less gaudy and effective than the Beat Movement further to the north, but a world with intense resolutions of its own, its own kind of lyricism and of social involvement. The people I knew and participated with were only one part of what was happening in Los Angeles. The poetic world of that city could never be contained by a single attitude or approach or known by a single person. It was peculiarly evanescent and diffused, like the weather and the odor of its hills of broken-up quartz and manzanita. I'll take its savage desolation to bandwagons of MFA's today and the hundreds of contests with their five and ten dollar reading fees. Poetry in L.A. when I was young was something like the flavor of a green persimmon in the mouth: acrid and forbidding. What only a Fool would bite."

Alvaro Cardona-Hine
Letter to Estelle Gershgoren Novak, October 1997

■ **Doomsday and Components**
there is more than one skeletal eruption
one brutal eyelash tattooed upon our sight
while hunger stretches off in vast horizons
this fat and blinded land prepares for war

in other lands the cross is not a cross
but a letter that all the children spell
backwards and upwards and in dreams
(of all our wars only this one is sacred)

who can the insistent teacher be?
never an A never a happy lullaby M
to remind them of their mother's breasts
always those t's and still more crooked t's

armies and generals are camped
beneath a momentary lull
they hold their breath they wait
they look through their binoculars

meantime those cemeteries shudder in the mist
those tombstones lie buried under moss

that moss under the morning dew
voices and laughter come cradled in the wind

in other lands if a crumb falls from the table
twenty hands snatch at it
one takes hold nineteen form a fist
only the fist holds hope

"Near the end of *Coastlines'* existence I became its poetry editor. Weekly, Mel Weisburd would bring me a box full of submissions. There was, in particular, a fellow in San Francisco who would send not just a fat envelope but two or three each week, stuff typed on an old cross-eyed typewriter, dreadful stuff. No matter what one said in response, the avalanche would persist. At first, in my enthusiasm, I would try and respond with individual messages to poets I felt could make it . . . but I soon found that I was resented for my opinion of their work and retreated to the printed rejection slip. Kiesel had been the previous poetry editor and had somehow infuriated a poet. At a party at Sandy Garrett's home in Santa Monica this fellow showed up threatening to beat the poetry editor. No one would admit to being such a person."

Alvaro Cardona-Hine
Letter to Estelle Gershgoren Novak, October 1997

### The Train of the Wounded

Miguel Hernandez

translated by Alvaro Cardona-Hine

Silence shipwrecked upon the silence
of lips sealed by the night.
Silence that won't cease throughout its length.
It uses the drowned language of the dead.
Silence.

It opens up roads of deepest cotton,
it muffles the wheels of clocks.
Oh, stop the voice of the sea, of the dove,
see if you can't move the night of dreams.

Silence.

The pluvial train of unfettered blood,
the fragile train of those who bleed away,
the silent, painful, pale,
quiet train of suffering.

Silence.

Train of mortal pallor which ascends,
paleness which reworks each head,
the sigh, the voice, the heart, the earth,
the heart of those so deeply hurt.

Silence.

They speed by shedding legs, arms, eyes,
unburdening themselves of stumps throughout the train.
They pass by leaving a trail of bitterness,
another milky way of stellar limbs.

Silence.

Hoarse, fainting, reddened train:
the coal expires, the smoke sighs
and the maternal engine groans
advancing like a long disheartening experience.

Silence.

She would stop beneath a tunnel,
that long mother, she would weep on the ground.
There are no stations where to rest a while
unless it be a hospital, a breast.
To live, a piece of flesh suffices:
in a little nook of the stuff a man will fit.
A finger by itself, a hunk of wing
lifts the entire body in its flight.

Silence.

Halt that agonizing train
which never finishes its run across the night.
Which, instead, remains barefooted to the horse
and mixes in the mire, hooves and breath.

# Stanley Kiesel

Stanley Kiesel, b. 1925—Stanley Kiesel is an Angelino and taught kindergarten in Pacoima for seventeen years; during that time he was the only male kindergarten teacher in the Los Angeles city schools. A playwright, Kiesel has had a number of plays produced in Hollywood and Minneapolis. He has published a book of poems titled *The Pearl Is a Hardened Sinner* and two books of young adult fiction: *The War Between the Pitiful Teachers and the Splendid Kids* and *Skinny Malinsky Leads the War for Kidness.* The former was a *New York Times* Notable Book and called "the most original novel of the year." He served as poet in residence for the Minneapolis Public Schools for twelve years, probably the only poet hired full-time and paid entirely by a public school system in the United States. Kiesel now lives in San Francisco.

■ **Gregg**

Gregg, you cork, speck of a great saint, I wish
    all your exits well.
The world's cold entertainment without you.
Never a detractor or an amuser, but a solid
    occupant of the actual,
What you gave me never graced your mind.
Modesty was your grandfather.
If indeed, you were a child, you were better than
    all the candy offered me,
Better than the apples because, Gregg, you were the
    bite itself.

A child like you is a clearing, the era's arable
    land;
Such a man that even your failures will find employment.
Gregg, there's no paper pleasure worth the thing you are.

### ◼ Joey

Ink, jam, chocolate, what does not pay you its
    respects?
There is not a grain of sand which has not been
    invited into your shoes.
Was a comb ever elected to run through your hair?

Pinching, pulling, prancing, puling, the whole
    day is prickled with you.
That small cluster of flexible parts which is
    you, Joey,
Avalanches down on everyone's goodwill.

Funds are dolefully paid out to keep you clean,
To punctuate your warm palms with pennies,
But vengeful and mucid, you spill and shriek,
And welt the water glasses with your greasy thumbs
And buy up even more land with your homeless anger.

Bernice Silberman, cover
drawing of Josephine Ain
(Chuey): *Coastlines* 5, no. 1 (1961).

## ■ Seven Children

David's eyes held his mind's reins so no thought stampeded.
Michael Dean gave his urine to secret agents and never
    washed his hands.
Virginia was alone among us all, the baggage car of her
    mother's care.
And Johanna was a sea that never conferred with anyone.

Where are you now, children? Rendered visible, I expect;
Wearing tight shoes, run over by a hundred trucks;
Terrifyingly suspect of planting aphids on your parent's
    roses.

Albert, you leaped off conversation's cliff and never did
    come back
Whereas you, Lynn, were the overtrained athlete of your
    mother's tongue.
And John—I remember you too—whose feigned deafness
Was all you had your mother could not bathe;
Your private mafia was the pants you filled from day to day . . .

To the mass-produced adult all children look homemade.
And so they are, who have not yet learned to do anything
    on credit:
The world is whatever they pick up off the ground.
We, who swallow our duties like medicine
Our salutes are always on time.

April, fifty six. Children, the future's good if you endure.
Do not shave off those sweet mustaches.

# Josephine Ain

Josephine Ain, b. 1916—Josephine Ain was born Josephine Cohen to a father from a rabbinical family in Damascus, Syria, and a mother from a family in Austria. She grew up in Ranger, Texas, between Forth Worth and Dallas. There she lived a rural life with no indoor plumbing and bathed in a tin tub. Ain was one of five children. She was nine when her family came to Los Angeles in 1926. She attended Los Angeles High School and Los Angeles City College, where she received an A.A. degree in theater, then spent a semester at the University of California at Berkeley. She was married three times, first to Gregory Ain, then to Michael Mark, and finally to artist Robert Chuey. Her first husband, Gregory, was an architect who worked with Richard Neutra. Years later Josephine and her third husband, Bob Chuey, would live in a house built by Neutra and hold poetry readings there for many of the *Coastlines* poets. These readings became a kind of salon, with her husband as cohost and his paintings and studio as part of the event. With her second husband, an actor and director, she helped build the stage at the Vagabond Theatre in Los Angeles. Josephine Ain was one of the finalists in the Yale Younger Poets Series in 1952, the year that W. H. Auden judged the contest. The manuscript she submitted was titled "Momentary Mountain." Although she never published a volume of poetry, she published in several literary journals, among them *Choice, The Kernel: A Literary Supplement*, where she was one of the editors; *Perspective: A Quarterly of Literature; Arts Tower's Smiling; Epos; Line; MS; Coastlines;* and in *Poetry Los Angeles, I*, the collection of the readings done at Barnsdall Park in Los Angeles. Ain also did readings on the radio for KPFK and KUSC, radio stations in Los Angeles. She was part of an experiment with LSD, as was Mel Weisburd, and she met with Timothy Leary and Alan Watts at her home. She also painted for a time and attended Jepson Art Institute. She was included in *Women Painters of the 1950s*.

## You There, Weeping

Between elms of shining water
A clock strikes. A dog barks.
A bird shatters the boughs.
And wavering in the furrows
I free myself to free myself again.

I have escaped to continue.

The bird continuously falling
The dew ceremonially shining
We are all in it together
All under the sky.

There is no other garden
And there is no other fate.
However disheveled your love
However distraught
Time will make intimate
Even your doubt.

And you will not surpass the clouds.
You there weeping, you will fall silent.

■ **Magdalen**

Vivid with impotence and sublime
Woman more woman than the universe is God
At last complete, at last discovered
Magdalen, stairway of plunder
Stands square circumference
About an octagonal thunder—
A frozen waterfall;
A parasol of rock;
Christ nailed between her hands;
She is the waking of an army.
She is the total tent.
Her hair spouts clots of blood;
Her feet are webbed;
Bludgeon of another's anguish.

She rears clumsy and incoherent
And magnificent.
Evocative of heaven
Dementia of her lids.
There is no saliva
And no spit.
Her robe rocks and is not rent.
This creature may walk backward in a minute.
She would displace the cross
And with each spike receive
Both Christ and Death,
Take life and perish.
Or rapt of mind be found
The morning of that time
Zig-zagging briar
About a crown.

## Don Quixote

Don Quixote like a tree walking
Out of his element, out of our world.
The blasted limbs like sour branches
Protrude a nectar of the bone.
Long nose of bleak and ravelled pride
Travels the foolish firmament.
Hail, the gaunt, the ripe eccentric
As wind blows tremulous on armor.
What if the eyes, besotted acorns
Sprout wistfully a thousand oaks?
He has Sancho and Dulcinea
And an island anchored to an antelope.
His bow of monumental mood
Is courtly and bizarre, more poignant
Than defeat, more elegant than wit.
Mounted, his yellow nag emits
The shrill alarm of prowess.
Imagination is atilt.
Against the errors of the world.
Beware the hollow cheek and winsome.
This madman moves invincible.
A spectre dusts the webbed horizon
In divine frenzy of elbows.
Huge hand descending
Salutes the impossible.
Takes purity and makes it breathe;
Takes love and makes it whole.

they think they are lost
so they are holding their breath
seven mimosa

a wild cucumber
the children cut it in half
for both their teachers

a slow butterfly
dips like a shadow below
the wing of a rose

humming birds tethered
in tiny stalls of blue air
champing at the bit

cats go out at night
you can tell by bells jingling
far down the hillside

just little puddles
yesterday has come to see
how it looks today

nunneries of light
telling their beads in water
the gilded poplars

■ Aspects
*I        Water*
How lakes resemble standing up
And pines a labyrinth of prone

Finally the fear
Falls like a star
To be wished upon.

Thru water, water is a
Stubborn dream,
An infant walking by a fountain,
Milk of a landscape of stone.

By the bridge one sees possibilities
And one is not disturbed.
Forever the lakes of trees rot in the clouds
And fester with birds
And one has not pity left
But the compassion of nearness.

From city to city there are only rivers.

## II   *Music*

Fate that is mine the music shades,
An exquisite husky elm.
I rise from being in the sound
Of sainted apparitions.
Enchanted clouds vanish invisible suns,
Corona without light
But meaning well.

And I surround the fragrant porch
With angels from a classic wood.
Transparent statues shine
In far indulgence.

The genuflections of the wind
Remembering the infinite
Of all beginning.

Repeat again, repeat the agony
Of true excuses.

A tree heavy in evening
An evening not available

Excess of sacred sense
Spain where we do not dwell.

## III   *Night*

Shadow where the song
Is like itself
Into which a lake may sink
And be remembered.

Shadow where all my privileges wait
A discreet distance like a lewd image,
Shall I refuse to sleep
Amongst kinsmen?

Shall I refuse to walk
After the sensuous shepherd?
Morning is a vision without shelter
Morning of an inexorable charm.

I have exacted what the night exacts
A lit dream, exalted silence.
Mine is the vow without sanctions
And without myself.

With what flowers the mystery colors
My stupidity.
I am not even humble.
For I am sleep.

---

**J o s e p h i n e   A i n**

## IV   Man

There is finally the rain
In its sheltering time
All things cease in want.

Only a man is different
Who is what he is not.

If you would save him, you must not despair.
He is in earnest with all his selves.

Accompanied by a sky
Correct with destiny.

And we pretend to understand
Why the angel should be afraid
And why the messenger should stammer.

Country-clad itinerant
Have you a road of your own?
You pass by cities
As one obsessed
By a journey.

You are manifestly lonely
On the road always a road
No matter what.

What if one day the excursion end?
Will the domain of your freedom
Extend even to death?

## V    *The Soul*

Who imagines that he lives
Imagines he becomes.

An image in a startled glass
Raising its doubled fist.

Tell me, oh frenzy,
What windows break?
Existence, you may not assault.

Anger is a tendency to bloom.

The antique vigor of a kiss.
The ancient house of a new birth.

Sometimes a longing is strong
To want perfection.

Where space its lucid shaft
Idiosyncrasy of light
Makes permanent the dark,
Where love seraphic asks
Am I not my own self?
Or am I not even yet?

Meaning to love forever
I must first become immortal.

Around the angels fountains gleamed
A lucid light of law.
For order was their harmony,
A grace of being so.

Rest in the raptures of the soul
Was like a journey of the whole.
Nowhere to go.

Leave me severe in morning pure.
The sensual adore God.

Lyric Mother, let love go.
After the dream of heaven
Only may heaven be.

The matter of fact blue
Of imponderable skies

This ever letting go
Of beauty and of God.

"Their house was a magnificent glass structure built above the Sunset Strip by Neutra, and Bob's paintings glowed against the white walls that did exist. The rest of the house was the immense Los Angeles night as it poured in through those huge windows. You could see all of Los Angeles pulsating with life below you and, on the other side, the almost-as-huge glow of the San Fernando Valley. The Chuey evenings are the nearest thing Los Angeles ever had to a salon."

Alvaro Cardona-Hine "Poetry in Los Angeles 1945 to 1975:

Part I: *Bach 12* 1978

"Josephine Chuey invited me to come to her monthly gatherings at her house atop Beverly Hills. That was the beginning of a custom that lasted from 1957 on through the early '70s. Many people read there, among them Curtis Zahn (who had his own salon at his home in Malibu and where people were encouraged to be discourteous to those reading), Fred Franklyn, Pat Minton (beginning to find her voice only to end in suicide), John Berry (husband of the fine painter Ynez Johnson), Frumkin, Kiesel. . . . One of those last Saturdays of the month, Stanley Kurnik brought Anais Nin."

Alvaro Cardona-Hine

Letter to Estelle Gershgoren Novak, November 1997

Arnold Mesches, cover:
*Coastlines* 2, no. 2 (winter 1956–57).

## Number XVI from The Flesh of Utopia

to Bob Chuey

at birth and steadily for one year
the afternoon concentrates on a beetle
it aids him buoys him feeds him his flyspeck lunch
calls him moose to his horns

and softly kindly the lights go on
as if the men at the switches were embracing
the corners gather momentum
                              efferent gentleness
the lime of a falling star catches you yawning
and crumbles into your mouth
you sit there at the curb
the rose-colored clay of your fingernails itching
the flavor of mahogany a river

I never saw him wear his hat again nor his fist
and he never made another wooden toilet in his life
laughing over my left-handed use of his tools

the maid said he was dead
and I hugged that word like a dirty old blanket
till he closed his eyes folded his hands
plowed the earth deeper than his oxen
and visited by dreams

at three the solitary sound
at four the smell of navigation
at five the field of strangers
but at eight
            at eight
                      oh pure universe
another one of your children holding onto her skirt
that he may be heard over the unfed birds

another one of your mountain paths
holding its breath a while
that the hill
and the wind
may sleep
—*Alvaro Cardona-Hine*

---

# Sid Gershgoren

Sid Gershgoren, b. 1937—Sid Gershgoren, the brother of Estelle Gershgoren Novak, the editor of this anthology, was born in Detroit, Michigan, and grew up in Los Angeles. He received his B.A. from UCLA and his Ph.D. from the University of California at Davis. Sid began writing poetry in the years before *Coastlines* was founded and has published several books of poetry, including *Through the Sky in the Lake* (Milkweed Editions) and *The Wandering Heron* (Red Dragonfly Press). He has also published widely in magazines and anthologies. His new book, *Symphony,* appeared in 2001 from Red Dragonfly Press. He is an avid listener to modern classical music and, besides having written a book of twenty-nine villanelles, is completing an anthology of formal poetry. He lives in Berkeley, California, with his wife, Patricia, a well-known medical geneticist.

## ■ The Frugal Repast

Here is the chained swan by the passive lake,
A swan of ivory, alive in its reflection,
Water tense as crystal, the sun,
The sun above a day's constant medallion.
And quieter than time we walked the shore
Near the green rust that had lain
Reflecting always on the shallows, and walking saw
Past the chained swan, the evening sink and rust
Into the grand canyons of our day.
We saw the stars rise and the voice of crickets
Painting the seasons with their constant static.
Light of innumerable gulls placid on the lake,
The quiet burns its huge swans of decay.

I talked to you of how your eyes were young
And you: 'My father never would let us marry.'
'He does not see,' I said 'how the world turns,
He is now blind with too much harvesting.'
'The cold comes very early,' I could say,

And that was all that I could say for fear,
Fear of nothing but the fear of her
Drowning amid the snows and foams of repentance.
The stars were white; the past seemed almost real,
But then I knew the tiger coughed for food.

Was it a cold reminder of our beginnings
Had brought us here under a mother of trees,
By the placid lake, did we already know
That we had lain with ragged generations,
The unkind, uncouth, kissed from even the beggars' gates,
The ragged outcasts of all generations?
And even a sea of creatures we never knew,
The first exiles from the warmth of seas.

But we were happy for the night, and covered
Our bodies with our cares and were content
To share the peace, carrying fantastic treaties.
But the night passed and the star left the sky
With no identity except the sun,
And saw the swan unchained lift to the air,
Borne away on time's miraculous wings.

Milton Gershgoren, cover: *Coastlines* 4,
no. 4 (autumn 1960).

## Cleaning Woman

Kneeling to no one she lights the empty lengths
of cooling halls that all doors open on—
the used up passion of abandoned places—
nightly: till her labor break through to daylight.

Kind now, she gilds each tarnished grace
to an impersonal perfection that glows.
Turns to compartments in their singular needs.
Over the magic lamps she hunts to brightness.

'But (roaring of seashell) she hollows out a room
and finds the shirtsleeves of a night's madness,
finds the unappropriated mirrors of a dream,
the lost manifestoes in the numbing light
of countless closets, and finally the paintings
cursing with no one in the empty room.'

But sick in a frond of lightbulbs explaining
a hallway, she will go home and there will find
the perfect order waiting on her doormat,
in the simple living that admits only one angel:
The small personal radiance of her desires
amidst the impersonal huge throats of her labor.

### The Trouble with the Times

Although the wood never laments
soaking in the wounds of varnished bars, judging
the broken bread full of static like a radio,
or judging those holding in the moon-alleys the cracked tennis ball,
wondering where the motion went,
or those poor souls that cry at the sight of chains—
the world caught between commercials leaves the night ajar,
and the rose of blowing sheets is never dead.
Therefore the horse perpetually winds a tunnel for a violin,
and the bones on melting snow find fires;
and a light oiled in winter's wound up sidereal lexicon
proves that the tautologies of tides are never useless.

And that hawk is not a mobile
(at night, as in proof, the moon cracks its cheap plaster)
He hovers over the always-cellophane fox-fields.
Oh, all is clear but blurred gold
and the country is only a barn, a talking tree,
a face of catcher's masks under strong wind
where no fox weeps for our Chanticleers
and the wanderer, sick with radios, has gone staring
off through the old valleys.

# Estelle Gershgoren Novak

Estelle Gershgoren Novak, b. 1940—. Estelle Gershgoren Novak, the sister of Sid Gershgoren and editor of this anthology, was born in Detroit, Michigan, to Milton (nee Yitzah Mayer) Gershgoren and Beatrice (nee Brocha) Rotman. The family came to Los Angeles when she was a young child, and she has lived there since. She attended UCLA, where she received a B.A. in English and subsequently an M.A. and Ph.D. Gershgoren Novak has taught at various universities in the Los Angeles area for over twenty-five years, among them USC, UCLA, and California State University at Northridge. In 1968 she married Maximillian Novak, a well-known scholar of eighteenth-century literature, and they have three children. In the late fifties she met Tom McGrath through her father, a Los Angeles artist, who had known Morton Dimondstein, the art editor of *The California Quarterly*, and the poets and artists of that group. Along with her brother, she began to study with McGrath and to associate with poets and friends like Bert Meyers, Stanley Kiesel, Gene Frumkin, Mel Weisburd, and Alvaro Cardona-Hine. She first published poems in *Coastlines* at the age of nineteen and subsequently published in *Ante, San Marcos Review, West Coast Poetry Review, Twigs, Colorado-North Review, Dakotah Territory, Poetry LA, Treasure House, Israel Today, California Quarterly, Judaism, Pemmican,* and other journals. A poem of hers was included in *San Francisco Renaissancen*, translated by Erik Thyssen and published in Denmark, and poems of hers have appeared in *Poets of Today*, edited by Walter Lowenfels, *Blood to Remember: American Poets on the Holocaust*, and other collections. She has published a collection of poems, *The Shape of a Pear*, that includes poems written as early as the sixties and as late as the nineties. Her second book of poems, *The Flesh of their Dreams*, will soon be published by Fithian Press.

## Legend

The sky is obese with red sun at mid-day
And the sun feasts on the salamanders of an ambivalent ocean.
The people can only feast on the beans in their bellies
Under an unhappy paper shack
With daisies in their hair
And the longitudinal meridians of time in their faces.

En Afrique
The elegant elephant
With his pointed trunk
Meets the waterhole
Halfway.

For the elephants—the mud
For the people under their paper parasols—the beans.

But the feast is leaner now in the sky
At the end of synchronized crossties
And the sun is taking the evening train out of town.


## The Time Machine of War

1.
1000 men were dead
before I caught my breath
and while I tied my shoe
5000 more had died
a million men were killed
who swore they would survive

2.
In the second it takes
To give you this kiss
Another man lies dying
In the moment it takes
To make a step
a child is born and screaming
In the time it takes
For my words to reach
Your ears beneath the wind
The world has spread its carcass out
And soldiers have stopped dreaming.

### Hiroshima Woman

August 6, 1945

She was born under the shadow of the great moon
Like a peach blossom she moved on the water
Floating into motherhood under a pregnant sun.

Her first born made a great scar on the earth.
In the afternoon of the burning heavens
The second son was marked on the sign of the mushroom
And the rain fell heavy that day.
The third son had ages in his belly
And the taste of death on the black of his tongue.

> On the day of the great mushroom
> That grew on the sky and exploded
> On the day of seven black suns
> The great moon grew horns.

In the burnt arm and belly opened to catch rain
No one watches, no one sees tomorrow written.
The print of the dress on the back flattens like paper
Between two scars, a woman sleeps.

### The Shape of a Pear

The shape of a pear is too much
like a woman's torso
to be eaten in public
and in summer when it's ripe
it is so sweet
though it may leave your tongue
dry at its tip
the juice drips on your palate.

Silence is kept where secrets are
apples blushing in their native green
grow ripe and round.
Peaches have a young man's beard
and cherries bleed where
they are cut by stone.

These silent forms keep secrets
and are eaten.
Only you who have tasted
the private form of pears
been stained by red cherries
kissed the peach
been caught between
the sweet and sour
can keep the secret.

### Scars

Autumn brings relief
The scars fall off our arms
like reddened leaves.

The tanks have exploded
Winter comes to cool
the flying sparks.

The guns have dropped
beside a corpse,
spring turns up a leaf.

Napalm falls below our skin
Summer burns
but not like this

# Ann Stanford

Ann Stanford, b. 1916–d. 1987. Ann Stanford was born in La Habra, California, and died in Los Angeles. She taught English and American literature for twenty-five years at California State University at Northridge. Stanford published numerous volumes of poetry: *In Narrow Bound, The White Bird, Magellan: A Poem to Be Read by Several Voices, In Mediterranean Air,* and a translation, *The Bhagavad Gita: A New Verse Translation.* She also published a study of Anne Bradstreet, *The Worldly Puritan: An Introduction to Her Poetry.* In addition to her publications in *Coastlines,* Stanford contributed poems to more mainstream literary journals like *The New Yorker* and *The Atlantic Monthly* and edited *The Women Poets in English: An Anthology.*

## ■ Pandora

Never, never again the house new or youth precise,
Or the fresh loaves of hay in the field.
And the tree bark shimmers black and white
Only after rain

The day rose clear-faced and quick
Breathing lemon and sage, undoubtedly crystal,
Fog was for coolness, not to get lost in, and the wicked
Rode to ominous music.

The box had been left, but I never suddenly opened the lid.
The day hung so full, time being happy and short,
No reason to fret over a dusty chest in a corner,
And I had given my word.

But nothing is changeless: while it was there in the house
Something crept out, buzzing and small.
I heard it at night, an insect whine in the air
Unseen in the light.

And the mornings were sad sometimes
And rising slow, and the day crumpled and worn

Like a picture handled too much,
And I indifferent.

Came haze outlasting the dawn
Between me and the fields, the horizon too close:
And bright days were full of objects
Not noticed before.

Love broke to a trinity, there were too many paths;
None seemed to be true, and in the oat fields the horsemen
Wore various guises, and which could I trust
On their spotted geldings?

I have heard of such things, but not for myself,
And the silver sifts from the box
On my hair and my tears, and the owner is gone, and I—
I shall never be rid of it.


■ **The Burning Glass**
There is a moment on which moments turn
And radiate to and from it as a sun:
So we concentrate with a glass to burn
All the warm rainbows of the wide spectrum,

So kittens jump at twigs and catch a string
To bring us proudly home the rats of hunting,
And telescopes of all the earth at once
Combine upon Mars' near coincidence.

The long years of learning ancient tongues
Compose themselves in buried cities when
Are used three verbs, three nouns, an ampersand
To read a cracked rosetta in the hand.

Under the klieg lights for a little space
A whole life converges in a face,
While I in dark go once more round the flame
And all my tongues expound a single name.

---

### The Weathercock

Wind shakes me
I am weak and spent
With every argument.
I doubt and hang
A breath disturbs me.
Sinewless and vain
The harsh and soft are one to me
Zephyr or gale, I turn my face to it.

North wind and south have whispered
And I go with each.
The dulcet evidence of bloom and spring
Or the cold reason of on-circling storm
Both have convinced me, and I yearn with them
Yearn as the smoke drift or the lifted leaves.

Yet I proportion my stance to the breeze.
Wind shall not take me
Though he shriek and bite
Frighten all other birds to leeward shade
Blow down the pigeons from the cooing lofts
Sail the hawk back downwind and send
Laborious eagles panting to their rocks.

I have set my claw
Deep in the roof's pinnacle,
There to hold
While solid objects knock about—
Each broadside thing—
Stiff in this hub to turn and, keen,
Broach to the wind a practiced waywarding.

Though the barn totters
And hay flies
And the wood is pierced by pebbles;
Till the ties of the timbers skew
With the beams ajar

And the shingles scatter
And the great roof falls

I crow though none may hear.
In the vast spinning world, I still point true.
I fly here.

■ **The Bear**

(From Grimm brothers)

Rose Red:

    We have once more caught

    This old humbug, sister.

    Here he lies in his shaggy coat

    Snug by our cordial fire,

    Claiming to be a prince, or a lost Christian in disguise.

    There are things of the chrysalis—the butterfly,

    Plots that must be hatched, deeds long in doing,

    But this is thorough bear, rumpled and earthen.

Snow White:

    Remember, sister, other miracles:

    The pellet seed, bursting to root and leaf,

    The hard green bud to rose,

    The thought newborn

    That pecks at the skull like a rousing chick.

    Great things from small,

    The pearl from the ooze,

    And the radiant soul

    Rapt from its prison in a broken spell.

Rose Red:

    Snakes drop their skins, but remain serpents still,

    And the moth, long harbored in its chrysalis

    Flies as a birthright to distorting flame.

    Leaves spurt from seed, but only for the season.

    No one has charted the sea-track of souls.

    Bears sleep in winter caves and wake up bears.

The Bear:

> The forest offers honey, hollow logs
> Streams fraught with fishes,
> Berries on the hills.
> Yet here I ponder.
> I am no common bear, for I have visions.
>
> I dreamed I was a prince;
> I walked in halls
> Brilliant with torches.
> Underneath this pelt
> I feel the hardness of the golden mail.
> Can such dissatisfaction offer proof
> I am enmeshed in spells too fine to ravel?
>
> Snow White and Rose Red, divert your clumsy wooer.
> Some day we meet the dwarf and force the answer.

## A Summer Walk

Love, the harsh fields declaim
Unchanging chaos where we walk tonight.
Cut in the stubbled hay the scent
Waits where it lies dissoluble in air
Spicing the season, calling the name.
It is the summer—pomegranate, heat, haze,
After acacia, wind, pine, fire, rain—
Come in its order, earth circle and sun,
Round the hem of a robe, pine, pomegranate, pine.
The oat seed perfect closes the leaf;
The warm air, raising the summer scent,
Lifts like a letter on the cooler wind.
Grasp the torn page, the preface, lest it be
Rosetta of the structure, unity,
The title, author, centerstone, or key.

I feel the dark wherein I shall not fear—
No dark of sense, nor light, nor warmth of hand,

Only a stillness that I shall not hear.
The residual spirit, naked, wakes again
Into a flame, a fire, a light, a world,
An abstract energy of mind on mind.
Ah, wombs that gave them life, can you decree
The spirits haunting immortality?

I once was young enough to dream and know
I was immortal since I wished it so.
But where the I who dreamed? The mirror frames
An aspect stranger to the face it wore,
Mortality grown constant as a chain,
Binding as water that is gone and flows.

From untouched outlands at the mountain's rim
The dove recalls us with a mellow cry;
The summer morning shimmers off to lose
Its sheer beginning in the ragged sky.
I see the curve of earth whereon is wound
The ever-present present, sanguine, loud,
The shade of oaks stretching across the ground.
The summer pressed on us when we walk
Through fields called fields, whatever else they be,
And we imprisoned in a hedge of years
Look for a province and a dynasty.

### The Window

'Thou hast a double kingdom
and I am set between.' Etched on the glass

Now two dawns rise—the locked interior sun
That wakes good morning, and the forest rung
With doves' halloo—grow into light's arrival.
The same pulsation shivers on lands spread
Beyond this glass and creeps across the red
Carpet, and joins tracery on the wall.

Two kingdoms lie beside this boundary
Jointed together like the ripened peach
Ready to break into the streaked and yellow—
Two shapes composited till now as one,
Yet each divided toward its destination.

Even as I, between the room I see
And that expanse of woodland that may be
A window's myth, untrue on which to close,
Move through a doubleness of hemisphere.
Nor does a solid sorrow give such tears
As the imagination gives to this:

If I dream out on darknesses that wheel
At the day's end, where out of change the still
Round of eternity rubs the half of time,
Through panes of cutting glass that must dispense
With both the hills and room and difference
To make duality again the same.

# Reading Poetry Aloud

## Peter Yates

Anyone who elects to read poetry aloud should keep in mind the facts of performance. Fact one: if you expect anyone to listen and enjoy it, better make sure that you are being heard. I gave a fine reading myself lately—if you have access to the tape and turn up the volume—; but I hadn't thought enough about the shape and area of the room, into which I was throwing my voice diagonally from a corner. My best friends didn't tell me until afterwards, and when I reproached them they explained: 'We were too busy trying to hear you.'

Kenneth Rexroth read here in November for Poetry Los Angeles to an audience of 300. He delivered his verses sonorously in a voice like sour red wine, with only one mannerism: just when you thought you had his meaning he would fade. World-weary but exasperating. He may have been relying on the mike to carry his message for him; when he had been informed it did not, he discarded the mannerism.

Fact two: Whether you are reading your own verses or those of another, try to give the impression that you understand them. A flat, arbitrarily separated patter of words, unaccentuated, unphrased, unrhythmed, may arouse subconscious linkages in the reader, while disturbing for the wrong reasons the listeners who are being verbally spattered. The recorded reading of Wallace Stevens affects me so*.

Fact three: remember that the communication of art is a delicate matter. A man who violently appreciates himself in public may be a good comic. Anyone is likely to be flattered by his first Haw-haw! from an audience, especially when he believes he may have said something to deserve it. So he tries for another. And the atmosphere for an evening of serious reading may be ruined.

More dangerous than inviting the audience to laugh with you is taking yourself so seriously as a bard the audience may laugh at you. It adds nothing to your message to strip off your clothes while reading, as a prominent young visiting poet did here some months ago, either literally or figuratively. The poet who delivers a poetic attitude or tone of voice as an adjunct to his words resembles the pitchman who sells his personality instead of a product. Several friends of an older generation have told me about listening through an evening of poetry read by William Butler Yeats. Each report agreed that the effect was first solemn, then serious, then, as the evening waded on while voice and manner did not change, provocatively near tittering. Yeats chanted bardlike on a fixed vocal tone in a compelling rhythm, imparting to every utterance a doomlike fervor. The fragment of his reading preserved for us on a *Caedmon* record could be the voice of Hesiod or the Ancient Mariner; when the manner conflicted for too long with the lyrical matter, a choking risibility set in among the audience.

Fact four: like it or not, reading aloud is a performance. Whoever would perform must practice what he intends to do. An unpracticed voice will not well up spontaneously to the proper pitches, control itself in making correct accents or mingle phrasing with silence to the best advantage of the poem. The reader should practice reading his poems aloud at a pace which allows the listener to hear them. This, let me assure you, is more difficult than it seems. Most of us, if we have not practiced, read too rapidly and stammer ahead where we should pace each grouping of two or three words by a modest insertion of silence. In reading as in music silence imparts tone, silence determines the fluency of phrasing which permits inflection of the component syllables, silence gives the listener time to comprehend, detail by detail, what is being done. As silence permits inflection, so inflection, articulation, particularly of the consonants, distributes silence among the syllables. A slower reading, well spaced with silence, will seem relatively rapid; a faster reading, if partially unintelligible, will drag.

This is not to say that a slow reading is necessarily good. Dramatic pauses should be used cautiously and seldom. Some readers clot their phrasing by leaving too little space among the syllables, then clot their silences by lingering on them too long. When a listener becomes aware of silence following on silence, he forgets to listen. In music or in reading the projection of silence is the supreme art. There is an article by R. P. Blackmur, *The Language of Silence,* in which he tries to convey the presence of silence as the background of esthetic expressiveness, building around this quotation from Lear:

O! how this mother swells up toward my heart;
*Hysterica passio!* down, thou climbing sorrow!
Thy element's below.

He points out that 'mother' may be only 'smother.' Some of us have heard old-style Shakespearean actors who tried to put over everything *hysterica passio.* There is also the opposite fault, in much contemporary Shakespearean acting, of letting everything come down to the nerveless pace of nervous speech. In either the reading dissociates itself from the drama: one is conscious of the actor. The words serve as a scaffolding for the emotion, for the silence, the 'element below,' out of which they emerge. There must be both passion and silence, outburst and waiting, 'smother' and 'mother.' No, you must rant a bit when ranting is necessary, but never let it rant away with you.

The great performer gives the impression of being so lost in what he is doing and feeling that he is artless; and the incompetent audience, believing him, believes that the greatest art is no art, it is just letting oneself go. It is because he has studied carefully, with attention to the text and the occasion, every motion of his art, every pause, has learned to project every silence, that the great artist can transcend the formality of his preparation, can appear transported in his action, while he is in fact linking every action by a predetermined continuity of art; and the perceptive audience, knowing this, will share his transport while trying to distinguish in its pleasure each detail of his method. When a critic informs you that in his opinion there was, yes or no, emotion in a performance, disregard him; pay attention while he is telling you what the artist did. If he can see that, he will be impelled to tell you; if he does not, he is a worthless critic.

Now don't run out on me and disregard the argument by claiming, in peculiarly American fashion, that you are no artist, you can't read, you are not a professional. Americans think of a professional as somebody who does very well, for big money before a big crowd in the proper season, something nobody cares much about otherwise. A professional is a name read about in the newspapers, seldom seen in action. For the person who enjoys reading poetry aloud there is no time or season, very little money, small following, and seldom reputation. I shall not go so far as to suggest that no one can be a poet who does not read aloud: some of my best friends would prevent that. A composer may be no instrumentalist and a poet before an audience may be dumb. Yet I do believe that every poet should prepare himself to read before others and read as well as he is able. He should work his poems over thoroughly, but for consistent practice he should read aloud the work of other poets, consoling himself among the less adequate by reflecting that by so much as his skill is greater there will be worse poets. Bridges generously miscomprehended Hopkins, who from the high reaches of his inspired intransigent amateurism patronized Patmore. While Patmore during his own lifetime was more popular than either.

Too many readers prefer to live among masterpieces, like the musical amateur who assuages his judgement by listening only to accredited performances of accredited symphonies on his phonograph. The reader who has learned to read aloud will find fresh work for his discrimination in bringing out the essential virtues of poems that do not, in his judgement, entirely stand up by themselves, lending his skill of articulation to the most meagre measures. Thus when he is asked to read in public he need not be concerned what is put before him. There are poems that live only in print on the page. And there are poems that are never quite at home in print, because they do not fully live until they are read aloud. I would gamble that over the long stretch it is the latter will survive.

My final fact is that if you are going to give pleasure to others by reading poetry aloud you must take pleasure yourself in reading it. This does not mean that you should enjoy the sound of your own voice and let it go at that. Listen not for the sound of your own voice but for the silence of good listeners. They may not know they are good listeners, but a skilled reading can make them so. The purpose of art is to create itself where it does not exist. Artiness pretends that art exists where you go to find it.

In reading the intense silence by which an audience, forgetting its condition as an audience, becomes one with the reader in a projected esthetic experience belonging to neither and to both is the ultimate reward. Even the most gifted of us will not find this experience so often that we can afford to disregard it. There is no substitute for it. Applause clatters away into nothing; laughs distort attention; weeping, less common in our astringent days than in another era, directs tearful attention to one's own inadequate emotions. Whatever distracts from the immediate response is less than the response. The good listener will never be aware how well a thing has been done, unless his perception is linked with his attention in a continuous awareness beyond the complacencies of enjoyment. Otherwise he may applaud, he may criticize, but he will not remember, as a part of his own inward knowledge of doing, what has been merely well done.

We wish to make Los Angeles a centre of poetry, a community where poetry as a living part of human existence is recognized and read, where poets are known, where new poetry is awaited. If we are to do this, we cannot do it halfway. Each of us who wishes to share in this poetic community must have an active part in it; the best way to have an active part in poetry is by learning well how to read it. Although you may intend never to raise your voice in public, you should know how this is done. Although you intend never to write poetry but only to share in the poetic experience of others, you cannot do so without an active poetic background. Looking at poetry on the pages of many books will bring you no nearer the art of reading poetry aloud. Criticism, even the New Criticism, avails nothing to apprehend a living art. And without that art there can be no living poetic community.

*I have chosen to criticize as readers only poets whose work I particularly admire.

# Two Poets
## on the Beat Fringes

# The Pocket Poet Series
## Reviewed by Thomas McGrath

There's a difference between San Francisco and Los Angeles which impresses everyone according to his needs.

To some, it is all that northern Old World Culture: the Tong Wars, the Vigilantes, the Barbary Coast, the Hungry Eye, bridges (G. G.: Bay and Harry), the Eastern Fox Squirrel (escaped or released at Menlo Park some years back and now spreading):

VERSUS

the Chinese Spotted Dove (released or escaped from Pershing Square in 1914 and now as far north as Santa Maria and Bakersfield), smog. The Industries, religion. Forest Lawn, plate glass bedrooms.

To others: the true and beautiful city

VERSUS

A congeries of silly middle western towns.

And:

Sentiment

vs.

Money

I suppose all of this is true; but I see it differently, at least for the moment.

What I see is Lucia, at the south end of the Big Sur country where the rational, pure, classical light ends in a romantic Franciscan fog: and where the pilgrim, bearded, bronzed clad in South African walking shorts, his ruck-sack bulging with books on Zen, marihuana, and the sacred writings of Henry Miller, is toiling toward Partington Ridge and Satori. Instead he gets to the bridge that Hart Crane never saw but which is Crane's honest-to-god Bridge; and begins to write poetry. And why not? The northern trek is a shattering experience.

Anyway: San Francisco is producing the only truly Romantic poetry in the country. It is poetry that is pretty much "committed": it is generally anarchist, pacifist, individualist, etc., etc. This is a Bad Sign to many people, to the Academy of the English Dept. and their institutional magazines, etc., etc. But it makes for a lively poetry—San Francisco is a city of energy at the very least.

The latest sign of this energy is *The Pocket Poets* series[1]. Taking them serially:

1. *Picture of the Gone World* by Lawrence Ferlinghetti (the editor of the series). Seems to me one of the best of the bunch. The subject generally is a perhaps too-easy kind of alienation: love, Paris, etc. But many of these poems have a wholeness about them even when they are slight; and I like the broken line he uses (of god knows what possible length) better than most "free" verse.

2. *Thirty Spanish Poems of Love and Exile* by Kenneth Rexroth. This book *really* has thirty two poems in it—San Francisco exuberance. They are translations of Albert Guillen, Neruda, Lorca, etc. No originals, but they are a pleasure to read.

3. *Poems of Humor and Protest* by Kenneth Patchen. It was always a toss-up which had to invent which: San Francisco Patchen or Patchen San Francisco. It is restful to have them united.

This book won't do much for Patchen's reputation—the poems are cuttings from the sundry gardens of this valorous invention—from seven of his books.

Perhaps it's harsh, but I've had an exasperated feeling that with Patchen it's usually the Children's Hour: he can write a psalm about God as fast as one on baseball, but the question always remains—*just Who's on first?*

But "Carnival at Night" has the fun of old automobiles, and "A true blue Gentleman" is a red blooded unamerican jape. There's a lot of fun in this book and whatever it hasn't, it's got more life than one can find in *A Little Treasury of Stuffed Owls.*

4. *Howl* by Allen Ginsberg. This is archetypal. The title poem is twelve pages long and mainly consists of a sentence:

"I saw (the good and the bad, etc. etc.): "who" (did good things, bad things, etc.); "And" (etc.). There is also a foot note of several pages.

When I first read it, this poem seemed to me very bad. (It has a commendation by William Carlos Williams, a thing that always makes me wary). It is a disturbed and disturbing piece of work. All it says is "pain" and "alone," most of it is predictable, and it doesn't grow and develop. On the page it appears to sprawl (Ginsberg does homage to Whitman, but I would have guessed Oppenheim) although that isn't necessarily the poet's fault: without some system of notation it's hard to know how a poem is supposed to sound—unless it's written in some fairly traditional form.

Since reading it, I've heard it recited by the author—a moving experience, one with a wallop. The poems turns out to have music, considerable metrical control, a painful sincerity beneath its stridor. It seems to have arrived so hard and fast that the poet hasn't had time to sort it out. I still think it is a bad poem, that it would not survive more than a couple of hearings, but I think, all the same, that it has an air of greatness to it. It is certainly worth a few Yale Younger Poems.

"Howl" is a poem to be read aloud—maybe that accounts for its strength and weakness. Other poems in the pamphlet are less rambunctious, and I think "Sunflower Sutra" is the best in the book.

All these booklets are worth having, whatever their limitations, because there is a vitality in them which is hard to find in American Poetry these days. They would be a lot better poems if they had more control; but perhaps that's too much to expect from such a rainy and romantic town. Anyway, energy is always holy.

—Thomas McGrath

[1]City Lights Bookshop, 261 & 271 Columbus Ave., San Francisco, 50¢ and 75¢

# Lawrence Lipton

Lawrence Lipton, b. 1898–d. 1975. Lawrence Lipton was born in Poland and immigrated to the United States. He was mostly known for his popular history of the Beats, *The Holy Barbarians*. He also wrote *The Erotic Revolution* and two novels, *Brother the Laugh Is Bitter* and *In Secret Battle*. His volumes of poetry include *Rainbow at Midnight* and *Bruno in Venice West and Other Poems*. Parts of *Rainbow at Midnight* were first published in *The California Quarterly*. Lipton published poems in *Coastlines* for many years, although he feuded off and on with its editors.

Lawrence Lipton on "America's Literary Underground"

"For the underground writer, emergence into the sun of recognition, fame and fortune is beset with hazards. . . . A sufficiently talented writer will survive anything, even Hollywood—if he gets out in time. But he is a very self-confident, or conceited one, who thinks he is robust enough to risk it. The Social Lie has many champions, and powerful ones."

"America's Literary Underground," *Coastlines* 2, no. 2 (winter 1956–57)

# rainbow at midnight

**AUTHOR'S NOTE**

Structurally *Rainbow at Midnight* (only one-third of which is presented here) is a travel diary, the narrative of a journey through time-space: the first fifty years of the Twentieth Century, with flashbacks into pivotal and pertinent times and places of the past, and an occasional glimpse into an imagined future.

Thematically the poem deals with the crisis of our time, which is examined in its twofold character: psychological and cultural, spiritual and sociological. The question that is raised is, to use a line from *Dead Reckoning:* What was it went awry? Where, at what moment in man's evolution, did he take the road that brought him to his present crisis? And what was "the road not taken"? The subject is debated by various "characters," e.g., The Pale Young Man and Joana of the Bound Hair in *Between Two Worlds;* Haggard in *Ritual of the Lights;* the New Barbarian as The Postulant in *The Ritual of Community,* etc.

The poem is in four parts. *Night Flight* states the problem in terms of recent history—wars, revolutions, the concepts of Progress and Decline, Challenge and Response, etc. Part Two, *Fanfare for a Delayed Exit,* examines the problem on the level of intellectual values. *Point of No Return* explores the implications of choice in terms of the individual's dilemma (as in *Between Two Worlds* and *And Choose You Must,* the latter not included here). Part Four, *Rainbow at Midnight,* employs the device of ritual drama to present an imaginary (post-world-revolutionary) therapy for the "healing of the lesion," the New Man (as The Postulant) seeking his way back to "the forking of the road" as a point of departure for other, more desirable destinations—a community in the functional, rational sense of the world. Three "rituals" comprise this section, of which the final one, *The Ritual of Community,* is presented here.

L. L.

## ■ Part One: Night Flight

### take-off

(Kitty Hawk, Dec. 17, 1903)

> *Henceforth space by itself and time*
> *by itself, are doomed to fade away*
> *into mere shadows, and only a kind*
> *of union of the two will preserve an*
> *independent reality.*
>
> H. Minkowski

1.

Twelve seconds, mark it well. In space and time
No longer than the first conceptual thought
That launched the brief millenniums of man,
Laid down the flaming measures of the mind
Yet left a morbid lesion still unhealed
A fractured Adam with an Adam's Fault.

No matter. Fallen but with Reason crowned
He scorns instinctual Eden, powers a wing
With charnel fires from Cambrian seas distilled
Storms heaven again with mathematic eye
And since that first abstraction split the mind
No longer asks the mythopoeic Who
Demanding only to know How, not Why.

The old faiths loosen, fall away. Look down,
The spiral of the centuries is coiled
Around an alp whose root is in the sea
Whose steps are measured eras ring on ring
Dividing reason from the mythic dream—
Evolves the wheel, the sail and now the wing.

2.
This was to be no ordinary century,
The very torque and turning point of time;
Keen bladed for the forward thrust, on wings
Prefigured by no prophet in his dreams
This groundling guns a path into the sky.

Computing drag and lift, resultant vector,
Finds new coefficients of the will
Explores the mind's dynamic and the soul's
Stagnation point; Bernoulli's theorem
Transformed into a common apothegm.

No omens and no auguries attend
The scene; the rite is secular and plain.
Man come of age succeeds to his estate—
Parthenogenesis of the cosmic egg
Self-conceived and self-inseminate.

3.
*Cogito ergo sum.* By taking thought
Man has added cubits to this stature
Creates himself, out of himself distills
Essential ichor of *elan vital;*

All things are possible. Our bright retorts
Precipitate a culture—now the word
Recalls to mind bacteria more than books;
If Newton's apple falls it falls *ad hoc*
In proof of Newton's law. A worthy cause.

The only ghosts we know are in the spectrum
Imperfections in diffraction grating;
It is better so. Our *ignis fatuus*
Is no foolish fire, no will-o'-the-wisp
But only methane gas: to be explicit,
Carbon-Hydrogen, four.

4.

Laboratorium, no longer meaning
Labor linked with prayer, now conjures up
No Ouroboros, no Hermetic dragons,
Only test-tubes, charts. Of all the gods
Only Eros is permitted wings;
New-fledged in Vienna, reapotheosized
In Zurich, de-sublimated in Chicago, lays
His Psyche on the analytic couch.

The pleasure principle is plain. The age
Impatient with Platonic nonsense, prone
And prurient takes its ease, al fresco in
The park; its bed the Sunday comic page.
Brancusi's bird, a hieroglyph of flight
Beside the primitive mask. In Grand Palais
*Donatello au milieu des fauves.*

*Dubito ergo sum.* Our Anthropos
Is logical to a fault. Our Athens needs
No Paul. The Unknown God is Truth.

5.

The Century of Man. His hand directs
The camera's eye, his mind seeks out, selects
Among the multitudinous footage, finds
A frame of reference in space and time.

Slow motion of the runner, there a point
Significant, a moment rare and beautiful
The diver dives and then, reverse, she rockets
Up again. You sweep away the grime
Of ages; see, the Neolithic potter
Fashioned these, and flung them in the teeth
Of time.

And speech, man's oldest monument; alive
Upon our living lips today is ancient man,
His gestures caught in breathing pictographs

Preserved as insects are in amber or
The mastodon in Pleistocenic clay.

6.
Restore the book of bones and beasts and men.
Jerusalem, her holy mountain. Rust
Is on the sacrificial knife; where priests
In blood up to their elbows documented God
And stoned the prophets. Let the tomb reveal
The saint his cloven hoof, the hero-god
His feet of clay. Unwrap the cerements,
Unseal the lips that to Osiris lied.

Unriddle all arcana, cryptogramic
Charts of secret and untraveled oceans
Sunken islands long since overborne
By ancient unimaginable seas.

7.
Restore the past. Knit word with word and bone
With bone. Fill in lacunae in the text.
Reveal the writing underneath the gloss
Lay bare the skeletal structure stone by stone

But gently, brother, gently. These are sign
And signet of the quintessential anguish.
Fear and wrath. Incunabula of men
Who ate the bread of trembling in their time.

And whether on reindeer cave or Karnak's wall
Etched out the selfsame hope. Set their stamp
On history's page, then died and left their bones
Between the battle-axe and the votive lamp.

8.
The word is Youth. The word is Progress. I
The heir of all the ages, from this height
Survey my world and godlike call it good.
Fiat lux, from chaos conjure light,
Create all things in my own image with
The automatic the immediate word
I blast the banal and I break the norm
Revaluing all values and all form.

And now behold the miracle of flight!
Across the bright meridian of noon
Wild horses storm unbridled to the sun
The world is young and life has just begun.

Then lock the door and file the script away.
The play is ended; if recalled at all,
Remember only with the long-drawn breath,
A poem of love remembered after death.

9.
Here is the curtain, dust enfolding dust.
The last prop, a folded fan, is left
Upon the boards where it fell. The gilt
Is scabrous on the royal box. No man

Has lifted hand to fly the final drop,
"A sylvan dell, with shepherds in the lower
Left, and at the right a well." The seats
Yawn upward to the high proscenium arch.

Dust is on the green tormentors, high
Under the iron beams the wings are greyed
With distance. There the door stands open for
The final exit that was never made.

Attention! Action! Let the worklight down.
Call all hands and let them set the stage.
The actors stand impatient in the wings.
Music. Lights. A new play for a new age!

# Poetry, Jazz, Etc.

Los Angeles now has poetry and jazz, and the bill at The Jazz Concert Hall* is a held-over success with plans in process for a new show to be mounted during holiday week. Also much heady talk about poetry being set to go with jazz in various bistros of the city. Also many records coming out, so that there is enough evidence around to build a case for or against it. Unfortunately the case can be built *either* for or against, depending upon what performances you think of, or what records you present as evidence.

So far the most satisfying performance I've heard has been that of Rexroth at the Tin Angel in San Francisco. Not necessarily because the poetry or the jazz was better than at the Jazz Concert Hall, but because Rexroth had had time to work with the band there, *and because he was on long enough for one to get used to the style of things*—the voice, the band, the kind of poems he was doing. Jazz Concert Hall offers the interest of variety, but the poetry is somewhat scattered among the other acts and, with the exception of Rexroth, no one is on long enough to give the full flavor of the thing.

After hearing the show at JCH a couple of times (the second time a much improved performance; there had been almost no rehearsal for the first) I'm left with somewhat mixed feelings and a number of questions. Concerning:

1. The audience. Who goes to these things? Everybody, it seems. In the audience at JCH the second time I was there was Stravinsky—and someone who was sitting beside me who started giggling uncontrollably when the pome-readin' began. Also what used to be called bobby-soxers. People with beards and sandals. And a lot of people who might have been found at the opening of an art exhibit, a concert or a poetry reading, i.e., Ciardi's 'person of (some) culture.'

It's certainly a fine thing to have a varied audience, but how many at JCH come for the poetry and how many for something else? I don't know, and I don't even know how relevant the question is, but it is a fact that the solidest hit of the show, to judge from applause, is Katie Lee, who sings some songs which are not all *that* witty. On the other hand, Rexroth, whose group of poems is the biggest single contribution in the poetry and jazz department, is received with some reservation, although that may be because he is the first live poet to appear on the stage. The question is: if you take away the big jazz names, will you still have an audience? Yes, you will—the fact that 300 or so turned out for Rexroth's reading at Poetry Los Angeles (probably the biggest crowd since the Poetry Festival at the Unitarian Church a few years back) is proof of an audience. But it probably will not be as big as attendance at JCH would indicate. There'll be a fall-out if the big jazz names are dropped and again when poetry and jazz ends its history as a fad and becomes an accepted form—supposing that happens. Still, there will probably remain a bigger and more varied audience than poetry has had in the past, and that is all to the good.

2. Gresham's Law. Bad money drives out good—will bad poems drive out the good ones? Maybe. There's a lot of junk being waxed these days, and some of them cats can't blow, not when it comes to words anyway. A good example here is Mingus's 'The Clown.' The music is fine, but the flat-footed prose of the voice-man (I don't care if he *is* full of red white and blue lemons) might have made a fair children's record, nothing more. Yet the record is being talked about as if it were really part of the scene.

Or to take another case. Sitting beside me at the Rexroth Poetry Los Angeles reading (how come always beside *me?*) I heard the small voice of rebellion: 'And they call *this* avant garde?'—in accents of indescribable contempt. Now it is true that most avant-garders tend to be a bit old-fashioned, ill-informed and square in a sharp way. But this has the sound of Thermidor. These cats have been feeding on raw meat for some time (and Rexroth has himself presented them with the catsmeat of certain bad San Francisco poets as if he were putting out nothing but straight God's-body and blood) and it is not surprising when they start calling for wilder music and for stronger wine. It is ironical that the cry should be directed against Rexroth in this case; and of course it is ill-informed: Rexroth finished long ago with a lot of things that are now paraded as avant garde. But what are you going to do with an audience which, in part, is already hunting the farther out? If poetry gets a bigger audience will it, following that grand old American culture-pattern, debauch-and-be-debauched-by its audience? There is no guarantee that it won't, and some evidence that such is already happening. But poetry is in such a state just now that such debauchery might be healthy. It can't really damage The Grand Old Girl. *But* people who have a hand in presenting poetry to this new audience have a responsibility to the Muse none the less. Let them remember that a poem should still be a poem. E. Guest might go good, but it wouldn't help the Goddess.

3. Performance. Performance can make a good poem bad or vice versa. This relates to Gresham's Law above, but also to itself. At JCH the best received poem was that of Saul White. I don't think that it was the best poem of the evening, however. Why best received? Partly perhaps because of certain esthetically irrelevant aspects of the performance, but *also and especially* because White suggested or created an organic relationship between the poem and the music—something which occurred, to my way of thinking at least, only sporadically in the other readings. To some degree this happened in Stuart Perkoff's 'Alba' as well—this too was very well received—although there the voice dominated the music, and there was little of the interplay which this form requires. Worst relationship of words to music was in one of Lawrence Lipton's poems 'How Jazz Was Born.' As one who does not believe that painting is about paint, I also do not believe that the proper poetry-and-jazz subject is itself; but the difficulty was compounded here because while the poem is talking about trombones, we are confronted by an excellent 'cellist. Not a trombone on stage—probably not even one on all Crenshaw Blvd.

That's a small point, certainly, and easily correctable. I am more uneasy about some of the other goings on. There is no reason, of course, why poetry cannot be used with or against any single instrument or combination of instruments, but I'd like to see poetry and jazz really worked out before people go to poetry-and-musical-effects. Rexroth has an interesting thing with two basses, but his poem—and Patchen's—cum piano is apt to remind one of certain disastrous Sunday afternoons spent in the parlors of people of (some) culture. These wild 'experiments' might have been left to the 'nineties or 'twenties or whenever they happened. A new sound? Then my name is Ethelbert Nevin. But the poems might go with a piano that wasn't pretty—Cow Cow Davenport, maybe.

Conclusions:

1. Poetry-and-jazz can be very moving and beautiful when it works.

2. It hasn't worked very often so far.

3. It needs a feeling of spontaneity—the feeling that jazz often gives even

when it is not truly spontaneous. This, I think, means that the poem can't be tied too tightly to the music.

4. To achieve this feeling of spontaneity and *ease* of performance, and at the same time to avoid the goofs that would be inevitable in anything really 'improvised,' the poet and the band have got to work together for some time— long enough to get to know each other's qualities.

—Thomas McGrath

*Los Angeles Jazz Concert Hall, 3020 Washington Blvd., First West Coast Poetry and Jazz Festival in association with Venice West Poetry Center, under direction of Lawrence Lipton, December 4–7

Announcement for jazz and poetry at LA Jazz Concert Hall.

## ■ I Was a Poet for the FBI

Murder, suicide, mayhem. Wow! The stories I could tell. See my agent.
  Even before God was insulted at Yale I was at the U of I picking up
  spondees and trochees in the Co-op and counting the condoms in the
  boneyard on Monday morning.
I was Ed Hoover's man at YMCA College collecting free verse in the ladies'
  room and once, disguised as Oscar Wilde, in the men's toilet. Cash
  McCall is my co-pilot.
At the Green Mask, in the very shadow of the Tribune Tower—may I speak
  freely? the beard of Henry Wadsworth Longfellow was burned in ritual
  orgy, hair by hair.
In Chicago I joined the Escalator Movement under the name of Gertrude Stein
  and nobody suspected anything. From a poet named Rexroth I learned
  about six different kinds of sex, all of them subversive.
In dives on Rush Street we lay on divans in mixed company and talked about
  modern art, waited on by naked African pygmies. We sat on the floor
  and read Edna St. Vincent Millay, aloud. I could name names and places.
On orders from Ezra Pound I infiltrated the *Saturday Evening Post* and planted
  excerpts from Edgar A. Guest. One night I broke into the *Saturday
  Review* and lopped off Literature from the masthead. Nobody noticed it.
Four times I escaped from behind curtains—iron, bamboo, dimity and
  shower, and once I barely made it by way of a bedroom fire escape clad
  only in pajama tops. Danger is my business.
I found an atheist in a foxhole and reported him to General MacArthur.
  Twice I was shot down in missions over Union Square, Waldorf Cafeteria,
  Camp Nitgedieget and the League of American Penwomen. Arthur
  Godfrey is my co-pilot.
I joined the Brownian Movement before it split with the Fourth Dimensheviks.
  Big Jim Openheimer was its Party boss. I would tell you about my affair
  with Tillie Zilch but that's still classified.
I was there when they dubbed the Communist Manifesto into the movie of
  *Charlie's Aunt,* and nipped the conspiracy to smuggle quotations from
  Karl Marx into the popcorn bags. Now they're plotting to foul up the
  rhymes in the singing commercials.
Ten grand buys my tale of horror at the Cotton Club when Louis Armstrong
  sang *Eli Eli* on secret orders from the Elders of Zion, and the
  borschtcapades in the Holland Tunnel with Mickey Katz on Walpurgis-
  nacht. Commander Whitehead is my co-pilot.

For an extra grand I'll tell all I know about free verse, free love, free lunch,
free wheeling and free pop at barbecues of the American Academy of
Arts and Letters, a Dadaist front controlled by Tristan Tzara and
Ogden Nash.
Now, back in the free world, with my unexpurgated copy of Ann Morrow
Lindbergh's *The Unicorn* and the complete files of the Soviet Ministry
of Culture I am Poet in Residence at *Time, Life and Fortune.* Zsa Zsa
Gabor is my co-pilot.

Your files will show, as mine do, that I have not submitted material to *Coastlines* since 1957, first because former editors disapproved of my activities in poetry and music and later because of their disapproval of my hospitality to the New Writing, then known as the beat writing. Political and literary-sectarian difference lay at the bottom of this controversy. Before that I had contributed a good deal of prose and poetry to *Coastlines* and before *Coastlines* to its lineal precursor the *California Quarterly.*

If you have kept up with my articles in the Calendar section of the Los Angeles *Times* (articles leading up to my forthcoming THE GROWING EDGE: The State of Culture and the Arts on the West Coast, U. of C. Press) you must know that I would have preferred to publish my work in *Coastlines,* a West Coast magazine, rather than in other periodicals where my work has appeared since then in the U.S. and abroad. I refer you, on this point, to my latest articles in the *Times* of last Sunday, Dec. 1, 1963, on the subject of publishing on the West Coast.

The poems I am now submitting are as yet unpublished, probably because in the case of two of them they are so long. But if you care to publish one of these long ones they will do, as far as I am concerned, in lieu of half a dozen shorter pieces. Since my collected poems will be coming out next year and will contain these poems I would suggest that this will probably be the last chance any magazine will have for prepublication.

Too bad it has to be your valedictory number. It needn't have been, in my opinion, if *Coastlines* had not pursued such a narrow sectarian policy. It may well have been *the* magazine of the West Coast renaissance since it was first on the scene, but editorial hostility precluded any such possibility. There is still room for such a forward-looking magazine (see the final paragraphs of my last Sunday article) in Los Angeles.

Sincerely,

Lawrence Lipton

# Charles Bukowski

Charles Bukowski, b. 1920–d. 1994. Charles Bukowski was born in Andernach, Germany. He married Barbara Fry, and they were divorced in 1955. He attended Los Angeles City College between 1939 and 1941 and over his lifetime worked at various manual labor occupations, including dishwasher, truck driver, stock boy, warehouseman, and post office clerk. Bukowski won the Silver Reel Award from the San Francisco Festival of Arts for a documentary film and a National Foundation for the Arts grant in 1963. He began writing poetry at the age of thirty-five and published in *Coastlines* early on. His early books include *Flower, First, and Bestial Wail* (1959), *Longshot Pomes for Broke Players* (1961), *Run with the Hunted* (chapbook) (1962), *Poems and Drawings* (1962), and *It Catches My Heart in My Hands* (1963), among many others published later. His early poems were collected in *Rooming House Madrigals.*

## Dow Jones: Down

how can we endure?
how can we talk about roses
or Verlaine?
this is a hungry band
that likes to work and count
and knows the special laws,
that likes to sit in parks
thinking of nothing valuable.

this is where the stricken bagpipes blow
upon the chalky cliffs
where faces go mad as sunburned violets
where brooms and ropes and torches fail,
squeezing shadows . . .
where walls come down en masse.

tomorrow the bankers set the time
to close the gates against our dam
and prevaricate the waters;
Shilitz, stiltz, bang the time,
remember now
        the flowers are opening in the wind
        and it doesn't matter finally
        except as a twitch in the back of the head
when back in our broad land
dead again
we walk among the dead.

■ everything:
the dead do not need
aspirin or
sorrow,
I suppose.

but they might need
rain.

not shoes
but a place to
walk.

not cigarettes,
but they tell us,
a place to
burn.

or we're told:
space and a place to
fly
might be the
same.

the dead don't need
me.

nor do the
living.

but the dead might need
each
other.

in fact, the dead might need
everything we
need

and
we need much,

if we only knew
what it
was.

and
it is
probably everything

and we
probably die
trying to get
it

or die

because we
don't get
it.

I hope
you understand
when I am dead

I got
as much
as
possible.

## MOVED ON

I find it interesting, if depressing, that the outlets for all the arts *but* non-commercial writing, are finding increasing support in Los Angeles. Reading requires no audience participation. It is a lonely occupation and does not excite the money-men as do theatre, music, art galleries, or politics. Though it can produce prestige, it has very little publicity value.

The former editors (and founders) left us with a good name. With the Los Angeles 'cultural explosion' the past few years, (including the appearance at the universities and colleges of genuine published, practicing poets as teachers), the new editors of *Coastlines* felt that we *might* succeed in raising the money to continue. If nothing else, *Coastlines* was the only such outlet in the city; and where did the unknown graduates of all those writing courses expect to be published? We spent a year and a half trying to raise the funds. We failed.

Perhaps there is much to be said for another view. *Coastlines*, before we took over, had a distinct personality, one that was often praised and sometimes damned. This personality belonged to the former editors and was not transferable. These editors and many of the writers they printed 'moved on' in the same sense as the writers in this quote from Michael Straight in *The Carleton Miscellany*.

'Of course money is important. But, for the small magazine, it is far less important than verve. *Le Banquet* was born when its thirteen founders threw ten francs apiece onto the editorial table. The thirteen included Barbusse and Gregh and Leon Blum—and Marcel Proust.

*Le Banquet* brought the earliest works of these men into print. They moved on, and *Le Banquet* folded—as it should have done. I'm appalled by the energy we devote to keeping alive institutions that have earned an honorable burial. Nonetheless, in the United States, one hundred and thirty francs will not start many presses turning.'

Ultimately the question is, how much of a sacrifice are you willing to make and where do you draw the line. Do you finally throw the remaining drunks out of the house after the *Coastlines* party is over, or do you leave them lay (along with the couple among the coats on the bed) and give them breakfast in the morning?

—Alexandra Garrett

NOTICE

Despite a year long effort, *Coastlines* was unable to raise the funds to continue. *Coastlines* will discontinue publication with this double issue which will count as two issues on our subscriptions. Subsequently, unexpired subscriptions will be filled by *Trace*, P.O. Box 1068, Hollywood 28, California. In case of duplication, *Trace* will be happy to extend your subscription if you will contact them. Most back issue of *Coastlines* are available in limited supply. These may be ordered through *Trace*.

Earl Newman, cover (final issue):
*Coastlines* 6, nos. 21 and 22 (1964).

# Coastlines: a Post-mortem

On Sunday, August 30, 1964 Robert Kirsch at the *Los Angeles Times* marks the demise of *Coastlines* in a little piece titled "*Coastlines*: a Post-mortem." Kirsch says of Coastlines: "The list of contributors, many of them poets and short story writers, given their first or very early publication in *Coastlines,* is imposing." He expresses what many in Los Angeles felt at the death of *Coastlines,* a sadness at its end, a feeling of loss for what the journal represented in Southern California. He ends his little piece by praising the quality of the journal: "More impressive in this final issue than the editorials on the life and death of the magazine is the level of the poetry and fiction printed." Someone at the *Los Angeles Times* had noticed *Coastlines* and mourned its passing.

## Complete List of Coastlines Contributors

Chester Aaron
George Abbe
Josephine Ain
Walter Albert
Daisy Aldan
Jack Anderson
Felix Anselm
Philip Appleman
Richard Ashman
Sonora Babb
Ray Barrio
Elizabeth Bartlett
Paul Bartlett
Lee Baxandal
Grove Becker
John Beecher
Jack Beeching
Michael Benedikt

Nelson Bentley
George Betar
Henry Birnbaum
Paul Blackburn
Melissa Blake
Maurice Blanck
Susan Blodgett
George Bluestone
Robert Bly
Charles Bukowski
David R. Bunch
Jean Burdin
Robert Burlingame
Rex S. Burns
Johanna Campbell
Alvaro Cardona-Hine
Arthur Carson
Mario Casetta

Arthur Castillo

John Ciardi

James Comorthoon

John Cooper

Paul Cordell

Cid Corman

John William Corrington

Gregory Corso

Henri Coulette

Judson Crews

Winifred Cullen

R. R. Cuscaden

Barding Dahl

Patricia Darrin

Genevieve Davis

David C. Dejong

Pierre Henri Delattre

Norman Disher

George Dowden

Charles Edward Eaton

Eleanor R. Edelstein

George P. Elliott

William Esher

Clayton Eshleman

Robert Eskew

Ray Fabrizio

Norman Friedman

Gene Frumkin

Jean Gancher

Alexandra Garrett

George Garrett

Jed Garrick

Stephen Geller

Estelle Gershgoren

Sidney Gershgoren

Barbara Gibbs

Morgan Gibson

Allen Ginsberg

Don Gordon

Scott Greer

Vahan Gregory

Seymour Gresser

Virginia Grey

Harold Grutzmacher

Charles Gullans

Lawrence S. Gurney

Menelaus Guskos

John Haines

Paul Haines

William Harmon

Barbara Harris

Leslie Woolf Hedley

Moss Herbert

Louis Hill

James Hiner

Jack Hirschman

George Hitchcock

Allan Hoffman

Harry Hooten

R. B. Irvine

Sylvia Jarrico

Judson Jerome

Louis Johnson

Duane Jones

Lenore Kandel

Walter Kerr

Jascha Kessler

Milton Kessler

Stanley Kiesel

Ralph Kinsey

Bill Knott

J. D. Koerner

Stanley Kurnik

Danial J. Langton

Carl Larsen

Myron Levoy

Jack Lindeman

Lawrence Lipton

R. Little

Joanne de Longchamps

Walter Lowenfels

Mary Graham Lund

David Lyttle

Derek Maggs

William J. Margolis

Robert Martin

Joseph Martinek

Jill Marx

F. X. Mathews

James Boyer May

Lachlan McDonald

Alice McGrath

Thomas McGrath

Roy McGregor-Hastie

Ken McLaughlin

Eve Merriam

Richard Merriss

Mike Meth

Bert Meyers

William R. Miller

William Millet

Ruth Finer Mintz

Marion Montgomery

Rita Mosher

Lowell Naeve

Helen Nonam

Margaret Nordfors

William Norton

Stanley Noyes

Ron Offen

Gil Orlovitz

Brian Parvin

Kenneth Patchen

Nancy Lou Patterson

Simon Perchik

Christopher Perret

Lory Petri

Nora M. Pettinella

Mary Alice Philips

William Pillin

Tom Poots

Byron Pumphrey

David Ray

Robert Reiss

Wallace Rena

Naomi Replansky

John Rety

Kenneth Rexroth

Tim Reynolds

Martin Robbins

Lee Robinson

Edwin Rolfe

Melvin Rosenberg

Larry Rubin

James Schevill

Norbert Schiller

Winifred Townley Scott

David Seidman

Ramon Sepulveda

Priscilla Shames

W. E. Sharpe

G. W. Sherman

James Singer

Fred Smith

Helen Sorrells

Merrill Sparks

Lawrence P. Spingarn

Ann Stanford

George Starbuck

Felix Stefanile

Arlene Steinberg

A. Wilber Stevens

Robert Stock

Barton Stone

Robert Sward

John Tagliabue

Idell Tarlow

Carl Thayler

John Thompson

Ralph Treitel

Martin Tucker

Lewis Turco

Robert Vaughan

Tom Viertel

Diane Wakoski

Dorothea Walker

Zack Walsh

David Rafael Wang

Irma Wassall

Jon Edgar Webb

Robert L. Weeks

Mel Weisburd

Philip Whalen

Marjorie S. Wheeler

Joan White

Ruth Whitman

Kingsley Widmer

Edith G. Wies

Miller Williams

Carleton Winston

Harold Witt

Peter Yates

Donald J. Young

Curtis Zahn

Lloyd Zimpel

Richard Zink

*Contributing Cover Artists:*

Mae Babitz

Frances Blaker

Mario Casetta

Morton Dimondstein

Angel G. Esparza

Milton Gershgoren

Sylvia Jarrico

Chris Jenkyns

David Lemon

Martin Lubner

Arnold Mesches

Lowell Naeve

Earl Newman

Manuel Santana

Bernice Silberman

# The Artists

**Mario Casetta** was an artist who, besides painting and drawing, specialized in woodcuts. He studied painting and drawing in Fontainebleau and Paris in the 1950s, then attended the Ecole des Arts Appliqués in Lausanne, Switzerland, where he studied graphic arts, winning several awards at graduation. He had exhibitions in Geneva and Berne before returning to the United States, where his work was exhibited in Los Angeles. In Los Angeles he also illustrated books and album covers and did designs for advertising art projects.

**Morton Dimondstein** began his study of art in 1937, when he enrolled in the American Artists School and the Art Students League in New York City. He continued his studies at the Otis Art Institute in Los Angeles. In 1951 he moved to Mexico, where he became a member of the Taller de Gráfica Popular and was staff artist and instructor for UNESCO. Between 1951 and 1956 he was art editor for *The California Quarterly.* During the 1950s and 1960s he taught at the Kann Art Institute, the New School of Art, the School of Fine Art, and USC. In addition to his painting and graphic art, he began to sculpt after he spent some time in Rome in the early 1960s. Dimondstein had paintings, prints, and sculpture exhibited at many museums and galleries, among them the Los Angeles County Museum, the Metropolitan Museum of Art, and the Pennsylvania Academy of Fine Art. His work is collected in the Library of Congress, the Seattle Art Institute, and the Pushkin State Museum. He died in 2000.

**Milton Gershgoren,** after immigrating from Russia as a child, attended the Pennsylvania Academy of Fine Art on a scholarship and the Jepson Art Institute. His work has been exhibited at many museums and galleries, among them the Los Angeles County Museum of Art, the Pasadena Museum, the Pennsylvania Academy of Fine Art, and the Library of Congress. Among other prizes he was awarded the Tom Gooch Memorial Purchase Prize by the Dallas Museum, the Motion Picture Directors Purchase Award in Watercolor, and the Sacramento State Fair First Purchase Award in Oil. His work is represented in the collections of the Dallas Museum, the Long Beach Museum, the Los Angeles County Museum of Art, the Richmond Museum, the New Britain Connecticut Museum, Occidental College, and USC and in many private collections. He painted and did graphic artwork in Los Angeles for most of his life. He died in 1989.

**Chris Jenkyns** enjoys a professional reputation as a talented producer, director, writer, and designer who has received international acclaim for his work. Jenkyns studied at Los Angeles City College, the Art Center School, Chouinard Art Institute, the New School of Social Research in Los Angeles, and the Academie Julian in Paris. It was in Paris that he became interested in filmic expression, and after a brief career as an advertising designer and illustrator he went to work for Storyboard, Inc., films in 1954 as a writer and design artist. Jenkyns worked continuously in film production from 1954. He worked for John Sutherland Productions, Ray Patin Productions, Jay Ward Productions, and Playhouse Pictures. Jenkyns has received over 150 major awards for writing/ direction/design from the Art Directors Clubs of New York, Los Angeles, Chicago, San Francisco, Detroit, and Atlanta and foreign honors at the Tours, Annecy, Cork, London, Edinburgh, and Venice film festivals. He worked on *Self-Defense for Cowards*, which was nominated for an Oscar by the Academy of Motion Picture Arts and Sciences in 1964. He worked on numerous television films as writer and designer, including the *Doctor Seuss CBS Special, Fractured Fairy Tales, The Rescuers,* and *The Bullwinkle Show* and was producer, director, and designer for *The Carol Burnett Show* in 1970. In addition to all these credits, Jenkyns has illustrated many books for children, among them *The Beautiful Things, Clouds, How to Lose Your Lunch Money,* and *Andy Says Bonjour,* the last chosen as one of the ten best illustrated children's books by *The New York Times* in 1954. He presently lives in Los Angeles in the retirement community of the Motion Picture and Television Fund.

**David Lemon** studied at the Art Institute of Chicago in the 1930s. During World War II he served in the air force. He and his wife, Frankie, moved to the San Francisco area and settled in Berkeley, California. He exhibited primarily in Los Angeles, originally at the Streeter Blair Gallery and then mainly at the Fleisher-Anhalt Gallery. His work is held in many private collections in Los

Angeles and in northern California. It was David Lemon who provided the cover for the first issue of *Coastlines* and for many issues that followed. He died in 1979.

**Martin Lubner** taught at the New School of Art with Arnold Mesches, Morton Dimondstein, and Ted Gillian. He also taught art classes through UCLA's extension program. Lubner has been a figurative painter, as he says, "an island not in the mainstream." He has taught at the Royal College in London and has exhibited his work in London, New York, and Los Angeles. Lubner is married to painter Lorraine Lubner and has three children.

**Arnold Mesches** moved to Los Angeles from Buffalo, New York, in 1943 and first studied advertising design at the Art Center School there. He subsequently went on to study at Jepson Art Institute and at Chouinard Art Institute and then began teaching at various places, including the Kann Institute of Art, USC, Otis Art Institute, and the New School of Art. He also taught at the Art Barn School in Salt Lake City but was fired for his political activity. In 1955 he went to Mexico to meet and learn from such great artists as Siqueros. There he lectured at the Taller de Gráfica Popular. In Los Angeles he exhibited at the Pasadena Art Museum, the Santa Barbara Museum of Art, the Ankrum Gallery, the Paul Rivas Gallery, the Landau Gallery, and many others while participating in group shows in New York and elsewhere. He currently lives and paints in New York City.

**Earl Newman** is a poster artist who paints his work on silk screen. He has created posters for the Monterey Jazz Festival, the UCLA Folk Festival, and other fairs. He currently lives and works in Oregon.

**Polia Pillin** was the wife of poet William Pillin and worked in ceramics and graphic art throughout her life. Her work is owned and enjoyed by many throughout the country but particularly in Los Angeles, where she made her home.

**Manuel Santana** was a student of Marty Lubner, Arnold Mesches, and Morton Dimondstein in the 1950s. Presently he runs several restaurants in northern California and has a studio in Santa Cruz, where he continues to paint.

**Bernice Silberman** was a student of Morton Dimondstein and Marty Lubner at the School of Fine Art and then became a teacher at the school. She kept the school running when Dimondstein and Lubner were out of the country. Afterward she developed her own studio and taught both there and at the Barnsdall Art Center for fourteen years and at the Otis-Parsons School. She also worked in animation for Victor Habush, a studio that did live action and animated commercials. She worked on one long animated movie, directed by Bob Mitchell, a parody of the well-known *2001: A Space Odyssey.* She has exhibited in Los Angeles at various galleries, including the Felix Landau, Zora, and Heritage. She has also worked in lithography and sold her lithographs in New York.

# Title Index

All the Dead Poets  /  63

Aspects  /  208

At the Station  /  96

Aubade  /  109

Bear, The  /  225

Because There's So Much Speed  /  142

Between Chicago and St. Paul  /  160

Bon Voyage  /  85

Burning Glass, The  /  223

Cleaning Woman  /  216

Clue, The  /  171

Complaint  /  78

Consider the Meaning of Love  /  97

Crow Black With Purpose, A  /  146

Debt, The  /  175

Dissenter, The  /  93

Don Quixote  /  207

Doomsday and Components  /  198

Dow Jones: Down  /  255

Dreamsong: a sirvente for Mel Weisburd  /  149

Editorial  /  150

Elegy for a Soldier of the Spanish Civil War  /  86

Elegy for a Tailor  /  168

Epitaph: 1945  /  104

Escape  /  66

everything:  /  256

Frugal Repast, The  /  214

Grammarian: Parts of Speech, The  /  136

Gregg  /  201

Head's Dark House, The  /  117

Hiroshima Woman  /  220

Housing Shortage  /  102

Idiot Joe Prays in Pershing Square and Gets Hauled in for Vagrancy / 91

I Dreamed / 141

imperial fragment, an / 132

In the Alley / 138

investigation, the / 94

Iowa, Kansas, Nebraska / 170

I Was a Poet for the FBI / 251

Jack of Diamonds / 135

Joey / 202

Legend / 219

Letter To An Imaginary Friend / 68

*from* Letter To An Imaginary Friend / 74

*Longshot O'Leary Says It's Your Duty to be Full of Fury* / 79

Magdalen / 206

Men Fail in Communion / 176

Mr. and Mrs. Foxbright X Muddlehead, At Home / 62

Middle Passage, The / 98

Migration / 116

Miserere / 114

My Father / 145

Night in the Funeral Range / 131

Night Prayer for Various Trades / 103

Number XVI from *The Flesh of Utopia* / 213

Ocean Park / 112

Officers, Gentlemen, Reluctant Violence / 123

One Star for "P.R." / 126

Pandora / 222

People's Choice, The / 120

Picture Framing / 141

Poem / 90

Problem of Creation, The / 118

rainbow at midnight / 241

Report From Evanston / 162

Ring Song / 101

Roads into the Country, The / 66

Rococo Summer / 134

Sabbath / 108

Scars / 221

Sentry / 84

Seven Children / 203

Seven Haiku / 208

Shape of a Pear, The / 221

Ship of Fools, The / 132

Southern California as the State of the Union / 128

Successions / 78

Summer Walk, A / 226

That which is good is simply done / 113

Three Personal Poems of Grandeur and Magniloquence / 190

Tijuana / 124

Time Machine of War, The / 219

Train of the Wounded, The / 199

Travelers, The / 94

Trouble with the Times, The / 217

Two Jewish Poems / 110

Unposed Photograph of I. I. Freitag, Esq. / 121

Vindication / 146

Waiting Room in the County Hospital, The / 168

Weathercock, The / 224

When I Go Down to That Sleep / 148

Window, The / 228

You There, Weeping / 205

You Walked a Crooked Mile / 104

# Index of First Lines

A crow, / 146

After split skies and tardy thunder, rain / 131

A gentle wind quiets his brow, / 86

Although the wood never laments / 217

Asleep, breathing like an enormous child, / 84

at birth and steadily for one year / 213

At noon an airplane, / 138

Autumn, and migratory birds begin / 116

Autumn brings relief / 221

Because there's so much speed / 142

Be nimble, Jill. The legends in your purse / 135

Between elms of shining water / 205

Bring me the evidence of the dead man. / 171

Colonels Oddbold & Fieldglove, and the / 123

Comes the murderer's evening, *ami du criminel* / 62

Consider the meaning of love in the time / 97

David's eyes held his mind's reins so no thought stampeded. / 203

Destined to be born and born to lead, / 120

Don Quixote like a tree walking / 207

"From here it is necessary to ship all bodies east." / 68

Gangrenous day! Caries / 168

Gregg, you cork, speck of a great saint, I wish / 201

He started from the nouns, the feeble names / 136

Here is the chained swan by the passive lake, / 214

how can we endure? / 255

How lakes resemble standing up / 208

How vainly men themselves bestir / 63

Hunting in the dark my father found me, / 66

I confront the star-spell of the esplanade! / 112

I dreamed of a light that kills: / 141

I had expected something quite different. / 160

I think of the young, of their disbelief in dying: / 98

I tried to live small. / 102

I will not endow you with a false glow / 114

In all that thin, squalid, exploited valley / 124

In church, from between artificial shoulders / 124

Ink, jam, chocolate, what does not pay you its respects? / 202

Iowa, Kansas, Nebraska, / 170

It is childhood's haunted house / 117

Kneeling to no one she lights the empty lengths / 216

Let us praise, / 91

Life, be fresh with daybreak! / 109

Love and hunger!—the secret is all there somewhere— / 74

Love, the harsh fields declaim / 226

Machinist in the pillow's grip, / 103

Many an outcast calls me friend / 90

Murder, suicide, mayhem. Wow! The stories I could tell. See my agent. / 251

My father, a laborer, forty eight, divorced three times, timid / 145

My fingers feed in the fields of wood. / 141

Myopic old tailor, you poked at life / 168

My spoon was lifted when the bomb came down / 105

Never, never again the house new or youth precise, / 222

Night where the Greyhound never stops, lizard's night; / 131

Not the prescribed movement of hands / 108

Noting here the lean burro leaning against / 118

1000 men were dead / 219

People will turn the middens we bequeath: / 93

Perhaps I met Thomas McGrath somewhere in Nicaragua at a time / 80

Permit me refuge in a region of your brain: / 85

'Professor, what are we doing in this institution?' / 136

Ran only in one direction, in childhood years— / 66

She was born under the shadow of the great moon / 220

Silence shipwrecked upon the silence / 199

Sing a song for Thomas McGrath / 79

Somehow under the stagnant air, / 162

Somewhere in his mind, / 94

Southwesterners / 128

Take what is at hand / 111

That which is good is simply done / 113

the dead do not need / 256

The endurable voyages are those I do not take. / 94

The Queen / 78

The rabbi noted: it is worse to violate / 110

The shape of a pear is too much / 221

The ship of fools moves down the burning world / 132

The sky is obese with red sun at mid-day / 219

There is a moment on which moments turn / 223

There is more than one skeletal eruption / 198

They fail in communion, a surplus of failure / 176

They say he could blow life into the F-holes / 121

they think they are lost / 208

this has happened lately / 194

Thou hast a double kingdom / 228

today a leaf and yes / 192

Twelve seconds, mark it well. In space and time / 242

Upwards now / 196

Vivid with impotence and sublime / 206

We have once more caught / 225

We speak again to all in the city built on a swamp: / 132

When I go down to that sleep / 148

When I go down to that sleep / 149

When I read of worms slipping / 175

when lemons bloom / 190

When that joy is gone for good / 101

Which way do the trains run? / 96

Whoever drives commands the speed that kills / 78

Wind shakes me / 224

With much laughter at ourselves, / 150

You walked a crooked mile / 104

POETS OF THE NON-EXISTENT CITY

# Works Consulted

Bolter, Michael, interviewer. *The Education of Alice McGrath.* Los Angeles: UCLA Oral History Program, 1987.

Boyer-May, James, ed. *Trace.* London: Villiers Publications, Ltd., October 1955, February 1956.

Boyer-May, James, Thomas McGrath, and Peter Yates, eds. *Poetry Los Angeles: I.* London: Villiers Publications, Ltd., 1958.

*California Quarterly,* Vol. I, no. 1 (autumn 1951–autumn 1956). Hoboken, N.J.: B. De Boer.

Cardona-Hine, Alvaro. "Poetry in Los Angeles 1945 to 1975 Part I and Part II." *Bachy* 12 (1978): 138–49.

Ceplair, Larry, interviewer. *Hollywood Blacklist: Donald Gordon.* Los Angeles: UCLA Oral History Program, 1988.

Ceplair, Larry, and Steven Englund. *The Inquisition in Hollywood: Politics in the Film Community, 1930–1960.* Berkeley: University of California, 1983.

*Coastlines.* Vol. I, no. 1 (spring 1955), to vol. VI, nos. 21–22 (1964). London: Villiers Publications, Ltd., 1955–64.

Crawford, Dorothy Lamb. *Evenings On and Off the Roof.* Berkeley: University of California Press, 1995.

*Epos: Quarterly of Poetry* (summer 1958). Lake Como, Fla.: New Athenaeum Press.

Funsten, Kenneth. "Bert Meyers (1938–1979)." *Bachy* (1979).

Garrett, Alexandra. *Alexandra Garrett Papers.* Special Collections, UCLA.

Gibbons, Reginald, and Terence Des Pres. "Thomas McGrath: Life and the Poem." *Triquarterly* 70 (fall 1987). Evanston, Ill.: Northwestern University, 1987.

Gordon, Don. *Displaced Persons.* Denver: Alan Swallow, 1958.

———. *Statement.* Boston: Bruce Humphries, Inc., 1943.

Hall, Donald, Robert Pack, and Louis Simpson, eds. *New Poets of England and America.* New York: Meridian Books, 1957.

Kirsch, Robert. "Coastlines: A Post-mortem." *Los Angeles Times,* 30 August 1964.

Levertov, Denise. "Bert Meyers." In *Light Up the Cave.* New York: New Directions, 1981.

Linnick, Anthony. "A History of the American Literary Avant-Garde Since World War II." Ph.D. diss., UCLA, 1965.

Maynard, John Arthur. *Venice West: The Beat Generation in Southern California.* New Brunswick, N.J.: Rutgers University Press, 1991.

McGrath, Thomas. *Witness to the Times: Poems by Thomas McGrath*. Los Angeles, n.p., May 1953.

Nelson, Cary, and Jefferson Hendricks. *Edwin Rolfe: A Biographical Essay and Guide to the Rolfe Archive at the University of Illinois at Urbana-Champaign*. Urbana-Champaign: University of Illinois Press, 1990.

*North Dakota Quarterly: A Festschrift for Thomas McGrath* 50 (fall 1982).

Rolfe, Edwin. *Collected Poems*. Edited by Cary Nelson and Jefferson Hendricks. Urbana: University of Illinois Press, 1993.

———. *First Love and other poems*. Los Angeles: The Larry Edmunds Book Shop, 1951.

———. *Permit Me Refuge*. Los Angeles: The California Quarterly, 1955.

———. *To My Contemporaries*. New York: Dynamo Press, 1936.

Stanford, Ann. Ann Stanford Papers, uncataloged. Box nos. 5, 67, 70, 71. Manuscript Collection, Huntington Library. San Marino, Calif.

Stern, Frederick C., ed. *The Revolutionary Poet in the United States: The Poetry of Thomas McGrath*. Columbia: University of Missouri Press, 1988.

Thyssen, Erik. *San Francisco Renaissancen*. Copenhagen: Sirius Press, 1973.

Wolf, Leonard. *Voices from the Love Generation*. Boston: Little, Brown, 1968.